# STRAWBERRY ROAD

# STRAWBERRY ROAD

## YOSHIMI
## ISHIKAWA

TRANSLATED BY EVE ZIMMERMAN

Kodansha International
Tokyo • New York • London

Originally published in Japanese as *Sutoroberī rōdo*.

Copyright © 1991 by Yoshimi Ishikawa. All rights reserved.

Distributed in the United States by Kodansha America, Inc.,
114 Fifth Avenue, New York, New York, 10011,
and in the United Kingdom and continental Europe by
Kodansha Europe Ltd., Gillingham House,
38-44 Gillingham Street, London SW1V 1HU.
Published by Kodansha International Ltd.,
17-14, Otowa 1-chome, Bunkyo-ku, Tokyo 112
and Kodansha America, Inc.

Printed in the United States of America

First edition, 1991
91  92  93  94  7  6  5  4  3  2  1

Library of Congress Cataloging-in-Publication Data
Ishikawa, Yoshimi, 1947–
[Sutoroberī rōdo. English]
Strawberry road / Yoshimi Ishikawa ; translated by Eve Zimmerman
p.  cm.
Translation of: Sutoroberī rōdo.
ISBN 4-7700-1551-8.
1. California—Description and travel—1950–1980. 2. Ishikawa,
Yoshimi, 1947–  —Journeys—California. I. Title.
F866.2.I8413   1991
917.9404'53—dc20      91-209
CIP

\*   \*   \*

*The text of this book was set in Fairfield Medium.*
*Composed by Folio Graphics Company, Inc.,*
*New York, New York.*

*The jacket was printed by*
*Toppan Printing Company (America), Inc.,*
*Clark, New Jersey.*

*Printed and bound by*
*R. R. Donnelley & Sons Company,*
*Harrisonburg, Virginia.*

*To my brother and all the people
who lived on the strawberry farm*

# STRAWBERRY ROAD

# 1

# The Road to America

Two days had passed since our first faint glimpse of the continent, and our ship was still inching toward the port of Los Angeles. A middle-aged passenger flicked his cigarette overboard, grumbling, "This ship is really getting to me. We've seen land and now this."

The year was 1965. Our journey had begun on a day in early April, after the cherry blossoms had scattered and all of Japan was turning green; friends and relatives had seen us off, showering us with best wishes and mountains of streamers. Our ship, however, was not a honeymoon cruiser, or fishing ship or battleship—it was an immigrant ship and had none of the luxuries of a passenger ship. We slept like sardines in its dark hold, unaware of how much this journey would change our lives.

Leaving Yokohama, we had traveled north along the bow-shaped islands of Japan, then headed east just off the Sanriku coast. For three days the islands of Japan were still visible, and no one returned to the hold; day and night people stood on deck bidding the country farewell. We asked ourselves whether we'd ever go home again and strained to imprint our last view of the islands in our hearts.

Fellow passengers grew close almost overnight, confiding their dreams to one another. Once the islands had disappeared, we felt awed by the expanse of the Pacific and the beauty of the stars overhead. But soon we grew uneasy as we made our solitary way through the sea, and grumpy at the monotony of the scenery. Week after week, we saw nothing but water. Eventually, we stopped going up on deck altogether and spent the days moping in the ship's dim hold.

Then one day a loud voice rang through the cabin: "I see America!"

We rushed up from our prison below deck and once again began joking and chatting.

But then: "We're just off Oregon. Take it easy, everybody." One cynic dashed our hopes.

"Listen to us," chimed in an elderly couple who had emigrated to America in the twenties. "We're just off Santa Barbara. Trust us, this is our fifth trip. It's only a day and a half more. You're going to love America."

Of course the crew would have given us our bearings if we'd asked, but we didn't, preferring instead to compare imaginary maps among ourselves.

Our ship, the *Africa-maru,* was making its last journey. It carried more than one hundred and sixty immigrants, a few businessmen, and five exchange students. Although the ship was destined for the immigrant regions of Paraguay, Brazil, and Argentina, it would stop off in America for the businessmen and the students. Among the immigrants were farmers from Tōhoku, the north of Japan, who had sold for a pittance farms that had been in their families for generations; a middle-aged couple with their children who had lost all their money in the construction business; and white-collar workers in their thirties looking for a new land because they could not live in Japan on their skimpy salaries. All had their own reasons for coming, but all had the same goal— success. We were poor people.

That year a huge economic boom started in Japan. No one on that ship would ever have guessed it; the people back home would have found it even harder to believe. Certainly, those of us on the boat who had graduated from high school had heard the slogans of the Ikeda cabinet—"double the national income" and "Japan with an income equal to Europe's by the next decade." Attractive words, but who really believed them? Less than a decade after the Tokyo Olympics of 1964, the impossible actually happened. The value of once inexpensive rice fields soared astronomically, and thousands of Japanese began to go abroad.

Were those of us who left Japan in the spring of 1965 short-sighted because we missed our country's economic miracle? Forget doubling our income—at the time, we were going to make ten times what we did back home. And as for growth, well, the sky was the limit. Aboard our sluggish ship, however, we could not have imagined that our dreams would go up in smoke. We were just people trying to make it abroad.

Before long, an announcement came over the loudspeaker: "We arrive in Los Angeles at noon tomorrow. Please prepare to disembark."

That evening the other passengers threw us a good-bye party. The singing and drinking lasted long into the night. When the ship docked in Los Angeles, the people bound for Latin America were not allowed off; after a few days anchored offshore, they faced another two weeks of life at sea. We must have seemed very lucky to them. "We want to work in America, too, but we don't have the connections," grumbled a couple bound for Paraguay.

Tomorrow? At last. That night I barely slept.

Anchan, my eldest brother, who had come to America to farm strawberries four years earlier, was supposed to meet me. My plan was to attend American high school and help him in the fields. I was eighteen and had just graduated from high school in Japan.

When I got off the boat, my brother was not at the pier. Four hours later I still sat there, drinking in everything around me. All I had was my duffel bag, a tangerine crate filled with books and clothes, and the one hundred dollars my mother had given me (at the time, one dollar was worth 360 yen). Sitting on my crate, I felt absolutely lost. From my vantage point I could see nothing that looked even vaguely like America. Now and then I could hear English spoken by black dockworkers who must have been six feet tall. I thought of showing my brother's address to one of them but felt intimidated by their size. Their English also sounded completely different from the English I had studied, which made me even more anxious.

Clutching my little red "English Conversation" book, I fought back tears. Nothing in the port reminded me of Japan—even the boats anchored there were foreign. The only familiar sight was the lonely Japanese flag hanging from the mast of the *Africa-maru,* and, looking at it, I began to weep. It was the first time in my life that I had cried at the sight of the Japanese flag.

"There *yuu* are!" A voice thundered behind me.

It was my brother.

"Let me introduce Mrs. Watanabe-san. Mr. Watanabe is your guarantor."

"*Howu aru yuu?* Welcome to America. You speak any English?" The matronly woman spoke strange Japanese.

My brother's face was deeply tanned, and his nails were stained with dirt. As he reached out to shake my hand, I shrank back from his abrupt, unfamiliar gesture, but he grabbed my hand anyway and squeezed it firmly. Grinning at me, he asked, "Are Mom and Dad all right?" I took a good, hard look at him. Could this be the brother I knew so well? And why was he calling me *yuu?*

"Sorry, sorry, I *mistaku* the time. I drove so fast I got a *goddamu tiketto.* Mrs. Watanabe came along to translate in case we had *torabaru* with immigration. My English is no good at a time like this."

Even though I would be struggling with English all too soon, I was bewildered from the start by the odd mixture of English and Japanese spoken by the *isei* and the *nisei,* the first- and second-generation Japanese, in America.

Dusk gathered over the pier.

"Well, we can talk more later. I bet you're tried. *Californi's* getting hot now, but it's pretty and there are lots of flowers. You came at a good time. In my field, the strawberries are at their peak. *Yuu* must be hungry. I know, let's stop in Japantown and eat Chinese to celebrate. I'll treat," my brother offered, as he loaded my luggage into the car.

I didn't know what to say, so I watched the scenery speeding past the window. America looked emptier than I had imagined— where were all the people? After half an hour we got off the freeway and found ourselves on an old street lit up with red and blue neon signs in Japanese. When we left the car, I saw lots of Japanese faces; people were milling about and speaking the same odd dialect as my brother. Seedy restaurants and shops, unlike any back home, lined the streets. Where the hell was America? Where were the high-rise buildings and the glamorous blondes? Everything looked wrong.

Seeing my vacant stare, my brother explained with pride, "This is Japantown. It's also called Little Tokyo. Japanese flock here on the weekends. Here, you can buy almost anything Japanese."

We entered a Chinese restaurant. "This is a good cheap *Chinamen*," he added.

When a disgruntled Chinese waiter approached our table, Missus fired away in rapid English, but the Chinese waiter made her repeat her order several times.

"*Yuu,* this is a celebration. Order a lot. The noodles and the vegetable chop suey here are specially good."

Looking at the menu, I couldn't tell what was what. I was having trouble adjusting to the flow of things, and my head was beginning to ache. A young Hispanic man who also couldn't speak English brought our meal, and, though the food was delicious, there was much too much of it. Eventually, a plump, black waitress appeared and began putting the leftover food into a cardboard box.

"*Yuu,* know what that is? It's a doggie bag," my brother explained, "for taking home food you don't eat. America is rich, but it's 'waste not want not' here."

Meanwhile Missus was examining the check. "Only five yen for three people. This is cheap. *Bery goodo.*"

"So, Missus, how about leaving one yen for the tip?"

"No, no. Fifty sen is *alrigh-yo.*"

I broke into the conversation. "Five yen for eating all that? I still have yen, you know. Can you really use Japanese money here?"

"No, no. Japanese in *Californi* call one dollar one yen, ten cents ten sen, and one hundred dollars one hundred yen," my brother said, smiling. "All of this is new to you, but you'll get used to it. Don't worry. America has everything—even samurai movies. The other day I saw a Kataoka Chiezo picture. There are bookstores, too, and you can learn anything here—even *shigin** and folksing-

* *shigin*: sung recitations of Chinese poetry

5

ing. But the most important thing is to pick up English. You won't get anywhere without it." For the first time that day Anchan spoke in the dignified tone of an older brother. We are fifteen years apart: he is the eldest of eight children, and I am second from the bottom.

We left the restaurant.

"Let me show you Japantown. I'll just put the doggie bag in the car." Anchan walked toward the parking lot, and Missus went with him.

I waited, looking over the town outside a bar of some sort.

"Everyone thought you were dead, Otomi-san, even the Buddha . . ." The strains of a familiar song drifted out into the night. Presently, the door opened and two customers staggered out, accompanied by a woman who looked like a hostess.

"Bye. *She yuu tomoroo.*"

She turned to face me. "Hi there. Wanna come in? *Kamu inu.*"

The bar's sign said GINBASHA. On the wall next to the bar were posters for Kataoka Chiezō's *Tarao Bannai,* a familiar sight in Japan, and for a Higashi Chiyonosuke samurai film.

Yen-dollars, samurai films, doggie bags, Chinese waiters, my brother's Japlish, familiar songs. . . . Where was I? Did America exist? Were there no Americans? Nothing in Japantown was either Japanese or American—just shabby. A strange emotion hovering between sadness and anger took hold of me.

It wasn't until much later that I realized that in-betweenness was simply one of America's many faces. At the time, I remember praying that my first day would end soon. Much to my dismay, however, more surprises awaited me at my brother's house, where I would live for the next four years. My first day in America was not over yet. But before I continue, let me go back to the two of us before we came to this country.

No matter what your nationality or age, America is a known quantity before you ever set foot there. An Englishman, for example, must go to Japan if he's curious about it. But if he wants to know about America, at least one family in his town will have sent somebody there and will be able to conjure up visions of America in the English air. The same would be true for a man in an African town. A story about America can begin in any small town and feature the average guy as its hero. Small-town people are the backbone of this country, and they are the ones who send information about America back home. American culture permeated my small island, so I felt quite familiar with America before I ever set foot here.

If you sail from Tokyo Bay on a clear day, a group of islands soon comes into view. These are the seven islands of Izu, or the Izu Shōtō. Izu Ōshima is the largest among them and the closest to Tokyo, with a circumference of approximately 30 miles. Mt. Mihara, a dormant volcano, rises 2,500 feet above sea level at the island's center. At the southern end of the island lies a little fishing port, Habu. In 1791 a party led by a doctor for the Shogunate government landed on Ōshima in search of medicinal herbs. An expert surveyor who was a member of the party noticed the volcanic crater and advised the government that it was the perfect spot for a port. Construction began in 1800 with the removal of the crater's southern wall, and by the next year, when the Pacific Ocean flooded in, the port looked as it does today.

Ōshima faces the Pacific, and a strong westerly wind blows on the island for three or four months a year, churning up the waves and blanketing the island in a white haze. During the rest of the year, the island, encircled by the Black Current, enjoys tranquil weather. For the past decade Ōshima's population has hovered at around 11,000.

An American naval base once stood on the western shore of Habu Port. When the Americans left, no one came up with any plans for the land, and it remained unused. Today very few islanders even remember that twenty American soldiers once lived among us.

I was born in 1947, just a five-minute walk away from the American camp. Like those of anyone in my generation, my memories of childhood are intimately connected with food. Because the volcanic soil of Ōshima is unsuitable for farming, our only abundant food was fish, and sometimes we had very little to go with it. On rare occasions, a mysterious assortment of plump American canned ham, greasy sausage, and *kusaya*—a smelly dried fish that was our local specialty—graced our table. I first met America through food.

Once a week a boat came from the American base at Yokosuka with provisions for the Habu base. This was a day we looked forward to. As the soldiers unloaded the provisions, they'd throw any loose cans of ham or chocolate to those of us waiting onshore with outstretched arms. Sometimes my spoils of war—ham or sausages—livened up our dinner table. The more agile adults made quite a killing, then went off and sold their prizes.

It was during this time that seven or eight *onlys*—mistresses of the American soldiers—came to live in our village, having followed their men from the mainland. One stood out from all the rest. She was seventeen or eighteen, had a perfect figure, and dressed with such taste and style that heads turned when she passed. Seeing her, the islanders would say, "Oh, what a shame, such a beauty taken by an American soldier." She was stunning. When we saw the other *onlys* with their sullen painted faces, clinging to soldiers' arms, we felt the inferiority of our defeated nation and hated it. But when we saw this pretty girl walking with her tall, handsome American soldier, we could say to ourselves: "See, some Japanese women are beautiful."

The islanders didn't ostracize the *onlys*. While their soldiers were working, the *onlys* stole time to visit and gossip with their acquaintances in the village. But the truth was that the villagers only befriended them for the armfuls of American goods they brought as presents. It was a time when everyone wanted things.

The American camp, we were told, was a Navy intelligence base, not an active combat unit. From the outside, life at the base did not look particularly hazardous, and the soldiers seemed to have plenty of time on their hands. During the summer they sunbathed on the beach, proudly baring their young flesh to the sun. When we passed by the base's seaside firing range, we could hear the *rat-tat-tat* of the gunfire, but, peeping through the fence, we'd see the soldiers treating their exercise as a game. Life on the island must have been incredibly boring for them.

Except for a few military dogs tied up out front, the base was not heavily guarded. We snuck in under their noses to pick cans and scrap iron out of the garbage and gather the empty cartridges from the firing range, then sold our finds to a nearby Korean scrap dealer for pocket money. Life in any Japanese village or town near a base probably didn't differ much from ours except that we didn't feel the oppressive military presence. The soldiers were just a bunch of guys who had little to do and who liked to spend time with their *onlys*. Perhaps we were wrong, but it certainly looked that way.

Even during the controversy that surrounded the Japanese-U.S. Security Pact, no one on the island made an issue of the base. The soldiers just seemed like vacationers to us. They lived in rounded barracks, many had private rooms, and, when we visited the ones we knew, they pointed out who was who in the photos of their families and girlfriends taped up on the walls. Good-hearted Americans, they were, like the ones we saw on television in "Father Knows Best" and, later, "Route 66."

Once or twice a year, the soldiers visited our elementary school to show us science films and cartoons. We rolled in the aisles watching *The Three Little Pigs*. Every Christmas Eve they handed out chocolate, chewing gum, cake, and Coca-Cola in the camp's meeting room and without fail showed us a western. Only children were invited, but when adults appeared the soldiers were too generous to turn them away. Although we looked forward to these days, our English teachers dreaded going to the base; they were embarrassed in front of us because the soldiers couldn't under-stand their English.

The young village men who worked on the base as launderers, handymen, or cooks picked up English naturally and spoke it unself-consciously, making the rest of us jealous. Their accents were very different from ours. "Don't say 'wara,' say 'wada,' " they told us.

Every kid learned some English. Vaguely I remember learning "wada" and "ice." Japan wasn't well off in 1955, but the villagers who worked on the base had plenty of food and wore cast-off jeans and T-shirts with USA printed on them. Fashions that are the norm now came to our island early; even as a child I wanted to put on worn jeans and strut around looking tough. Today, of course, looking tough is the rule.

9

Around this time Anchan, who craved the riches of the American soldiers, began to work on the base as a cook.

Yet Anchan didn't work on the base just for himself. As the eldest son, he had to help support the family. Like my father, he was a carpenter, but there was little demand for construction during the time of shortages. Young as I was, I didn't understand all the details; I was just happy that Anchan worked at the base. Having him there meant I was free to come and go as I pleased. Every day at lunchtime I casually dropped by for cola or juice. It also meant that he brought home new American products and proudly taught us the English vocabulary he had learned that day. It was his salary, however, that made my mother happy.

"I'm studying English. One of these days, I'm going to America," Anchan announced at dinner one day. In those days, nobody went farther than Tokyo. We were shocked.

"Are you crazy?" my mother asked.

"No," my brother answered quietly.

American food spiced up our meals, American soldiers walked through our village, America was a part of our lives, but our parents felt angry and confused at the idea that a family member might actually go to the United States. In the end America did pull the family apart, and four of the five brothers would live there. At Anchan's declaration, I, too, felt drawn to that country across the Pacific.

In those days we loved reading the comic books *Akadosuzunosuke* and *Posto-kun,* but we also scanned old issues of *Life* and *Look* that we had picked out of the base's garbage or gotten from the workers. Japanese magazines were cheap and rough to the touch, whereas American magazines were so incredibly shiny I had to squint while looking at them. Glossy shots of New York City at night inflamed my dreams.

Japanese movie stars in magazines looked beautiful to me, but I found it almost painful to look at the actresses in American magazines, with their breasts spilling out of their clothes. Their bodies looked as rich as the country. I tore out pictures of buxom blondes and secretly passed them around among my friends. Though I was still a child, the sexy pictures fired my imagination, and I had many a sleepless night.

10

Curiously, although twenty American soldiers lived on our small fishing island for years, people can't remember when the soldiers arrived and when they left. Ōshima lies exactly at the point where the cold northern current meets the warm southern current, so the island had long been a port of call for drifters, exiles, and fishing boats from all over Japan. Half of its inhabitants originally came from other places anyway—Okinawa to the south, Hokkaido to the north, Sadoshima, Saipan, and even the Chichi and Haha islands in the nearby Ogasawara chain. To the islanders, American soldiers seemed more like foreign drifters than members of an occupying army. I remember my mother, unable to communicate with words, gesturing as she offered pickles and *kusaya* to American soldiers who stopped by our house.

There were, however, two incidents that forced me to see the soldiers for who they really were. The first occurred in April 1952, when a Japanese plane crashed into Mt. Mihara. I had just turned five, but I vividly remember my fear of the jeeps filled with guns and soldiers rushing past our window to the crash site. Suddenly I realized that these men were soldiers who would kill on command, not just Americans who made love to the *onlys* and gave us chocolate.

The second incident occurred in 1960, when a right-wing youth named Yamaguchi fatally stabbed the socialist Asanuma Inejirō. Asanuma was from Miyake, one of the seven Izu islands, and he was popular among the people of Ōshima. Perhaps the Americans feared an uprising, for when I stopped by the base on my way home that day, I saw soldiers readying their guns.

One day in May 1958, Anchan abruptly told my mother: "In two months, I'm going to America. I haven't said anything till now, but I just passed the test. All I have to do is get a physical. I'll be back in two years, when my contract's up."

My brother had decided to go to America as "a short-term agricultural trainee," in other words, a contract laborer, since California was recruiting them at the time. Talk of going to America when he was practically supporting us completely upset our household, but my mother and father ignored the issue as much as possible. Maybe that way, they seemed to think, my

11

brother's passion for America would cool and he would give up the idea altogether.

But external circumstances worked to his advantage. Two years earlier, a woman from our village named Akiko had married an American soldier and gone to live near New York. She wrote frequently, and, although she sounded lonely, the packages of cake and chocolates we got from her twice a year enhanced our visions of American wealth and splendor. The cakes were packed in color comics from American newspapers, which we flattened with our hands and read voraciously. Akiko was a close friend, and her reports of America carried weight. "See. Isn't it just like Akiko says? America's great, I tell you."

My brother also got encouragement from other quarters. One of his classmates, a technician, went to a little island between Australia and New Zealand to teach artificial ice making, and another man, who had emigrated to Seattle before the war, came home a success. Soon after returning, this man appeared in the local primary school and handed out souvenir pencils with his name on them. Anchan often went to his house to stock up on information about America and, according to Anchan, he left a lot of money there.

"I passed the exam," Anchan said one day, showing no sign of relenting. He attended the training sessions for farmers in Fukushima and Shizuoka diligently, and at home read his English book aloud and practiced his English vocabulary.

"Oh, it's awful. That's all you'll be able to speak when you come back from America." My mother made a face whenever strange words popped out of my brother's mouth.

Half-joking, he replied, *"No, no, mazaa."*

Those were her last words of protest. My mother must have felt empty losing a child to America, but she was also angry at the country that had invaded her home. She wasn't the only one who felt this way. The issue in postwar Japan was how much people should allow American culture to invade Japanese society. Our household was so poor and so envious of America's wealth that my mother must have feared the issue would split our family. Her fears were well-founded. Later, Anchan would have children with a white woman, and my mother would be called "Grandma" by

12

grandchildren who couldn't speak Japanese. To her, the postwar period was the time when her sons were snatched away.

As the day of my brother's departure drew closer, she told him repeatedly, "The one thing I don't want is a blue-eyed daughter-in-law."

"It's a two-year contract—I won't have time for that. I'll be back soon. I'll send you lots of money. Some guy before me made a million yen before he came back." So went my brother's defense.

My brother got to the United States despite the complications of American immigration law. Japanese immigration to America had been virtually prohibited by the immigration law of 1924. In 1952, however, Walter McCarran's immigration law was passed, giving Japanese in the States the right to become naturalized citizens. At the same time, although the channel was still a narrow one, the limits on Japanese immigration were relaxed slightly. Of course, other immigrants were allowed in, but it was just after the war and everybody knew that it was most difficult for the Japanese.

There was one other way to get into America. Postwar America, especially California, had been blessed by an unprecedented economic boom and was short of manpower. In the early fifties, the state began hiring 350,000 workers a year from Mexico under the *bracero* program. As migrant workers, the Mexicans became the backbone of American agriculture. When Japanese farmers heard about this, they sent Hiroshi Nasu, the chairman of the Japan International Farming Friendship Association, to America to ask that Japan be allowed to join the bracero program. After some initial setbacks, they sent their first contract laborer to America in 1956.

Although Anchan had no hopes of settling in the United States for good, he looked forward to the flight over the Pacific. It was the age of the propeller plane, and they would have to stop twice to refuel before they reached San Francisco. Everyone in the group wore blazers with Japanese badges on them, which made them look like members of an Olympic team. My brother looked unusually tense.

A month later, I got my first letter from him. He was working, he wrote, in Stockton, a little town in northern California. Nowadays overseas mail automatically means "airmail," but in

13

those days airmail was too expensive, and my brother's letters took weeks to reach us by sea. There were times I wanted to write to him but had no address because he kept moving from one farm to the next.

With a map of America spread before me, I tried to find the farming towns he mentioned in his letters, but they were too small to appear on the map. He described how big and wealthy America was and how much delicious meat and fruit he could get. But the work, he said, was much harder than he had ever dreamed. His salary was seventy cents an hour—about 250 yen at the exchange rates then—which meant that he could make as much in a day as college graduates in Japan did in a week. And every month without fail my brother sent my mother fifty dollars.

"Thank God. He sent it again." Even now I can see the tears in her eyes.

My father had almost no work. I was just starting middle school, yet I well understood how this money was supporting the other nine members of our family.

After Anchan left for America, I kept visiting the American soldiers. Since I was approaching adolescence, I could now understand what interested them most—women. I became friendly with a soldier who was about nineteen and had as his *only* a worn-out looking woman who was pushing forty. They made an odd couple as they walked through town. But, he told me through energetic gestures and rough sketches, he had fallen for one of the village girls and wanted me to play go-between. The adults had, at times, been suspicious of the Americans, but I felt only sympathy for them because they wanted just what we did.

A scandal broke out when the prettiest young *only* got pregnant and her boyfriend dropped out of the Navy and abandoned her. "Oh, you know how it is. You can't trust Americans. Isn't it awful? Such a nice girl, and now she's damaged goods. What's going to happen to the baby?" whispered the village gossips. After this, the mothers in the village strictly forbade their daughters to visit the base. That was how America introduced me to sex.

As I write this account, I'm afraid that I'm painting a sad portrait of our lives during the Occupation. But the truth is that food and sex are universal concerns, whether one's country is occupied or not. That's all there is. I began to see that the American soldiers made moves on our women because they truly desired them.

When my brother came home loaded down with presents at the end of his contract, I was in my third year of middle school. His face was deeply tanned, his arms muscular, and he looked every inch the farm laborer. My mother cried for joy when he appeared in the doorway, chewing on a cigar and wearing jeans that smelled of America.

Night and day my brother told us about his life on American farms. A group of curious villagers constantly surrounded him. "Anyway, it's big. Especially compared to here. I'm amazed that we had the nerve to fight them. Did I go to New York? What? Do you know how far California is from New York? Triple the distance from the top of Hokkaido to the bottom of Kagoshima and then some. The cucumbers are huge—like this—they call them *kyukanba,* which sounds like *kyūri* in Japanese."

Anchan tirelessly answered the villagers' questions, his eyes sparkling. But one day after being home for about a month, he suddenly blurted out: "Mom, I married a white woman over there."

Silence.

"Look, here's a photo of her," he said, taking one from an envelope.

"What?" Mother stammered. "Sons are so much trouble. . . ."

She was in shock. We all were. It was so sudden. According to my brother, he met his bride while working on a farm in San Diego.

"Did anyone besides you—a short-term farmer short on brains—get married?"

"No. Just me. But I'm serious, Mom. I'm going to settle there. On the two-year contract, I could only do work that they gave me, but if I marry and settle there I can do whatever I want. I have carpenter's hands. Whites are clumsy, but a Japanese carpenter can make lots of money. Listen, a carpenter can make two dollars an hour. Two dollars! That's seven hundred yen. How much does

Dad make in a day here? About six or seven hundred yen, right? If I get permanent residence, I can become an American citizen. Then anybody in my family can get permanent residence, too. It's fantastic," he explained feverishly.

"What do you mean you'd become an American? You're Japanese. You're not planning to turn white, are you?"

"No, no. You can become American even if you aren't white, even if you weren't born there."

"You left your mind somewhere back there. You're Japanese. Why would you want to be one of them?"

My parents and my brother talked at cross-purposes. His secret marriage created tidal waves in our household.

"If you love her, there's nothing to be done. But do you really plan to live in America all your life?" my mother asked him. Apparently that idea bothered her even more than the marriage. "And you've just gotten home," she added with chagrin.

When my brother left for America again, we saw him off at Yokohama. This time he took an immigrant ship bound for Brazil. Four years later I boarded the *Africa-maru* on the very same pier. And not just me. In the end, two more brothers left for America, too, and it was always my mother who saw us off.

Back in America, Anchan hardly ever wrote to us. My mother often complained, "Something must have happened. I bet he's turned American."

During my third year of high school, I was having trouble deciding my future when a letter came from him. Although I was very busy studying for my college entrance exams and no longer went to the base, the letter drew me back once again.

"Come to America. Come to this great, big country" were his closing words. The letter arrived during the Tokyo Olympics, when "The Eastern Witches," a women's volleyball team led by Ōmatsu Hirobumi, was very popular. Things had changed completely since my brother had left three years earlier. The Japanese were becoming more and more familiar with foreign cultures, and anti-American views appeared in Japanese media and public opinion because of the escalation of America's intervention in Vietnam. There were reports on television and in the newspapers about the growing student movement in the United States. The Beatles and American rock and roll had also reached our island.

The times had grown more turbulent. I began to feel the animosity that most Japanese educated in the 1960s felt toward the United States, yet somehow America still attracted me. At the end of that year, I made up my mind to go there.

# 2

# On the Farm

My plan was to live with Anchan for a while, and, though I had come to America on a four-year student visa, I had no idea how long I would actually stay.

After dinner in Japantown, we drove Missus home and switched over to my brother's car. "This car is a piece of junk, but it runs pretty well. I bought it for a hundred yen," he explained as we headed toward his house on the farm, hurtling down the freeway so fast I was paralyzed with fear.

"So, you're really here," he kept repeating. In principle, nothing should be happier than a family reunion. But I couldn't think of what to say, so conversation was spotty.

After an hour, the car stopped in front of a house in the middle of nowhere. In the pitch darkness, I couldn't make out our surroundings but could just see specks of light from other houses off in the distance. Finally I gathered up enough courage to ask the question that had been on the tip of my tongue all evening. Anchan had not mentioned his wife once since my arrival. "Anchan, will your wife mind if I live with you?"

"Umm . . ." My brother faltered for a moment and then continued, "She's not here anymore. When I got back from Japan, she was gone. It took six months for my visa to come through, so . . . I went to her parents' place in San Diego, but they said they hadn't seen her. . . . That's just the way it goes. Thanks to her, I'm here. I should be grateful for that. I didn't want to tell Mom. It wouldn't be fair to make her worry even more. That's why I didn't write."

"But . . ."

"Well, no worry. It'll turn out OK. You and I have to join forces. America's the land of opportunity. Here we are. This is my house. It's divided in half; Mexicans live on the other side, but you've got your own room."

My brother opened the door and switched on a light. A scuffed-up table sat in the center of the room, and muddy work boots and work clothes rose in a pile next to a sofa riddled with holes. Shovels, old tires, and carpentry tools were scattered everywhere. The walls were crumbling.

"You must be tired. Sit down. I'll make you some coffee."

"I've got some *kusaya*," I offered, opening my crate.

"Well, let's have some."

As Anchan cooked, the smells of coffee and *kusaya* filled the room. When the fish was done, he picked at it with his fingers while sipping coffee—maybe he felt sentimental about a food from home that he hadn't eaten for years. It was nearly midnight. "You must be tired. Sleep late tomorrow. We can talk later."

My brother showed me to my room, and I threw myself down on the bed. What an awful house, I thought, it looks more like a storage shack. How had Anchan managed all by himself in this little house in the middle of nowhere? His sunburned face, thick arms, dirty nails, funny Japanese, lost wife . . . Thoughts of how much he had changed ran through my head and kept me awake. When I realized that I would be living here, a wave of homesickness washed over me.

The next morning when I woke up, it was already nine o'clock. My brother had gone to work. Once again I noted how dingy the house was. Where were the riches of America he had described in his letters?

Outside, a wide expanse of field stretched all around me. For a moment I shrank back from the sun, which was noticeably different from the sun on Ōshima—it was a white light that pierced everything it touched. All around me were strawberry fields with pickers busy at work. In our garden, rosy oranges as big as fists weighed down the spindly branches of the trees. An overpowering scent of oranges and strawberries filled the air. Our house sat smack in the middle of the field.

19

The strawberry pickers were Mexicans, and I could faintly hear them talking in Spanish. The farm itself was huge and bore no resemblance to the small, crowded farms of Japan, where rice plants grew in one field, cabbage in the next, spinach in the next, with persimmon trees thrown in for good measure. Our field went on for hundreds of yards and contained nothing but rows of strawberries. The pickers kept their eyes to the ground as they plucked the ripe, red fruit, placed it in boxes, and loaded the boxes onto small handcarts. Anchan had written about being a farmer, but I had never imagined that the fields in America could be so big. After all, I had only learned about America from the Americans on Ōshima, the movies, and my history teachers.

If a samurai with a topknot had appeared in the middle of a field in Japan in 1965, people would simply have fainted. But if a cowboy on horseback or a group of covered wagons had appeared at that moment in the field, I wouldn't have blinked. Not even the sight of an Indian with a bow or an outlaw with a gun picking strawberries would have surprised me. I strode into the rows and plucked a ripe, red strawberry. Its sweet juice flooded my mouth.

Around noon my brother returned in a large muddy truck with a white farmer.

"This is Charlie," he told me. "He works in our field."

"Daiku, is this your brother?" The small man shook my hand with a smile.

"Anchan, why is he calling you *daiku?*"

"It's my nickname here. *Daiku* is the Japanese word for "carpenter," right, and I was a carpenter back in Japan. When I'm not farming I fix sheds and stuff for people. Anyway, I taught Americans the word for carpenter in Japanese, and the name stuck. Daiku Ishikawa. Not bad, eh?" My brother seemed pleased with the name. "White guys, when they get friendly with you they'll ask you how you say something in Japanese. Then you've got it made. Make friends with them and you'll learn English fast."

Charlie spoke to me rapidly in English, even though I couldn't understand him.

"Did you try a strawberry yet?" my brother asked. "Aren't they good? This crop is sweeter than most years. It'll fetch a decent price. After lunch, we'll go see Frank Machida, the owner of the farm."

Anchan opened his big refrigerator and began to fry up ham and vegetables. There was enough food in the refrigerator to keep us going for more than a month. For lunch Anchan ate steaks twice the size of my hand. His car was old, but at least he had one; the house was falling apart, but it did have a bath and hot water; and why wouldn't a farmer wear cheap, sweat-stained clothes? Still, looked at with a cool eye, my brother's life was a mixture of extravagant wealth and grueling poverty.

Frank Machida's office was a ten-minute drive from our house. Anchan drove the truck slowly through the fields, sticking his head out the window and shouting encouragement at the Mexican pickers: *"José, ándele! Antonio, pronto!"*

"Your Spanish is good."

"You have to know Spanish in the fields, because all the workers are Mexicans. They're illegals."

"Illegals?"

"Yup, about nine-tenths of them—wetbacks they call them. You'll learn about these things. I get along with the Mexicans; they're fun people. By the way, you've got to get a driver's license. You can't even get a cup of coffee here if you don't drive."

We stopped in front of a building, and a short, sturdily built man of about fifty emerged and waved us over. He had a round face and a bald head; energy radiated from him.

*"Werucome, werucome.* Ishikawa's brother? You look just like him. Body looks *alrigh* too. Great, a new pair of hands. *Bery goodo.* You can call me Frank."

"Thank you very much for everything," I mumbled.

Frank wore a short-sleeved military shirt and an expensive watch; a cigar dangled from his mouth. Completely in awe of this odd stranger, I could barely mutter my thanks. He had paid for my passage to America.

Frank was a nisei. At the age of six, he had gone back to Wakayama, his parents' home, and had graduated from middle school before returning to America. I knew he was Japanese because he was speaking the language, but somehow it just didn't

21

fit. Could growing up in a different environment transform the language so much? Charlie was a foreigner, but I didn't feel ill at ease with him because I knew who he was from the beginning. Instead, I was tongue-tied with my own flesh and blood and with Frank, who had planted himself firmly in front of me. Much later I came to understand why.

There are two types of Americans: natives and people who are trying to become American. The Chinese man I saw in Japantown that first night, my brother, and Frank were all part of the latter group. You might say that this is true in any country. In Japan, Vietnamese immigrants and Korean residents study Japanese diligently, eat Japanese food, and imitate Japanese ways of life. But they aren't doing these things because they want to *be* Japanese; they are doing them to survive. In the United States, tens of thousands of people who want to become Americans are waiting in the wings. But these people do not enter into Japanese images of America. To the Japanese, Americans are white people who speak English. When I lived in America, I always felt uncomfortable with the "wanna-be" Americans.

"Ishikawa's *buraza*," Frank continued, "America's a great place. *Yuu* gotta work hard and be *biggu shotto*. Come see me later. I'll teach you how to drink *cafe*."

Be a big shot—what a way to talk to me, I thought, and his pretentious pronunciation of coffee made me want to laugh.

"Ishikawa, take the rest of the day off. Take your brother downtown this afternoon and eat a good meal. Here." Frank handed my brother some money.

"Thanks. Well, let's go. I'll just go tell the *Mexis* what to do. If I'm not there they slack off. Wait for me here—I'll be back in half an hour." My brother rode off in the truck.

Frank had an office in a loading station in the middle of the field, and trucks drove in and out continuously. The strawberries were taken as soon as possible to a market in Los Angeles. Because the market closed at three, the trucks had to leave the field between one and two in the afternoon. Strawberries picked in the afternoon were taken to market the next morning.

I went into the office. A white woman sat there typing. "Hi," she said, smiling at me. Americans smiled at everyone. She immediately served me coffee and cake, and a moment later winked at me and began pointing toward Frank's private office, indicating that I should look in. I could hear Frank on what seemed like a very long phone call, but I knocked anyway and peeked in.

"Oh, doctor, I feel it, oh, doctor, I feel it," Frank said in Japanese. He lay on a long sofa with the phone to his ear, his eyes squeezed shut and his face screwed up in a grimace.

"Oh, doctor, it's working good today. The pain's going."

Although sweat poured down his face, he looked quite contented. What was this man doing?

"Oh, Ishikawa's *buraza*."

"Yes, umm . . ."

"Doctor, I think that's enough for today. *Sankyu, sankyu.* See you tomorrow. How about lunch at that Chinese place?" Frank hung up the phone.

"What were you doing?" I asked.

"The telephone doctor was sending me healing energy. I worked too hard when I was young, and it gave me a bad back. I went to lots of doctors, but nothing helped."

Frank told me more about his youth and how he had made his money. It was when his bad back had gotten chronic that he had met the telephone doctor. Now, when the telephone doctor sent him energy over the phone, he said, his back felt instantly better.

"How does he . . . I mean, what does he say when he's sending the waves?"

"Nothing. He just places his fingers on the mouthpiece and projects his spirit. Like this." Frank wiggled his fingers back and forth. "He used to be a spiritual healer in Japan. Got any aches and pains—he'll take care of you."

Frank was dead serious. Japan has its sham religions and weird beliefs as does any country, but, I thought to myself, supposedly we are in the most culturally advanced nation on earth, and a Japanese healer is projecting his spirit over the telephone?

The whole thing sounded dubious, yet it had a ring of truth to it. If people had strange obsessions that couldn't be laughed away, a telephone doctor seemed as good a cure as anything.

23

Outside I heard my brother's horn. As we drove, I told him the whole story.

"He pays a lot for it, and he's always pushing me to do it," Anchan replied. "But tell me you can get your back cured over the phone. It's famous around here—his obsession with the telephone doctor. The *Mexis* call him Telephone Frank."

"He seems a little funny in the head."

"That's true. When you work so hard in this heat, your brain goes soft. Life is just work, food, and sleep. But you're here to study. Today is Friday, there's no school tomorrow or the day after, but on Monday we're going to register you."

After a day in America, I had completely forgotten about school. "School?"

"What's wrong?"

"I don't think I'm up to it."

"You'll get over it."

"Anchan, I want to walk home. Let me out of the car. I need to think. Can we eat at home tonight? We have plenty of time to go out later."

"OK, then I'm going to do some shopping. You know, it looks close, but it's a thirty-minute walk."

"I want to walk."

I got out of the car. At the end of April it was already over 85 degrees. I walked along a small path through the strawberry fields, finding that the smell of the fruit and the stench of hay made it difficult to breathe. Now and then, the young Mexicans glanced at the stranger in their midst, then quickly returned to picking. Women and children were also hard at work. As I walked along the narrow path, I thought to myself, So this is a strawberry field, pretty impressive. I held my head high. My walk down strawberry road had begun.

It was decided that I should begin high school on Monday. My brother took Saturday and Sunday off and drove me around so that I would become familiar with the area. Our farm was in a town named San Dimas in Pomona Valley, about 80 miles southeast of Los Angeles. With a population of about two thousand people, the town was bigger than the whole island of Ōshima. But it wasn't really a town; it was all fields.

24

"A lot of Japanese farmers work in these mountains. About three hundred Japanese *blanketo-men* worked the lemon fields here in the tens and twenties."

*"Blanketo-men?"*

"You know *blanket,* right? Well, migrant workers moved from farm to farm, each one with his own blanket. That's where the name came from."

Anchan pointed at the orange and lemon fields on either side of the car as he spoke. "This is Highway 66. It's not that big, but it's famous. If you keep on going, you get to Chicago via Las Vegas."

"This is Highway 66? It's tiny."

"If you drive along here at this speed for twenty-four hours, you still won't get to Chicago—that takes five days. And the East Coast looks totally different. The towns we're driving through now aren't even on the map. It's amazing, how big America is." Anchan's tone was severe. I had only expressed disappointment at the size of the road, but he thought I was being overly critical.

From what I had seen of my brother over the last two or three days, he didn't seem very happy, nor did he appear to be living well. Still, when I criticized America even slightly, he jumped down my throat. Either he experienced the stirrings of patriotism, or he felt like a fool if anyone criticized his new home.

I use the word *patriotism* advisedly. No other nation or people has more complex variations on the theme of patriotism than America. The people who want to become Americans are also deeply patriotic. They may resent America because they have been mistreated in the process of becoming citizens, but they often turn into outspoken patriots to prove themselves.

African-Americans are a typical example. Circumstances have made it impossible for them to love America. Yet even though they cannot love a country that kidnapped and persecuted them, they have created an America for themselves that they can love. The only problem is that, like so many others, theirs is an invisible America.

The patriotism of those who want to be American makes their presence felt by the majority. Yet they have gone overboard to prove themselves, and their patriotism affords a glimpse of America's darker, turbulent side. Invisible Americans, like my brother, are everywhere.

Wherever we drove, the roads were empty but in good condition. "What a waste. No cars, no people, and still they build a road all the way out here."

"You have to have a car here, so it's natural they invest in their roads. It's like this: the car is the husband and the road is the wife." My brother's choice of metaphor struck me as odd considering his domestic situation.

"You mean in America it's OK for the husband to run all over the wife?" I joked.

"No, no, just the opposite. If you lift a hand against your wife, she'll divorce you. Women wear the pants here."

Since childhood Anchan had worked to support our household. With no exposure to books about America, newspapers, or radio and television, his only knowledge about America had come first-hand. Yet his America seemed real to me.

"You have to go to high school on Monday and learn English. After that—college. What're you going to study?" he quizzed me.

I couldn't come up with an answer—I knew nothing about American schools.

"I know. We'll go see your school. No one's there on Saturday, but we can have a look at it."

My brother swerved around, leaving the desolate plain and taking us back toward La Verne. Lemon fields gave way to clusters of houses. My school was a long, narrow, one-story building, a complete contrast to a Japanese high school, with a large sports field behind divided into separate areas for baseball, soccer, track and field, and so on. Not a soul was in sight.

"Big, isn't it? Just like everything in America."

"What's that over there?" I pointed at the high wall behind the baseball field.

"Oh, that's a drive-in movie screen."

"Drive-in . . . ?"

"Yup, in America you can watch movies from your car. You sit in your car, hang a speaker from the window, and lie back. Whites are lazy. That's not all. There's a drive-in church where people hear prayers in their cars. I bet that makes God mad. Speaking of

Christianity and religion, everybody here goes to church on Sundays. You'll have to go sometime."

Preposterous! I couldn't believe that the words *Christianity* and *religion* were coming out of my brother's mouth.

"No, thank you. I don't believe in Christianity," I declined.

"That's the wrong attitude. The first thing an American's going to ask you is, What religion are you? Do you believe in God? Church is the best way to make friends with them. At least everyone's nice to you while you're there."

We started driving again.

"Well, we're getting into downtown now."

"Downtown?"

A banner with the words WELCOME TO OLD WEST TOWN, SAN DIMAS suddenly loomed into view. Downtown San Dimas wasn't much to write home about; it had about twenty houses and a lone supermarket and looked like the movie set of a western. The banner only drew attention to the town's seediness.

"You know," Anchan said, "no matter how small a town is, people always want to show how proud they are to live there. But this is really too much. I mean, our village has this many houses." He laughed grudgingly at the boastfulness of Americans. Then he shrugged his shoulders like a white man.

Horseshoes, antique guns, and a few old buggies were on display underneath the banner. Beyond this was a shiny hamburger stand, and in the vacant lot next door, a tractor was flattening earth for a foundation. A large sign announced the construction of a shopping center. I wondered if the Wild West would still exist if more big cities were built and more highways strung between them. As in all of America, the past, present, and future existed simultaneously even in San Dimas.

# 3

# Samurai on Campus

Monday. Time to register at school. Although I had just graduated from high school in Japan, I planned to spend another year in an American school to learn English. Pete, Frank Machida's brother, took me. He was pure second-generation Japanese and had learned Japanese from his parents. Shaking my hand, he asked, "Ishikawa, *speaku?*" Oh no, I thought, not more weird Japanese.

The school was fifteen minutes away by car. Classes were about to begin, and students were pouring into the building wearing short-sleeved shirts, T-shirts, and jeans. Were they allowed to wear anything as long as it was clothing? That was unimaginable in Japan. This was the first time I had been in a place with lots of Americans, and they seemed to sparkle under the spring California sun. Some of the girls wore clothes that showed off their breasts. Black kids, Mexican kids, and some who looked Asian—all talking up a storm. Wow, that incredibly fat girl, was she a high school student, too? Her chest looked two feet wide. And there was a blond boy who looked like Troy Donahue. What had I gotten myself into? I began to feel very self-conscious.

"Ishikawa, *thisu way*," Pete said.

In the office where I was to register, I spread out my transcript, an ID photo, and immigration papers. I was told that my papers were in order but that I had to have a physical. Then I was taken to the school infirmary.

A fleshy doctor swathed in a white uniform saw me in his office. Though I couldn't understand any of his questions, he seemed to be telling me to strip, and I took off everything except my underwear. The doctor checked my eyes and listened to my chest with a stethoscope. Then, without any warning, he stuck his hand into my underwear and began squeezing first my right and then my left testicle. His eyes were on me, and I thought to myself, Oh no, you can't be one of those. Or was he checking the size of my balls? Maybe they wouldn't let me in if they weren't big enough. I couldn't compete with Americans. This didn't look good. Why did he have to do such an embarrassing thing? He continued to grope at my private parts, and I was filled with shame. Finally the doctor left the room and began talking with Pete.

"Hey, *yuu*. He's . . . how do you say it? . . . checking to see if your *dicku* has any disease."

"*Dicku?*"

"Yeah, the thing men have."

"You mean he's checking for venereal disease?"

"Venereal disease. Is that the word? Yeah."

I was about to tell him that I was a virgin, but then a genteel-looking counselor named Mrs. Baker arrived and escorted me to her office. As usual, I couldn't understand the torrent of English.

"Ishikawa," Pete interpreted for me, "your high school transfer papers are in perfect order. If you want to go to college here, you must take the subjects that are required in California." Of course I could only guess what he was saying as I strained to catch his Japlish. "Mrs. Baker says that you must take these subjects." Pete showed me a schedule covered in small English letters that looked like hieroglyphics. I pointed out to him that I wanted to take subjects that wouldn't require much English—subjects like math, phys ed, and art.

"*I shinku sa.* Good idea. But take speech class. It'll help you learn English."

Here lay the root of all my troubles. To me "Speech" meant English conversation practice, but actually it was a class for learning major dramatic pieces from both classical and modern Eastern and Western theater. This class would put me through agonies.

"You find the classroom by looking for the number here." Pete showed me. "See, math is in Room 15. The teacher will hand out textbooks when you get there."

I wanted to ask him to come with me just the first day, but the words stuck in my throat.

"Classes start soon. Let's see, first period is shop. I'll take you there, but then I gotta go. Take Bus 15 in the parking lot at three-thirty. It stops right near the farm."

Was he joking? I had only been in America for a few days. Pete showed me to the door of the shop class and disappeared into the parking lot with a last *"Goodo luck."* It was just before class, and the students were chattering away at the door as they waited for the teacher. I decided to find a seat as far back as I could. Once or twice my eyes met those of a cute girl who would flash me a white, toothy smile. I forced myself to smile back, not wanting to look unfriendly.

The teacher finally arrived, and class began. I looked down, hoping no one would notice me. The teacher began to take attendance but didn't call my name—perhaps he hadn't heard about the transfer student yet. At that moment I should have gone right up to him and announced myself, but I didn't have the courage. I could feel his eyes looking in my direction. Why didn't he ask about this strange student—an Asian at that—who had wandered into his classroom? Was he oblivious? I felt like an utter nonentity. A few moments before I had been bemused by Americans with their big, bright smiles, but now I felt they were being so cold to me that I had to stop myself from running out of the room.

When the teacher had finished taking attendance, the students began to work on their own projects with saws and planes. I had nothing to do, and, resigning myself to my fate, I went over to a red-haired boy and held the edge of the board he was cutting. He began to speak rapid gibberish to me, and, not wanting to hear any more, I grabbed a nearby broom and began to sweep up the room. It was absurd, but I couldn't very well sit at my desk by myself. I wandered around the classroom this way for an hour.

Math during the second period and American history during the third were the same, and I felt very depressed. Lunch came next, and after that I would have gym. With the money my brother had given me, I lined up in the cafeteria.

"*Gibu mee hambaagu.*"

I repeated my request, but no one understood me. Eventually a big student barged in front of me, shooting me a hostile look. Wishing that I no longer existed, I shrank to the back of the line. Then it was my turn again.

"*Gibu mee hambaagu,*" I pleaded.

The serving woman couldn't get what I was saying, and once again I moved to the back of the line. Finally, after everyone had bought lunch, my turn came again. I stood all alone at the counter, repeating, "*Gibu mee . . .*" Suddenly, the woman's face lit up. She put pieces of sliced ham in a bag and handed it to me over the counter.

When a foreigner orders sushi in Japan he might say "osusushi" or "osuishii," but a Japanese person will understand him. The Japanese have a spirit of service, and they will make the American customer an extra big piece of sushi, thinking it cute that a foreigner is trying to speak Japanese. I couldn't believe that the woman got "ham bag" when I meant "hamburger," even though my pronunciation was terrible. Hatred toward America welled up in my heart. I was only halfway through the "ham bag" when the bell rang.

The gym teacher had been stationed at the Tachikawa military base and, introducing me as a transfer student from Japan to everyone on the field, he began to pronounce the few Japanese words he knew. I was feeling worse every minute.

"*Fujiyama, geisha girl, tempura, sayōnara, can-can musume, anpō . . .*" he recited, sounding as though he had some sort of nervous tic. But I knew the teacher was only trying to be friendly; he meant it as a gesture of friendship. Amused by his words, the boys on the field burst out laughing, and I, of course, felt sure they were laughing at me. Suddenly the teacher barked a command. From his hand gestures I could tell that he was making some of the students run around the field in punishment. As I watched, two students to the right of me broke into a run. Unable to ask whether I should run, too, I chased after them. But when I returned to the line out of breath, still wondering why I had been punished, the other students were bent over double laughing. I had made a mistake and stupidly run almost half a mile around the grounds. By the end of history class, I was so exhausted I felt nauseated.

When I came out of the classroom, three students were waiting for me. They were reporters for the school newspaper, one wearing a camera around his neck. The three explained slowly why they wanted to interview me; they had many second- and third-generation Japanese at school, but I was the first transfer student from Japan—I was the real thing.

"OK, OK," I agreed. They repeated each question slowly, and I did my best to answer yes or no. The interview took thirty minutes, and the photographer snapped lots of pictures. When we had finished, I realized that the school bus had long since gone.

"Now I've had it," I said to myself. What could I do? I couldn't remember my own address, and my brother didn't have a telephone. The only thing I knew was that we lived in a strawberry field along Route 66. The students departed, some in their own cars, others picked up by their parents. Throwing pride and reputation to the winds, I began to ask for help. But all I could say was *"My housu isu sutroberi fieldo. Kurosu to ruuto sixty-six."* People gave me funny looks; no one would stop to talk to me. I began to feel desperate. I didn't even know in what direction to start walking—only that the house was fifteen minutes away by car and a couple of hours on foot. A Mexican guy stopped, but he didn't seem to understand my English.

"Route sixty-six? No way, no way," he said. No way? Was he telling me that there *was* no such road, no Route sixty-six?

By six o'clock the campus was empty, and the sky was growing dark. A vast expanse of land stretched out to the east, ending in a dramatic mountain range. As the sun sank in the west, it dyed the mountains a purple-red. Gradually stars began to glimmer here and there in the sky. All alone I lay down in the neatly pruned grass by the parking lot and began kicking my feet in frustration. Another thirty minutes passed; then I heard a car! I got up; Anchan and Pete were walking toward me.

*"Whato izu za matta with yuu?* What are you doing?" asked my brother. What did he think I was doing? This was the last straw.

"*Yuu* missed the bus right?" Pete added.

"Well, get in the car," my brother ordered.

In the car I told them all about my day.

"Ha ha ha. You're learning. That's how a body learns things." Anchan's response seemed very cold. He began to talk heatedly about all his experiences—funny and otherwise—during his time in America. I was furious.

"You say people learn through their bodies, but it's also important to learn with your brain. Besides, why should an American squeeze my balls?" I wanted to prove him wrong by telling him about my shameful experience that morning. The truth is, dear brother, this is all your fault. I came here because you kept saying that America is such a great country. I felt like spitting the words at him.

"You shouldn't be so mad because someone squeezed your balls. You'll never make it here with such a thin skin."

"That wasn't the only thing. . . ."

"You're young," my brother said dismissively.

The next week passed in a flash. At the end of class that Friday afternoon, the school newspaper was distributed with my photo and an article about me in it. When the students in the class noticed it, they all turned to look at me, but not the way they usually did—now they were staring.

I began to pore over the paper with the aid of a dictionary. It said that I was the descendant of a samurai and that I had promised to come to school dressed in a kimono with a sword next Friday. I had no recollection of ever saying such a thing: the only words I knew were *yes* and *no*. Now I was caught! When I got home from school, I ran out to the farm. The shift ended at five o'clock, and the Mexicans were expending their last bit of energy on work.

When I got to Frank's office, the four of them—Pete, Ted (another nisei supervisor), my brother, and Frank were there. I held out the newspaper.

"What's this?" said my brother.

"*Letto mi shee*," said Ted, reading. "Hey, this is great. Are you really a samurai?"

"Why did you say you would do it?" My brother's face wore a troubled expression.

"I just answered questions in an interview for the school newspaper, and this happened. What am I supposed to do?"

"Wait a minute, Daiku. *I wanto shee samurai.*" Ted's attitude suddenly changed.

Ted didn't know anything about Japan. His dead parents had apparently been ardent Japanese nationalists who would slap the children if they ever spoke English at home. Once when Ted and his brothers were speaking to each other in English on the way home from school, their father caught them and berated them, saying, "Do you want to be barbarians?" Ted hated his parents, but when the family was interned in one of the American camps for Japanese during World War II, he began to understand his father better. Although he thought of himself as an American, they evidently did not consider him one, and, during his time in the camps, he concluded that Americans did dreadful things. It was then that his father told him about the brave samurai of Japan.

"I don't like whites—can't trust 'em—but I like samurai." Ted knit his brow. "Ishikawa, you should do it. Make a splash. Give them a taste of Japanese spirit."

I hadn't promised to give Americans a demonstration of Japanese spirit by playing samurai. It had only happened because I couldn't understand English. But Ted was dead serious. Although Ted had been born in America, Japanese blood ran through his veins, and, when he wrote Japanese characters, he felt himself to be a member of that culture. The sad thing was that if Ted went to Japan, he wouldn't be accepted. Having a name which he could write in English or in Japanese characters merely meant that he would continue to walk a tightrope between the two cultures.

"I'm not an American," Ted exclaimed.

A person can move to a new place, even have children and grandchildren there, but he can't escape his origins. Although it was difficult to acknowledge these three men as Japanese, they bore the weight of Japan on their shoulders.

"But what are you going to do about a sword and a kimono? Oh, you can wear my *yukata*. Mom sent it to me a long time ago." Now my brother was cheering me on too.

34

"Hey, they sell toy swords in Japantown. That'd be *alrigh*," suggested Frank.

"So," my brother said, "tomorrow's Saturday. You want to go shopping?"

That was how I came to school dressed as a samurai. It makes me blush just to think of it now: me parading around in a white *yukata* with a red fish-and-wave design that the Habu Minato Fisherman's Association handed out at summer festivals, a judo belt of my brother's, and a bamboo sword from a general store in Japantown dangling at my side. My high school crew cut was just beginning to grow out, so my topknot was a pitiful bundle of short hair in a rubber band.

Amazingly enough, my classmates didn't show much surprise or interest in my getup. Only a few gave me curious looks or asked me questions. One obnoxious white boy stuck out his middle finger at me, but the majority of the students uttered blasé comments like "What's going on?"

Once again I was ignored. But what really depressed me were the puzzled looks on the faces of the nisei and sansei Japanese students. They had been cold to me before. In the beginning I'd felt that we were all in the same boat, and I'd imagined them helping me with English and being my friends. After all, we had the same bodies and faces. They might call themselves Americans, but it was hard to see them that way among the radiant blondes at school. They might call themselves Americans, but they didn't look that way to me. Next to the blondes, the Japanese kids weren't very attractive, so I assumed that they would naturally prefer to make friends with a Japanese from Japan. But when I spoke to them at school in Japanese, they barked back at me, "I don't speak Japanese. You're making a big mistake." They acted ashamed of having Japanese blood and Japanese names. Many times I felt pained by their servility toward whites, their feelings of inferiority, and their scornful looks at other Japanese people.

If I couldn't get on well with Americans, perhaps there was nothing I could do about it. But why was it so difficult to get on well with Japanese Americans? It was a long time before I understood.

That day I felt as though I were performing a historical drama in an empty theater.

"*Yuu*, are you from Japan? Are you really a samurai? Can you do kendo?"

I looked around; a small, dark boy who looked Japanese was standing there. "I'm Frankie Noda," he said, extending his hand.

He didn't look like a nisei or sansei, nor did he speak English like a white person. But he also didn't seem Japanese like me—his Japanese was very coarse.

"Are you Japanese?" I asked timidly.

"Me? Yeah, I'm Japanese. I was born in Yokohama and came here in the fifth grade."

We walked along and introduced ourselves. His father was a nisei cook on a Pacific cruise liner who had married a Japanese woman he met in Yokohama. After finishing fifth grade in a Japanese school, Frankie came to America with his mother. He started telling me about the way the school worked, the teachers, the best sports, and how to improve my English.

"You're dressed like a samurai. Was your grandpa or somebody really a samurai? That's what it said in the paper. Can you teach me kendo? I like samurai. Sometimes I go to the samurai movies in Japantown. If the white guys think you're weak, they beat up on you. I want to learn karate or kendo."

Frankie had taken my act seriously. He chopped at the air like the famous wrestler Rikidōzan.

"No, it's just that they didn't understand my English. I've never done kendo. I did play baseball in high school in Japan though."

Frankie's face fell. How much worse it would be for someone like Frankie, who had come to America in primary school and been placed with white children when he couldn't speak English—he couldn't have been very happy. He was also small. Probably his greatest desire was to be strong.

For the first time since I had arrived in America, I was making friends with a Japanese person my own age.

"*Yuu*, do baseball then. If you *puray* good, you'll make lots of friends. You got to stand out in America. If you don't raise your hand and *speaku* something in class, no one will hang out with you."

He was right. For three weeks I had kept my head down in all my classes. No wonder nobody talked to me. All I got were friendly smiles and the occasional "Hi."

"That's easy for you to say. I don't speak English."

"Even if you don't *undastando*, you got to *speaku*. *Yuu*, you'll be real popular if you can play baseball. There's one really good Mexican guy on the team, and he doesn't speak English. He's very popular."

Frankie chuckled to himself and continued, "By the way, are you any good at math? I bet you can do Japanese math. Will you teach me? I don't get it."

The thick textbook he showed me was a mass of squiggly English letters, but I could recognize the math when I saw it. It wasn't difficult.

"Sure, if you translate English for me, I can do this kind of problem." It was the first time I had felt confident since my arrival.

*"Bery goodo."* Frankie laughed happily. "OK. See you later. Teach me *nexto time*. I have math now. What do you have?"

"English." I said it in English on purpose. "Next time we meet, please talk to me in English."

The truth is that I felt ashamed because I felt no warmth toward anyone in America, whether white, Japanese American, or first-generation Japanese. I had spent time with Americans on Ōshima, but once I had arrived on the mainland I felt confused and a little frightened by the tremendous variety of people I found there.

In spite of my sufferings, the days flew by. Every morning my brother left for the fields early to spend his day with the Mexicans, while I went to school on the eight-thirty bus that stopped near the farm.

The American kids at school seemed to flourish at school, while I withdrew more and more into myself. My internal sense of time had stopped. Although I felt that I had to learn English as quickly as possible, when I was handed textbooks as thick as telephone books for each subject and told to read so many pages per day, I knew that it was impossible. I decided to give up on my classes for the most part and figure out how to learn English by comparing books in English and Japanese.

"That sounds like a good idea," my brother said approvingly. "Plus, school English and farm English are different. There's a bookstore in Japantown. You should go get busy with something."

That weekend we went to Little Tokyo. The bookstore Anchan took me to, Japanese Books, was on the southern edge of the district, and there were some very old-looking books on the shelves.

"Look how many books they have. Remember, one hundred yen means one dollar. This magazine is two hundred and fifty yen, so it's two fifty," my brother explained conscientiously.

Casually I picked up a book. The back cover had a rubber stamp that said "MADE IN OCCUPIED JAPAN"; the book had been published in Showa 22 (1947).

"Anchan, what does this mean?"

"After Japan lost the war, we were occupied by MacArthur, right? That's why it says 'Made in Occupied Japan.' See, this more recent book says 'Made in Japan.' "

My brother picked up another magazine.

"Did all Japanese exports to America during the occupation say 'Occupied Japan' on them?"

"Sure. There are still things for sale in Japantown that have that stamp on them. Nowadays they're harder to find with all the new Japanese things, but you still see it on chinaware."

Next I had to search for a book that had been published in English, so I could compare the two versions. Seeing a set of classics and an intellectual history of the world on the shelves, I said to my brother, "They sell some really difficult books here."

"*Yuu*, not all the Japanese here are farmers. Before the war, a lot of smart people emigrated here. You know the politician Miki Takeo. He's dead now, but he was at USC. There was also this society of leftists in Japantown called the Tokyo Club. It might have been a gang or a secret group, I don't know for sure, but it was there."

As we were browsing for books, Japanese circulated inside the store talking to each other:

"Hello. *How ah yuu? Doo desu?* How's the Mrs.? *Zattso fine.* Summer's almost here so don't overdo it."

38

"Mister, is the January issue of *Wife's Helper* sold out? Isn't there anything you can do? I came all the way from Tennessee. Even just the household planner insert—that'd be *alrigh.*" Behind us a Japanese woman was speaking. She was with a black man.

"War bride," my brother whispered.

"What?"

"War bride. She's with that black guy."

"It's June. No wonder they don't have the January issue," I whispered back.

The war bride pleaded with the store owner. "I've been using the household planner from *Wife's Helper* for three years. I just won't feel right without it. A friend was sending it to me 'cause there aren't any Japanese bookstores in Tennessee, but this year we bought a new house and moved."

The woman's husband had no idea what his wife was saying to the store owner, and he thumbed through back issues of *Heibon Punch,* grinning at pictures of half-nude Japanese women.

"Why would anyone need a household planner from *Wife's Helper* here?" I asked, unable to understand her enthusiasm. Having grown up in Japan, I knew how popular the household planner, an insert in every New Year's issue of *Wife's Helper,* was among women. But I never dreamed that I would hear the name of that magazine in a bookstore in America.

"It's because you lose all sense of the seasons in America," my brother explained. "Sometimes it feels like time has stopped. There's no New Year's celebration here or Festival for the Dead, and you never go picnic under the cherry blossoms—everything's a muddle. Plenty of things happen, but they don't seem to relate to you. When people talk about who won the election in this town, it sounds like they're talking about some faraway country to us immigrants from Japan. I've lived here four years, but it feels like ten. She probably wants a household planner for a little relief. When I lived by myself in that little house, I was desperate to write things down in Japanese. Imagine what it would be like for a Japanese woman in Tennessee." My brother's voice was filled with sympathy.

Eventually I decided on two books: *The Stranger* by Camus and

*The Communist Manifesto* by Marx, because I knew that I could also find them in English.

The high school students of my generation in Japan were known as the "castaways," and we all knew the names of Camus and Marx. Many high school teachers all over Japan had been involved in the struggle over the Japanese-U.S. Security Pact during their student days, and they gave a leftist slant to our education.

"You bought some pretty hard books. But is this OK—*The Communist Manifesto?* Isn't it a red book? This country hates reds. You shouldn't even say the word *communist.*" Anchan had a serious look on his face. "The war is getting more serious, and students are demonstrating against it everywhere. The only thing on TV these days is news about the riots. Last year at this school called Berkeley there was a big antiwar demo. Something about free speech. Anyway, don't use the word *red* in America. Be careful." My brother looked serious.

I couldn't understand the television, but I could see that students were demonstrating on campuses against the Vietnam War. I also knew that the antiwar movement was spreading from campus to campus and that the flame of the student movement had been burning brightly at Berkeley since 1964. I could not understand, however, why Americans believed that the student movement was communist and why they hated communism so much. Was it such a dangerous thing? The communism we had studied in high school social studies in Japan had seemed to us an ideal model for mankind.

"Why do Americans hate communism so much?" I asked my brother. "In the communist system, everybody's equal, and you get what you work for. Don't you think it's a good idea?"

"No. Everybody here wants to earn a lot and get rich. Me, too. I don't want to work hard and end up equal. Takes all the pleasure out of life. The best way to live is to work hard and make yourself a pile of money."

After the bookstore, we went into a Japanese market, where we stocked up on tofu, miso, pickles, and pickled plums.

Night had fallen. Japantown had filled up with Japanese, and I could hear snatches of their conversation. These people probably spent their days cutting hay on a farm or working for white people.

In 1965 Little Tokyo still belonged to the first generation of immigrants; every shop smelled like incense.

The next day I borrowed English versions of *The Communist Manifesto* and *The Stranger* from the school library and set about studying with the English and Japanese versions and the dictionary lined up on my desk. I didn't expect any great improvement in my English; I just wanted to begin something.

One day I was sitting in Basic English class, a course designed for the children of immigrants that began with the ABC's. There were Indian, Guatemalan, and Thai kids in the class, and some of them didn't speak English, so this was the only place in school where I felt safe.

The teacher had just graded an exam we had taken that day, and he was staring at me. It had been a fairly easy test: write three words that begin with *E* and three words that begin with *B* was one question, and I was expecting a perfect mark. But the teacher kept staring at me quizzically. When the bell rang and all the other students had left, the teacher asked me to stay behind to talk with him.

"I don't understand you. You barely speak a word of English, but you do well on tests. In fact, you know vocabulary words that American kids don't know."

The teacher couldn't understand the answers on my test. He continued, "If I say give me three words that begin with *E*, most students will write 'eat, egg, evening.' That's a good answer 'cause it's practical—you can make sentences like 'Eat an egg in the evening.' But you write 'exodus, existentialism, and establishment.' "

I wrote *exodus* not because of the story of Egypt in the Old Testament but because I remembered the name of a movie with Paul Newman; I knew the word *existentialism* though I didn't know what it meant. The teacher said that he couldn't understand how I could write down words like *exodus* and *existentialism* without making any mistakes yet be unable to answer when someone asked me how I was.

"You took *The Communist Manifesto* by Karl Marx and *The Stranger* by Albert Camus out of the library, didn't you? I was looking for *The Stranger*, but somebody had it out. Can you imagine my surprise when I found out it was you!" The teacher was shocked by the fact that a Japanese student who couldn't understand English would try to read such a difficult book.

Come to think of it, the Japanese are a mysterious people. Japanese high school students read quite broadly in the major works of Western philosophers and writers. But when these same students get older and better at English, they might discuss Steinbeck and Faulkner with an American without realizing they are talking about American writers—a sign that they haven't read the books thoroughly after all. The same holds true for movie stars and jazz musicians, some of whom would be astonished by their fame in Japan. Japanese are maniacal about a certain type of knowledge. They will discuss democracy and socialism just for the fun of it, though the conversation has no bearing on their lives. Knowledge is paradise, and it doesn't matter how you get there; the Japanese just want to know as much as they can.

"How come you know Camus and exodus?" my teacher questioned persistently.

"It's common knowledge for the average Japanese high school student," I somehow managed to communicate to him.

"Existentialism . . . common sense in Japan, huh?" my teacher asked, and then shrugged. "Where do you live?"

I told him that I lived with my brother on a strawberry farm. My teacher said he loved strawberries, and he promised to come to the farm that weekend to buy some. He also invited me to visit his house sometime.

This was my first genuine conversation with an American, and I desperately wanted to make myself understood. But I also felt that no matter how well this teacher understood my words, there would be many things that we couldn't communicate to each other.

As he had promised, my teacher showed up at the farm that weekend in a battered old station wagon.

"*Yuu*, give your teacher the best strawberries," my brother advised, "and maybe he'll give you an A. Gotta cover your bases."

In a red T-shirt and jeans, my teacher looked like a Californian, without an existentialist bone in his body.

"Best strawberries I've ever had," he said smoothly.

After a few more years teaching, he wanted to buy land and become a farmer. By his looks, driving a tractor would suit him better than sitting in a classroom. But most Americans I'd seen looked more fit for physical labor.

"Ishikawa, keep it up. Anybody who can grow such good strawberries *should* be a farmer," my teacher said as he left.

What did he mean by "good farmer"? I hadn't come to America to be a farmer. There were plenty of farmers rotting away in Japan. I wished I'd told him I'd come here to study existentialism and Marx.

Over a hundred Mexicans worked furiously, groaning in the heat. Just standing in the field was enough to make your head swim. The white sun beat down mercilessly on our heads, bringing the temperature up to 95 degrees, and we felt smothered by the smell of overripe strawberries. June was fast drawing to a close and with it the school year; my first summer vacation was about to begin.

Having already graduated from a Japanese high school, I should have been making plans to go to college, but I was told that because of my English I would have to do one more year of high school. My brother complained: "That's terrible—you're going to stay in high school?"

He had to be joking. A person who came to America not knowing his left from his right could hardly be expected to learn enough English in two months to go to college!

"*Alrigh yo*. Just try hard next year and get into college. This summer you should work with me and save up."

I had expected to earn my own tuition.

The day after school ended, Frankie invited me to go to the beach for the first time. During my three-month summer vacation, I would have to work on the farm, so I wanted to go to the sea just once.

Frankie said that he was bringing three or four girls with him. This aroused my interest. Although I had been in America for two months, I had never done more than exchange hellos with the blond girls I longed for.

"American girls have huge tits," Frankie explained with a leer.

At the beach I would get a chance to see for myself. That prospect was the first thing that popped into my mind when Frankie invited me.

On the day of the outing, Frankie came to our field just before noon in a large station wagon with four high school girls sitting in back. Two of them had been in my class, and they seemed to recognize me.

"Cathy, this is Yoshi. Yoshi, this is Cathy." Frankie had shortened my name. Each girl shook my hand in turn.

"Is it all right to pick some strawberries? The girls love strawberries. We'll take some to the beach with us."

The strawberries had passed their peak, but there was still plenty of red, ripe fruit left in rows. But when the six of us went into the field and began picking berries, all the Mexican pickers who had been bent over working stood up.

"*Mira, mira. Bonita, muchacha.*"

"*Ai, ai,*" someone whooped, and one man thrust his hips back and forth. The Mexicans around him let out a great laugh. The sight of four white girls suddenly charging into their field was just too much.

"Shit. Dirty Mexican," one of the girls said, glowering.

"Frankie, what does 'shit' mean?" I asked.

"Ssh. Don't say that in a loud voice, see. It means *unko.*"

"How could she call him that?" I was stunned that such a sweet-looking seventeen-year-old girl could utter such an insult.

"Listen. . . . It's an expression. She doesn't mean that he literally *is* shit."

The girl's words were like setting a match to gasoline; comments from the pickers came thick and fast. Undaunted, the girls hurled insults back at them. Unnerved by the girls' forcefulness, I said to Frankie, "Come on, let's go."

We left the farm behind and moved onto the freeway, opening all the car windows while Frankie cranked up the radio. The girls' long hair danced in the wind. Many cars were heading for the coast; one of the guys in a carful of nearly naked young men gave the finger to the girls. A woman in a bikini driving a red convertible sports car with the top down drew up alongside our car. Her bronzed skin was barely covered, and I could see the swell of her breasts. When she noticed that I was staring, she flashed me a smile, winked, and accelerated quickly, disappearing among the cars ahead.

We got to Santa Monica Beach in an hour. The ocean spread out endlessly before us, and hundreds of people were walking along the beach in bathing suits of every size and shape. Many had portable radios and were dancing crazily to rock 'n' roll music. Sprawled in the sand, the older men pursued the young girls with their eyes.

The hot sun made me squint. Each girl we had come with was wearing a bikini. My eyes kept settling on their breasts. This was the best I had felt in a long time.

Dozens of yachts floated in the water. If I could only swim across the ocean, I thought I would reach my beloved Ōshima. I stripped down to my bathing suit and ran toward the water. A cold current flows by Santa Monica, and I jumped back when I touched the water. Steeling myself, I dived in and felt my body contract in shock. I came up near a beautiful blond girl in a bikini that clung to her breasts. With her smile she could have stepped right out of one of the glossy magazines I had seen at the base. I had finally found America. Very happy, I dived back into the cold blue water of the Pacific.

# 4

# Strawberry Days

The day after our trip to the beach, I started to work on the farm.

Wages for farm work in California are paid in two ways: the piecework system, which pays on commission, and the day-work system, which pays by the hour. On the piecework system in those days, for example, a picker got forty cents for every box of strawberries. Twenty boxes a day would net him eight dollars. Although day work depended on experience and age, it paid around a dollar twenty an hour, the minimum wage at the time. A farmer had to juggle these two systems wisely. At the peak of the season, when the workers could make a lot of money, he would pay on commission; daily wages were for less busy times. Of course it would be more profitable to pay by the hour during busy times and on commission when there was less to do. But if you paid by the hour when the workers could make more on commission, you could end up with a manpower shortage. This situation developed because more than 90 percent of the workers on the farms were Mexicans, and most of them were illegal. If working conditions did not suit them, they would move on to the next farm or city. California agriculture depended on the caprices of these Mexicans for its survival.

Every night my brother gave me an insider's view of farm work. My brother and Frank Machida, the owner of the farm, both told me that practically all the pickers were illegals, but at the time it was hard for me to believe it. Was it so easy to slip into a country illegally, and even if you did, how could you work openly in broad daylight with a hundred other illegal aliens? Their cheerful looks and life-styles didn't match my image of illegal aliens.

But, in spite of my impressions, I grew to like them. They fascinated me more than any of the Japanese, nisei, whites, or blacks I had met here.

Anchan and I shared our dilapidated house with two Mexican men, González and Antonio. My first impressions of them were formed about five o'clock on a Sunday morning around the time of my first miserable days at school. I woke up to the loud squawks of the chickens in the coop behind the house.

"Anchan, the chickens are making a lot of noise. Is it a wolf?" I went to my brother's room, rubbing my sleepy eyes. The farm stood on the edge of the wilderness and sometimes we saw deer and coyotes early in the morning.

"Goddam, the *Mexis* are at it. Stay here," my brother ordered, going outside in his pajamas.

I looked out the window. A group of Mexican men were chasing the chickens around in the coop. One man caught a chicken. Was he going to have it for breakfast? But the man's pants were down.

"What the hell!" I gasped. My brother was yelling something at the men. When he came back in, I asked him to confirm what I had witnessed from the window: I couldn't believe that a man had been screwing a chicken. "Forget it," my brother said, and went back to his room.

I knew about screwing chickens from books and from talking with friends. But these accounts had never been more than figments of our overactive adolescent imaginations. Witnessing the real thing was a shock. At the same time, there was something indescribably comical and sad about the guys next door running around with their pants down, holding on desperately to little chickens.

But there is a sequel to this story. A few days later two of the Mexican guys came over. They often brought us beer, but that day they brought eggs from their chickens.

"Mexicans are murderers. You are terrible people," my brother said when he received the eggs. Our guests were stunned.

"You can eat eggs that have your seed in them? Your kids are in

47

here." My brother lifted an egg up to his ear. "González, this one has yours in it. It's crying 'Papa, Papa' for you."

"*No, no, Ichikuwawa, mentira.*" González, a man with droopy eyes, sounded uneasy, but he seemed partly convinced.

"When you tell Mexicans stuff like that, they believe you," my brother told me.

One night the men came over when my brother was out. Although I couldn't communicate in English, mysteriously enough we made ourselves understood through hand signals. They called me "Ichikuwawa Junior."

"Is a Japanese woman's thing really horizontal?" they asked many times, with the aid of pen drawings.

The annoying rumor that Japanese men have huge penises—which isn't true—has been convincingly traced to the depiction of men's bodies in the *ukiyo-e,* prints of the floating world. I do not know the origin of the myth about Japanese women's vaginas. The "feared horizontal women" of Japan could not possibly have found their way to the farms. The birth of such a story, however, is not so strange when you consider the way Mexicans and Japanese lived together. It was a topsy-turvy world; no one could tell how ideas were altered when they were passed on.

A day on a California farm starts early. We finished a breakfast of coffee, sausages, and eggs by six and headed out to the field before sunrise. During the summer, with daylight savings time, six o'clock is actually five o'clock. White-collar workers enjoy daylight savings time; for them it means outdoor activities after work. But to the laborers working in the fields, it is "killer time," because work does not end until it gets dark, and the sun sets late in the west anyway. Daylight savings time makes the pickers' hot days even longer.

The supervisor's job was to get the field ready so that the Mexicans could get right to work at seven by placing empty strawberry boxes and drinking water at strategic points around the 2½-by-1¼-mile area. Before the workers arrived, we drove around the field in small trucks and split up on our own, hurriedly setting up for them.

At seven o'clock sharp, buses driven by the coyotes, the agents who handle illegal workers, pulled up. Mexican pickers tumbled out and ran to the fields as fast as their legs could carry them. Since on the piecework system the more you pick the more you make, much depends on what you can do before it gets hot.

My first job on the farm was to check that the strawberries were ripe and to judge whether they would bring a good price. Since the farm paid by the box, some pickers brought in boxes with green strawberries on the bottom and just a layer of ripe ones on the top. I had to take out the green ones and consolidate the boxes.

Then, while the pickers moved straight down the rows of strawberries, I had to go across the rows, checking their work. During the morning I walked more than six miles. The temperature climbed, heat rose from the earth like steam, and a hot breeze came up, barely stirring the air. I began to feel dizzy.

"Farm work's tough, you know. I wonder if you're up to it," my brother mused. After half a day I thought I had sunstroke. My throat was parched, but I had no energy to walk the half mile to the water station.

Even in this heat, the Mexicans were crouched down picking the red fruit with lightning-fast hands. Sometimes a man called out to his neighbor or a guy hummed while he worked. A man took off his shirt and tied it around his waist; another wrapped a water-soaked towel around his head. Their muscles jerked; the sweat poured off them.

After the afternoon shift, I trudged back to the office where Frank, Pete, and my brother were gathered. I was on the verge of collapsing.

"You're definitely Ishikawa's brother," Frank commented. "You work hard. We were talking about you just a minute ago."

His younger brother, Pete, also seemed satisfied. "Yeah, last year an exchange student came here looking for a job, so I give him work and he retires after half a day! You did great."

"*Californi* even makes farmers from Japan weep," Frank added.

These men believed in physical labor; they drew their strength from it.

As far as I knew, the word *farmer* in Japan was a synonym for poverty; the smell of poverty clung to farms in Japanese novels and films, a sad expression haunting the face of the farmer. But the farming I was doing now seemed more like a test of physical

49

endurance. Frank, Pete, and even my brother were happy, confident in knowing that they had pushed their bodies to the limit.

That day they were testing my character. These men were immigrants or immigrants' sons, and they had come to America to work; they were not about to accept an exchange student who came with naive ideas and neat theories. Everybody had to do the same punishing work they did. If you could bear it, you were one of them. The immigrants' belief system demands that the original group test the newest arrival; the trial became a test of allegiance, a rite of passage to become American.

Immigrants who came to this country during the seventeenth century or during the revolutions of the twentieth century were exploited at least once by their own people. An Italian immigrant, for example, joins an Italian community, then learns how to become American. In the meantime, he offers himself up as cheap labor to support his community. The same pattern has been repeated in almost every community down through the generations. The man who immigrated two hundred years ago and the man who immigrates today can both call themselves Americans because they have had similar experiences.

According to Daniel Boorstin, the historian, America is built on the "Everywhere Community": "A new culture [America] found a new way to bind people together. Rather than by creeds or belief, traditions or origins, people have been joined together by similar efforts and experiences, ways of life, and individual ways of thinking. They have been brought together not by their desires but by necessity, by the things they make or buy and by ways they make sense of their experience."

According to Boorstin, becoming an American is actually a process of learning, by having the same experiences as the next man. American democracy is different from all other forms of democracy because it is able to unite people from different generations and nations in the common experience of being an American. In comparison, the Japanese notion of democracy, whether personal or political, is lacking something.

Back on the farm I felt that they were beginning to accept me as an insider. Frank's voice had grown kind. "For the first day on

50

the job, you were on your toes. Just keep it up and you'll make a good farmer. Then you make it to big shot," he said, taking off his glasses and squinting. "OK. It's lunchtime. We got everything—fried chicken, Mexican food—eat whatever you want."

"What I really want is a Coke," I said, and gulped down a can the size of five ordinary Cokes. The dark brown liquid filled my mouth, making my body tingle. Had I ever tasted anything so delicious?

"Good, huh?" asked Anchan. "There's nothing so good as that first Coke after a day on the farm."

My first Coca-Cola . . . at the American base when I was a kid . . . I spat it out immediately because it tasted so mediciney . . . it was *the* American drink.

The next day and the day after I worked on, scorched by the white-hot sun and made dizzy by the heat that seemed to emanate from the ground. Far from getting used to the work, my feet swelled up and my back felt as though someone had hit me with a big stick.

"You seem to be holding up OK. Farming's hard work, isn't it?" My brother commented every morning before work over our breakfast. My brother always made breakfast.

"Coffee, sausages, and eggs alone don't make a great meal," he would say, serving up homemade pickles, sweet scallions, and beef that had been steeped in miso paste. "If we eat all the *kusaya* in one shot, who knows when we'll get it again. Just got to eat it little by little." Anchan was hoarding the *kusaya* I had brought him from the island. Smells of coffee, scallions, miso, and pungent *kusaya* always filled our kitchen.

At seven o'clock one morning we all gathered in front of the office as usual. "Two more rounds and we'll be done for this year. Then we move to jam," Frank announced to the supervisors.

There were only about ten days left till the end of that year's strawberry harvest. The quality of the fruit was going downhill. Nobody would buy the remaining strawberries at the market, so we would make them into jam.

"Today, maybe very hot, I think." Frank pointed at the mountains behind us. Unlike most early mornings, the air was already terribly dry and heavy with heat. "Look over there. At the haze.

We're going to have a scorcher once that gets here. Today might be the end of the strawberries. Anyway, do your best, everybody."

Slowly the pickers walked into the rows.

"*Yuu* could pass out today. Wear a hat or you'll get sunstroke," my brother warned me. "I feel sorry for them. It's so hot somebody could get sick."

He headed toward the loading station in the center of the field. As Frank had predicted, the temperature shot up fast, and I could feel the water being wrung from my body. The strawberry leaves had wilted in the heat, and the big strawberries were hot to the touch. It was still before eleven in the morning. How hot could it get? According to Anchan, as high as 110 degrees in the summer. I had never experienced 110-degree heat before, and I was worried. Pushing my cart in among the pickers, I began to pick strawberries from rows to my left and right.

The heat struck the usually cheerful Mexicans silent. They packed strawberries into boxes without a word. If you stood up, unable to bear the pain, a wave of dizziness washed over you. The workers knew this, so they would sit down on the ground, stretch out their legs, and rest awhile. Here and there people were already sitting.

A breeze blew up. You'd think a breeze would be pleasant, but it wasn't. Blowing masses of hot, sluggish air to test our endurance, the wind clung to our skin and sucked our bodies dry.

Suddenly a clamor broke out in the silent field. Somebody ahead and to the left of me had fainted. Nearby, Ted yelled, "Ishikawa Junior, lend me a hand. A girl fainted."

I ran up to him and saw that a young Mexican girl had collapsed. Crushed strawberries stained the sides and front of her uniform.

"Give me a hand. You take that side. We'll let her rest in the office." I wondered how often this happened in the field—Ted seemed to know just what he was doing.

Supported on either side by me and Ted, the girl rose unsteadily to her feet. When she shifted her weight over to my side, I was struck by the smell of strawberries mingling with the smell of a woman, and, though I was supposed to be helping someone in trouble, I remember feeling strangely excited. We got her to the office and lay her down on a crummy old bed. Ted wrapped ice from the fridge in a towel and laid it on her forehead.

"You, take care of her for a while," he said to me.

"But, but . . . I don't know what to do. She's Mexican, and I don't speak a word of Spanish."

"*Alrigh yo*. If you keep her head cool, *puri soon* she'll be fine."

"But . . ."

"Don't worry, she'll be *alrigh*." Ted left without waiting for my opinion.

Even inside the office, the temperature didn't differ much from the outside. But being out of the sun helped a lot. A few moments later, the girl seemed to pull herself together.

"What is your name?" I asked her in English.

"María, María Mendoza. *Señor, muchas gracias, muchas gracias*."

"María, *yuu* OK? *Yuu* OK?" was all I could say.

María's neck was soaking wet, and a pool of sweat was gathering on her collar. Gingerly I dabbed her skin with the towel, starting at her neck and moving down to the top of her chest, where her workshirt was fastened by a single button. The touch of something cold on her chest must have startled her, for she jumped with an "ah!" At that moment her blue workshirt popped open, and for an instant I could see her breasts, incredibly white next to the tanned skin above them. María seemed to guess by my flustered look that I had just seen something, and she looked embarrassed. The sensual smell of sweat blending with her own sweet scent were so stifling that I couldn't bear to stay a moment longer.

The back door opened, and Frank came in. Above white-rimmed glasses, sweat poured down his forehead, and his cheeks were bright red; he looked just like a boiled octopus.

"Goddam this heat. If I don't get some of that good stuff from the doctor, I'm gonna kill someone. Ted told me a girl passed out. Is she *alrigh*?"

"Yes, I think she's much better," I answered.

"*Zatso* fine. This girl, she's quite a beauty. There are lots of pretty Mexican girls," said Frank, walking over. "She was here last year, too. They're illegal."

"This girl, too?"

*"Zatso raito.* They all sneak in. Her parents were here last year too. Come to think of it, I haven't seen them this year."

Frank turned to María and said something in Spanish. María answered weakly.

"She says that her parents were caught by immigration this year when they were crossing the border at San Diego, and they were sent back to Mexico. A coyote brought her here alone," Frank explained.

A few minutes later, María sat up slowly, checked the button on her shirt, and said something to Frank.

"This girl says she wants to work more, but that's it for today. I'll give her extra money 'cause I don't want her doing more. If she went back out in this heat, we'd have real trouble on our hands."

Frank gave María a wrinkled five-dollar bill, and she happily tucked it away in her shirt pocket.

"I gotta get the doctor to do his thing. My back started hurting again in the heat."

Before our eyes Frank dialed the phone number. "Doctor? This is Frank. Yes, yes . . . that's it!" Telephone Frank was back. María seemed to have heard about Frank's telephone doctor madness from her friends, and her white teeth flashed in a smile.

She was very cute. Long black hair, big dark eyes, and a hint of long legs visible even under her work pants. Her breasts heaved under the coarse work shirt. Could such a beautiful girl be an illegal alien?

"Doctor, oh, coming, coming," Frank yelled.

As María watched Frank's antics quizzically—he lay groaning on the bed with the phone to his ear—I watched her, feeling a bit like a voyeur. I was strongly attracted to her. Our lives on the farm were made up of nothing but dirt, dust, and sun—María's young body seemed to wake up something in my flesh that I had forgotten.

When I led María out of the office, the oppressive wind engulfed us again. I explained everything to Pete and was about to help María into the car when she paused, seeming to want to thank me. She hugged me lightly, and her cheek brushed mine. For a moment I could feel her firm breasts pressing against my chest.

*"Muchas gracias, señor,"* she said as she got into Pete's car, which sped away.

A glance at my watch told me it was just about noon, time for lunch. The workers had left their little carts in the field and were trudging slowly to the office. As the large group of pickers walked toward me, I could see a shimmering haze rising from their midst. My brother returned with Ted.

"Whew, this heat is awful. If it keeps up like this, I don't know what kinda summer we're gonna have."

*"Thatso righto,* Daiku," Ted echoed. "It's gonna be a long, hot summer."

Long, hot summer . . . that was the only way to put it. The Mexicans had gathered around one of the big trees near the office and were opening the lunches they had brought, but no one looked very hungry.

"You lose your appetite in this heat," my brother said sympathetically. "You must be beat, too. Even I'm feeling fuzzy." Anchan was trying to express his appreciation.

"I've got Ōshima blood in me," I countered. "You think this is going to bother me?"

"If you're tired, it's OK to say so. You're stubborn like Dad," he said, unconvinced of my bravado.

"If you can stand this heat, you can make it through a summer on the farm. Sometime soon, I want to lease our own land and grow strawberries. I've been here about six years altogether. I'm not getting any richer as a hired hand. I make one yen and twenty-five sen an hour. Looks like if we don't get our own farm, we won't be able to send money to Mom. It's hard enough just feeding ourselves."

"I don't know about farming, and I have school, but it sounds like a good idea," I said, aware my brother had originally come to America to make money. "But you've also got to look for your wife, don't you? You know, Anchan, you're still legally married."

"Yeah, that's true. I've been so busy working I haven't given it much thought. But one of these days I'll go try her parents again. They might give me a lead."

After lunch we went back into the field. By the boss's orders, we were allowed to stop work an hour early. When the day was over, I was so tired I could barely talk. After dinner, I went for a walk alone; it was impossible to stay still in a house without an air conditioner or a fan. The sky had turned a light purple. Was it the aftermath of the hot noon sun? That night the farm landscape looked brighter than it did most nights. Holding a cold can of Coke in one hand, I headed toward the field where I had worked all day long. There wasn't a soul there now, but I could hear the coyotes calling.

I walked into the rows of strawberries. Ahead of me I could see the silhouettes of deer. Little puddles formed from the leaks in the pumps that brought water up from below ground, and the deer materialized in search of these puddles. I heard a rustling at my feet—a group of rabbits bounding along in search of water. The heat that day seemed to have threatened the lives of many creatures, and now they came looking for water in our field. We assumed that we had changed wilderness into farmland, but these animals had other ideas.

The image of María's ample white breasts floated up before my eyes. Pressing my hands to my chest, I felt where they had touched me. Would she come to work tomorrow? A sweet sense of breathlessness from María's image came over me, and, tearing off some strawberries, I hurled them at the rabbits with a yell. The strawberries landed in the dark field with a soft thump, startling little creatures who scuttled away. This hot land would scorch everything to death; I gulped for air, the wilderness and my wild feelings becoming unbearable. The first day of the long, hot summer was drawing to a close.

Working on the farm, time seemed to have stopped. Hearing no news about what was happening in the outside world or how other people lived, I picked strawberries day in and day out. If time passed at all, it could only be measured by the darkening of our skins in the sun each day.

Even the change in seasons on the farm didn't start the clock running again. What finally did was the day immigration officials made a surprise raid. All of a sudden, authority asserted itself. Our routine was shattered and we suddenly realized that the farm was just another manmade place to work.

It was early July, just after the afternoon shift had begun. Cars we didn't recognize pulled up at the side of the office, spilling out robust men with guns.

"Immigration! Immigration!" somebody screamed.

The pickers threw down their strawberry boxes and scattered in all directions. Parents who had brought children searched for them frantically in the fray. The Mexicans ran fast. In the blink of an eye the field was empty. But immigration still managed to catch twenty people.

"They got us again," Frank said. "I thought there wasn't going to be one this year. Well, the harvest's almost done, so there won't be too much damage."

"Do they come every year?" I asked.

"Last year, they got us once in the spring and twice in June, at the peak of the season. I had a lot of trouble getting workers."

Right in front of me, the Mexicans were being asked for identification, and the people who didn't have it were loaded into a truck. Among them was José, a young guy I often ate lunch with. He turned toward me and yelled something.

"What's he saying?"

"He's saying 'I'll be back soon,' " Frank interpreted.

I did a double take. María was among the ones who'd been arrested. She had come to work the day after she collapsed, and since then had always spoken to me when we met. In the midst of the drudgery of farm work, just the sight of María made me secretly happy, though we couldn't communicate with each other. Once or twice we had even eaten lunch together in the shade of the big tree near the office. I had never longed so much to be able to speak English or Spanish as I did those days. Every night in bed I fantasized that if I could only speak to her I might be able to caress her full breasts.

María looked very frightened as the immigration officers pushed her into a car. Frank, guessing my feelings, said, "That girl will be back. You know, *Californi* farmers call the *Mexis* pigeons."

"Why?"

"Because pigeons always come back."

"But how can you be so sure? They were just arrested. They can't get back that fast."

"They're taken to the border and dumped somewhere. Then they come back. But take care of the field for me, will you? It's a mess."

The immigration car with María in it disappeared in the distance. Thinking that she would never be mine, I heaved a sigh. Then I set about cleaning up the strawberry boxes and the overturned water tanks. The lives of people here were really quite violent. Americans still lived in the wilderness, even if they did drive huge tractors and luxury cars and have electric appliances in their kitchens.

"*Yuu*, did you see that?" my brother called from behind to me. "Wasn't it unbelievable? Like hunting Indians."

González, our next-door neighbor, was with him.

"What happened to him? He wasn't caught?"

"He's one smart *Mexi*. He knows how to hide. He dived into the basement of the office."

One moment González was smiling, the next he yelled something.

"Anchan, what's he saying?"

" 'Fuck America, this is our land'; that's the gist of it. These guys don't think this is America. It used to be governed by Mexico. Tonight, I'm going to take you somewhere interesting. Nobody's going to show up here tomorrow. The harvest's almost over, so it doesn't matter, but we still need to hire about twenty people. We'll take care of it tonight. We're going to buy people at a place where illegals hang out."

Buy people? I asked myself.

After supper, while it was still light, Anchan, González, and I drove along the narrow dirt farm road. The breeze blowing through the car windows cooled our skin. The sun had set behind a distant mountain range. Nature had drawn quietly back into herself. Now that the cries of the pickers and the rumble of the trucks over the field had faded, an air of melancholy hung over the farm.

González turned the radio to a Latin station and began singing along with the music. The raid that morning seemed quite forgotten; he was back to his old cheerful self.

"These guys love singing. If they have any free time, you can bet they're singing. And they're good," my brother said.

"What kind of songs?"

"Funny ones. 'I'm head over heels in love with you, I adore you.' Sweet stuff, embarrassing to a Japanese."

"So González is singing one of those love songs?"

"Yeah. I'm so in love with you my heart is going to burst. Just once let me kiss your slender fingers. That's the gist of it."

"Wow, what a song."

I stole a look at González; he was beating time on his thigh, moving his head up and down with his eyes half-closed, completely in tune with the music.

"You find this kind of guy in Mexico." My brother pointed at González.

All this time I thought the Mexicans were unexcitable, but actually they held the monopoly on love. They were certainly ten times more passionate than the Japanese.

Thirty minutes later we stopped in a town with nothing but tacky bars and cheap apartments and the strange name of Chino. We got out of the car and went into a place that looked like a bar. The air was ragged with smoke. Music blasted from the jukebox. I guessed the place had about thirty customers in it.

"This is a boardinghouse for the workers. It's supposed to be a bar, but that's just a front. When I get people here, I have to pay the manager five dollars a person. If we take ten tonight, that means paying the guy fifty bucks. Every route to illegal workers has its own rules." As my brother explained this to me, a fat man who looked like the owner came up and embraced him. They launched into conversation.

"Farmers are his best customers, so this guy's big on flattery. He says you're good-looking. OK, we've gotta find some good boys. Maybe I'll leave it up to González tonight. He's pretty good at it."

González seemed to be known; he went around the tables shaking hands and talking. There were only Mexicans in the place.

"Are all these people illegal aliens?"

"Yes."

I looked around curiously. After a while González returned to our table with some people. My brother had explained the situation to him in the car, and he had gone right to the point—they needed pickers for two weeks.

"That's half of them," González said proudly.

"*Muy bien, muy bien.* But they're pretty young, aren't they? Can they do the work?" My brother looked the young men over carefully, like a horse trader examining his wares.

In a heterogeneous society, the employer must base his hiring decision on the interview because he cannot measure the employee's background.

Over many years, hundreds of thousands of workers have settled in America and been absorbed into various jobs. Perhaps the most crucial factor in any of these situations has always been whether a worker can complete the tasks set by the employer. Prejudice and choosing among people begins in the workplace. Racial prejudice in America—especially toward people of color—certainly originates in the superior attitude and self-importance of white culture. But there is another possible cause: the old American looking at the new American with the eye of the horse trader.

"They're young," said González, "but they have green cards, so they're asking you for work."

"Green cards!" Anchan laughed.

Sometimes we just called them Greens because they were printed in green ink. Anchan looked at the cards the men were holding out and burst out laughing again.

"Fakes. I can't believe these guys carry these things around. Listen, this one says he's seventeen, but if you count back from the birth date, he's twenty-three. Look at this. Would immigration let him use a photo showing all his teeth on this kind of document? He just stuck an instant photo on here." I could see he was right. It was a small photo, but the man was smiling widely. As though he had understood, he pulled out another green card.

"These guys are amazing," my brother exclaimed loudly. He was used to Mexicans, but even he was surprised.

"Well, what do you want to do? Hire them?"

"Sure. They look strong. They'll work hard."

When this decision was reported to the Mexicans, they beamed and shook our hands. Two of them were young—seventeen and eighteen—just like me. But they had sneaked into America illegally to look for work. Their courage unnerved me.

"Well, I feel a little better. Now we've found some people."

González told my brother that he wanted to stay and drink awhile and that his friends would bring him home. My brother looked happier than he had in a long time. But even so, the line between a worker and a boss can never be crossed. We decided to leave, and on our way out we passed a white farmer.

"See, he's looking for Mexicans too. Immigration arrests them, and American farmers hire them. Strange country, this one," my brother quipped.

It was ten o'clock when we left the town—the road was so dark that squirrels jumped across the path drawn by our headlights.

"Is that how you always find workers?" I asked my brother.

"Yeah. But there are other ways, too. I feel sorry for them—we're going to work them hard tomorrow." There was a note of sympathy in his voice. "The boss worked me hard, too, at first. And the same thing happened to him when he came here. It's like a game of Old Maid. Next year I want to have my own field. Frank says he's going to sponsor me with the bank. You forget what you're suffering for if you're always working for someone else. Oh, this is wrong. I came too far."

We were on a farm road without any signs in pitch darkness.

"Well, we turned here, so we might as well stop in at Jiisan's place. He should still be up."

"Is he Mexican?" I asked.

"No, no. I told you about the old Japanese who lives on the hill. He's a great old man."

Jiisan lived in a small shack on top of a hill at the southern corner of our field. A light bulb shone brightly at the entrance to the house, drawing a cloud of insects. Our house was awful, but it couldn't beat this one.

"*Goodo ebuningu,*" Anchan yelled. "Hey! Jiisan. Are you there? It's me, Ishikawa."

After a good while the door opened and a small, frail old man appeared. His bathrobe was open at the chest, and the belt was loose, so every few moments the tip of his penis emerged.

"What are you up to—at this hour? Come in."

61

"I brought my brother to meet you. He just came from Japan. Sorry it's so late. *Sleep shite itan jya nai no?* [You weren't asleep, were you?]"

"No, *alrigh yo.*"

Junk was strewn all over the room. Dishes of partly eaten meat and vegetables sat out on the table, and the tablecloth was dotted with coffee and milk stains. Springs poked out of the sofa.

"Do you want anything to drink?" The old man opened his refrigerator. Whenever he moved, his penis peeked out of the bathrobe—I didn't know where to look.

Anchan told the old man a little bit about me. He had leased five acres of land on the hill and was growing strawberries like we were. "America's great," he said to me.

But there are no junky shacks like this anywhere in Japan, I thought. How could he think that when he was living in a place like this?

"Jiisan, when did you come to America?"

"In the twenties. It was awful then."

With this the old man began to talk as my brother made coffee. Jiisan and a brother two years his senior had stowed away on a boat going to Brazil, intending to sneak into the country. But Jiisan had been discovered when the boat stopped at Acapulco, and, leaving his brother aboard, he had dived into the sea and swum to shore. After a year of wandering, he crossed into America the wetback way.

"Lots of Japanese got into America through Mexico," the old man said.

I had assumed that only Mexicans were illegal aliens, but now I discovered that many Japanese had immigrated illegally before the war.

"I was small, so I couldn't get much work—life was hard. Every day I lived in fear of immigration."

Anchan poured coffee. His look told me he had heard the story before.

"So did you ever see your brother again?"

"Never."

"And Japan?"

"Not in forty years," the old man answered disjointedly.

62

Running out of things to say, I looked around the room. Next to the window was a small household altar with offerings and a photograph of what must have been the old man's parents.

"Well, I think it's time to get going," my brother said. "We just stopped by to say hello. You'll have plenty of other chances to talk with Jiisan."

"I want to hear more. You go on home, I'll walk. I know the way through the field, so don't worry," I reassured him.

After my brother left, I lost myself in the old man's talk. He told me that he was born in Okinawa and that many immigrants had come from Okinawa. This was news to me.

"I was lucky. I didn't go to the camps. All the Japanese—even the Japanese Americans—in California were sent to the camps during the war. But not me."

"What camps?" ·

"The desert camps—Japanese here were enemy aliens."

Ted had told me something about the "wartime facilities for Japanese Americans during wartime." In recent years, movies, TV programs, and books on the camps have appeared, but in 1965 not many people in Japan were aware of them. Although the camps are now called internment camps, during the four years I lived in America—1965 to 1969—the Japanese Americans called them removal facilities. Quite likely it was the Japanese in Japan who started calling them internment camps. Not until the seventies, when the media in Japan started to publicize the discrimination against Japanese immigrants in America did the people who had been detained begin to censure American injustice. People have trouble discovering the meaning of their own experiences; they feel more conviction when others do it for them.

"Do you feel like going back to Japan? I'm sure it's changed a lot in forty years."

"No, I don't want to go back. I wouldn't know anybody, and Okinawa was damaged in the war. I spent my life working . . . America's good . . . but my life doesn't amount to much."

I left the house and started to walk. When I looked back, Jiisan was still at the door watching me.

The next day the Mexicans we'd bought came to the field on time and started working. New people had replaced the old ones,

but life on the farm didn't change. Struggle with the heat . . .
pick strawberries . . .

"Ishikawa, thanks for finding workers. Usually after immigration comes, the *Mexis* are wary, and it's hard to find people. But
we're OK this time," Frank said with satisfaction. "After lunch I
want you to go and buy fertilizer. We'll be done picking in a week.
Then we have to get the soil ready for next year—turn it over, put
down fertilizer, and let it rest. I would go with you, but my back's
hurting more than usual."

After lunch Anchan, Pete, Ted, Ramón (a Filipino), and I
headed for the store.

To get to the main road we had to pass Jiisan's field, where five
Mexicans were working for him. He had put up Japanese scarecrows to protect his strawberries. The sight of Japanese scarecrows
on a California farm with all the latest in farm equipment was
indescribably funny.

The old man was picking strawberries unsteadily. The night
before he had told me he'd never had a wife and family. Was this
all there was to his life? A crow swooped down, and he shooed it
away feebly.

"The farmer plants seeds, and the crow digs them up. That's a
true saying." My brother laughed.

On the last day of the harvest, we finished work by noon. In the
afternoon Frank threw a good-bye party. My brother and I contrib-
uted a couple dozen chickens we had marinated the night before
in soy sauce and garlic. Barbecues had been set up near the office,
and there were snacks to go with beer. The smell of roasting soy
sauce wafted over the field, and the smoke from the fires drifted
lazily toward the sky, where the sun shone down more gently than
usual.

"Thank you, everybody. We had a good crop and made a profit
this year. Take next week off, then we have to plow the field,"
Frank announced.

"Good job. You're even starting to look like a California farmer,"
Ted said, passing me a huge piece of chicken. It was true that I
had developed some muscles.

"Hey, you guys, how're you spending the vacation? How about

the horse races in Del Mar? They start soon. I won a lot last year." Ted loved horse races.

The Mexicans gulped down beer and filled themselves up on barbecued chicken. Five or six big buses were waiting for them by the office, and after the farewell party a coyote would take about fifty of them to work on a grape farm in central California. For each person the coyote would get $5 from the grape farmer—$250 for fifty people. The coyote made a good living. Mexicans could find work by themselves, but it was very difficult. Workers without cars ended up totally dependent on coyotes.

Anchan told me a story about the economics of the border: "The ones who made a lot of money are going home. The illegal who made the most money this year is a guy who runs a ranch in Sonora. On our farm he gets about fifteen dollars a day. He says that it pays the daily wages of ten men on his ranch in Mexico. Isn't that amazing?"

The party was nearing an end, and Frank went around shaking hands, saying, "Please come again next year." I shook the hands of the men I knew and said the same in English.

As the Mexicans piled into the buses, one man yelled something out the window.

"Ted, what's he saying?"

"He's saying 'I shall return.' "

"Sounds like MacArthur," said my brother, who was standing next to us.

"They'll be back. Ishikawa-kun, María will be back next year, I *thinku*," said Frank.

By three o'clock all the Mexican "pigeons" had disappeared. The sun poured down on the silent, empty field.

"It's lonely when they go. Wherever you look, just fields." At my brother's words, Frank, the boss, and all the supervisors— Pete, Ted, Charlie, Ramón, González, and Antonio—gazed out at the field where they had been working for the past year. This was the time of year when thousands of Mexican workers left the farms around LA and headed north.

"I remember when I first came here. Wandering from farm to farm, every man with his own blanket," Frank reminisced.

"Are there any Japanese blanket men left who migrate with them?" I asked.

"Probably a couple hundred," Frank explained. "They didn't come this year, but usually three or four show up. It's tough—moving all over the place with everything you own in your car. All the Japanese were blanket men before the war. You met Jiisan from Okinawa, who lives on top of the hill. He only got his field three years ago. When you sneak into the country, immigration won't catch you if you keep moving. There are *mebi oba* million illegal aliens working in this country. Without them, American farms would go broke, so they overlook it."

The next day I slept late for the first time in ages. We no longer had to get up at five or six to begin picking. After I finished some easy cleanup work that day, I would be on vacation for a week. The plan was to go to San Diego in two cars, see the horse races, go shopping, and take a drive around the area. Having been in America for only three months, I couldn't wait for my first short trip.

At seven, my brother still hadn't emerged from his room. His exhausted body must have known that it only had half a day of work to do, and it wasn't about to wake up early. "If you're tired, rest." Ordinary words popped out of my mouth while I was making coffee.

González and Antonio must have still been asleep—there wasn't a peep from next door. All alone, I opened the door and went out. By this time yesterday, the Mexicans would have been gathering and talking and we would have been working the tractors, but now the field was empty and even the air seemed purer than usual. I bit into a few shriveled strawberries, but a rotten taste filled my mouth, and I spat them out immediately. Strawberry season was definitely over.

At about ten o'clock, I headed to the field and began to clean up—gathering strawberry boxes and tidying farm tools. Some of the berries in the field still looked worth selling, but they would be left for a week and then turned over by a tractor.

As I was eating lunch under the big tree next to the office, two strange cars, one a large station wagon, pulled up. In spite of the heat, the two Japanese men who got out of the cars wore suits. No one could mistake them for farmers.

"Bank guy," said Frank, stuffing a sandwich in his mouth. "Sumitomo Bank, Japantown."

The man called out to Frank.

"How are you, Frank? Hear you made a lot of money this year. How about joining our fixed savings plan?" The bank man looked and sounded like a Japanese salaryman who's just been sent abroad.

"The boss is one of their biggest accounts," Anchan told me. "Once I went to that bank in Japantown with him, and I couldn't believe my eyes. We were taken way to the back—"

"They come all the way from Japantown just to collect deposits?"

"Obviously. No American is going to save in a Japanese bank. So the bankers have to collect deposits of five or ten dollars from the Japanese on the farms. That reminds me. You made some money this summer, so you should put five dollars away every month—they'll come and get it for you."

As Anchan was explaining this to me, the man in the station wagon took an armful of electric rice cookers out of the car and spread them out on the ground. "This is the latest electric rice cooker. Now you can make perfect rice automatically." The salesman began describing the efficiency of the cooker in great detail. He was from the Matsushita Electric Corporation I knew so well—NATIONAL was written across his boxes.

"Anchan, do these Japanese businessmen come all the way out here to sell?"

"Yeah, sure. Whites don't use electric rice cookers. Besides, Japanese products have a bad reputation because they always break. You remember that broken-down car we helped fix last week? It was a Japanese car. The driver was so mad—'How's a car supposed to run when it doesn't use much gas?' he asked me. Japanese cars have weak engines 'cause they don't use a lot of gas. You can't drive on California freeways without power. The only clients these guys have is us."

Japan had just started exporting cars in the early sixties, and the first year they sold fewer than two hundred cars. Even by the summer of '65, not many Japanese cars were on California roads. The broken-down car was the only one I had seen.

"If we don't buy Japanese products," my brother said patriotically, "they won't be able to send dollars to Japan."

"*Thatso righto, Daiku.* If we don't buy Japanese things and save in Japanese banks, our country will be in trouble," Frank echoed.

Stirred by the patriotic sentiments of all around me, I decided to deposit five dollars a month in a savings account. My brother indulged himself in an electric rice cooker.

I still can't forget that scene. Only twenty-five years have passed since then, and when I think of my five-dollar deposits and of the men who drove over sixty miles to pick up small amounts of money at isolated farms, I am amazed by the growth of the Japanese financial system. Nowadays, four Japanese banks rank among the top ten in California. At the same time, Japanese money is buying up skyscrapers in Los Angeles, San Francisco, and Manhattan.

What happened in twenty years? Of course, one is tempted to say that everybody and his brother in Japan worked very hard, while Americans only thought of enjoying themselves. But were Americans really taking it easy in those days? As a person who lived and worked in America at the time, I would definitely say no. For example, the Mexicans who frequented our farm, my brother, Frank, Ted, the Filipino Ramón, and the white man Charlie worked themselves to the bone. And it wasn't just the people on our farm. The neighboring farmers, the schoolteachers, and the factory workers worked very hard too.

But America had a problem in the sixties that couldn't be solved by hard work alone. America had to move forward shouldering a new burden. After President Kennedy launched civil rights reforms, blacks, Mexicans, and other minorities who had been almost like slaves began entering various enterprises and participating in the social framework of the country. The established social order began to creak on its foundations. America in the sixties was frantically trying to adjust to these changes.

I clearly remember blacks from the South driving up in junkers looking for work on the farm.

Far from being lazy, Americans were willing to confront racial problems that the Japanese would never touch as they struggled through the sixties.

From the vantage point of a farm in California twenty-five years ago, however, Japan's rapid growth seems more than a miracle to me. There's nothing to be done if people say, "Japan is doing something unfair." Our country simply progressed too fast.

After the businessmen had left, my brother became nostalgic and began to sing a commercial jingle. " 'Happy National. Happy National. Radios, televisions, everything's National.' *Yuu*, remember that song? It takes me back. It was on the radio all the time in Ōshima. And now the same National is here."

"Tomorrow is San Diego," Frank said. "Let's stop for today."

"Yeah, tomorrow we get to play with Mexican girls," Ted said lightly.

My heart skipped a beat.

That night my brother went to Japantown by himself. Going to San Diego meant visiting the parents of his runaway wife, and my brother had to take them a present—preferably something Japanese—so he drove all the way to Little Tokyo to shop.

I planned to write letters to my parents and friends from high school, so I stayed home. I hadn't written them for a long time, because the last thing my tired body wanted to do after a day in the field was pick up a pen. When I finally did begin to write about my life, scene after scene of the Japan I loved rose before my eyes.

Overwhelmed by a rush of homesickness, I wasn't able to write another word. As I stared into space, longing for Japan, I could hear a woman's voice coming from next door. González and his buddies must have brought their girlfriends back. Again I heard the woman's voice, but this time it didn't sound like she was laughing; it sounded passionate.

"No, they couldn't be doing that."

I put down my pen and pressed my ear to the wall. There was no doubt about it. They were doing it. With my ear to the wall, I could hear everything clearly—the woman's gasps blending with González's moans. The bed was creaking.

My heart began to pound.

I remembered Ted saying that he was going to "play with the

69

Mexican girls." I wondered if I would get the chance, too. Could I find someone like that cute María? The sight of María's unforgettable body lingered before me.

The voices next door grew even more frantic. I couldn't bear to stay in the house any longer and ran out. A blue moon lit up the field. Trying to calm the desires boiling inside me, I ran down the road.

When I reached the middle of the field, I turned back; there in the distance was our little house, with the lights still on in the windows. Someone was making love to a woman in the next room.

Visions of a sexy woman materialized before my eyes and faded away. I looked all around me. Nothing. The only thing I could see was the blue light of the moon bathing the western edge of the field.

Soon my hand was loosening my belt and slowly caressing my hot, swollen penis. María, an image in shadow. Faster and faster till white liquid spurted out over the strawberry rows—bright for a second in the moonlight.

Still holding myself, I let out a sigh and sat down weakly in the field. I could feel something wet on my bottom—probably squashed strawberries. I lay down spread-eagled in the dirt and gazed up. The moon shone so brightly it was unnerving. Rabbits jumped through the rows.

Being all alone at night on a farm is too cruel for the body of an eighteen-year-old. I could hear the coyotes howling off in the distance. I, too, began to cry.

# 5

# Borders

We set out for San Diego in two large station wagons. I rode in Ted's car with Ramón the Filipino, and Charlie the white guy. Anchan, Frank, Pete, and González went in the other. Rather than go along the coast on Interstate 5, we decided to cut across the mountains on back roads.

"*Guddo* view this way. You'll get to see small towns and dairy farms. Ishikawa's *buraza* doesn't know how big California really is, so we'll take the mountain roads," Frank said as we left.

Off the freeway we drove at about 50 mph, which seemed incredibly fast to me. Through the front window I had a great view of the plain spreading out before us as we drove past huge eucalyptus trees on either side of the road. We drove on and on, our line of sight stretching out to the horizon. It was summer, and the green southern California land of April was now a withered yellow. It occurred to me that it hadn't rained once since my arrival.

"*Yuu*, dry, eh? If you lit one of these bushes, the whole place'd go up. Lots of brushfires around here—there's always some joker who wants to have fun," explained Ted as he drove.

"It's dry as a bone. Does it ever rain here?"

"Hmm. *Ocutoba meibee* it'll rain. This year there wasn't nothing but rain toward the end of March. So it's *sebun monsu no rain.*"

"Where do you get water from?"

"From the Sierra Nevada Mountains. Plus we use *undawara*. *Yuu* saw pumps in the field, right? They draw up the *undawara*. If the *undawara* dries up, no more *farma jobu*. Water's like gold in

71

*Californi,"* said Ted, teaching me the farmer's ABC's. *"Yuu* probably know this already, but we have to depend on wetbacks, on mountains hundreds of miles away, and on *undawara* we can't measure. We got water now but, what if all of a sudden, *no wara camzu outo.* What would we do? Or if the pigeons don't come back next year, *shinku whato wiru happun."*

While I was talking to Ted, Charlie and Ramón were talking to each other excitedly in English. Every once in a while, I heard the word *girl,* and assumed that they were referring to the girls they would pick up in San Diego.

Charlie was forty and came from Nebraska. Four years back, he had divorced his wife, left his family behind, and driven alone down Route 66 looking for work in California, which he found when he stopped at our field. He was a small and friendly man.

Ramón was well over fifty. During the Pacific War, he had suffered terribly at the hands of Japanese soldiers on his native island, Luzon, and he didn't hold a good opinion of us. Sometimes he made nasty remarks about us in the field. But today he was in a holiday mood. *"Ay, yai, yai, yai,"* he yelled, baring his yellow teeth.

"So," Ted continued, "that's why us farmers always say *famingu isu gambur.* That's the long and short of it."

At that moment our car was surrounded by about ten motorcycles ridden by long-haired youths wearing sunglasses. There were about ten of them.

"Goddam. Hell's Angels. Fuck you." Ted swore loudly.

The men in headbands were trying to slow down our car.

"Hell's Angels?"

*"Autobike curazy yo.* You've seen them on the freeway, haven't you? Young people nowadays, *curazy.* I know they're upset about the Vietnam War, but . . ."

The Hell's Angels was first formed by motorcycle aficionados in 1950 in San Bernardino, about 40 miles east of Pomona. In the 1960s, under the leadership of Ralph Sonny Burger—a biker with great charisma—the group turned into something like a religious cult. While America was rushing headlong into a tumultuous era of civil rights, black power, the antiwar movement, and sexual freedom, some young Americans protested against the establishment by making over their motorcycles (their symbol was the "chopper," a bike that had a small front wheel and a large back one) and joining up. There were Hell's Angels all over the country, but many were in California. They would drive past our farm on Route 66 making enough noise to wake the dead.

"Fuck you!" screamed Ted.

"Uh . . . Ted, what does 'fuck you' mean?" Since coming to America, I had heard people say *fuck* in conversation all the time without understanding what it meant. But this time I asked.

"Fuck is, well . . ." Ted sounded a little bashful.

"Fuck is *omechoko* in Japanese. What a girl has."

"Huh? . . ." I was flabbergasted.

"So you just said to those guys—you *omechoko*?"

*"Zatso raito."*

"It's incredible—what you say in English."

"What? You don't say 'fuck' in Japan? I wouldn't know 'cause I've never been there, but *omechoko* is OK for 'fuck,' right? Is there another way to say it?"

"Well, uh, the truth is it's better to say *omanko*." A word that I had never used in Japan slipped out of my mouth.

"Oh, it's not *omechoko*, but *omanko*?"

Ted emphasized the word *omanko*, which caused Charlie, who was sitting next to him, to ask, "What's *omanko*?"

Ted explained in English.

"What'd you say, Ted?" asked Charlie again.

Oh no, I thought, but it was too late. Next Ramón said *omanko* in his funny accent. Then Ted started again. The car was abuzz with four-letter words.

"OK, everybody, we got to do *omanko* tonight. Did I get it right?" Ramón yelled coarsely after he finally understood the word.

Unable to stand another volley of these words, I kept my mouth shut. At the same time, I found it interesting that people of all nationalities were fascinated by four-letter words. In the midst of this commotion, the Hell's Angels had disappeared.

"Ishikawa, tonight I find you a nice girl," offered Ted.

I had started it all by asking him about *fuck,* now the whole group was in the mood.

"You're not a *cherri boi*, right?" Ted asked.

"*Cherri boi?* You mean a young boy?"

"No, no. *Cherri boi* is . . . how do you say it? . . . a boy who never fucked a girl."

"You mean a virgin? No, I had a reputation in high school," I said, feeling compelled to bluff in front of the veterans. "Yeah, I had a couple of girls."

Still talking, we arrived in San Diego. In the harbor, warships of all shapes and sizes were moored tightly together.

"Wow, it's incredible. If you had this many warships, you could beat any country," said my brother.

"Nice breeze," said Frank, the sweatiest member of our group. "I wonder how much cooler it is here than on the farm."

The sun glittered on the water, making it impossible to stare at the sea for long.

"The sun sets over there. It's gorgeous. All that hard work on the farm just melts away. Listen, everyone, I want you to have a good time in San Diego, so I'm giving you a bonus," Frank said, handing out fifty-dollar bills to all of us. "I've been invited over to a Japanese farmer's house nearby, so maybe I'll stay there tonight. My friend is coming to pick me up soon. Tomorrow we'll all go to the horse races together."

"I'm going to visit my wife's parents. *Yuu* coming?" my brother asked me.

"No, I won't understand them, and I don't know what to say to them either," I replied.

"Well, get Ted and those guys to take you shopping in Tijuana. I might be back late. Her parents did a lot for me once."

We left our luggage in the hotel and got ready for the business of the night. Ted, Charlie, Ramón, González, and I decided to go to Tijuana. It took only thirty minutes to reach the town on the Mexican border, and at five o'clock it was still light; we had plenty of time to enjoy ourselves.

"This is the border town," Ted explained. Mexicans were selling various goods at outdoor stalls. "Everything's cheap here. That's why the whites come here to shop. Look! See that fence—that's the line between Mexico and America. The Americans go shopping over there with dollars. Like *yuu*, how much does a haircut cost in

America? About two-fifty with tip, right? But across the border you can get a haircut for about twenty cents. *Puri guu.*"

"But is it that easy to cross?"

"Sure, it's open twenty-four hours, and you don't need a passport or a visa. It's like having a free pass. But if you're Mexican, forget it. They get in big trouble if they come over here. I bet all the *Mexis* would move to America if they could."

We walked over to the fence that marked the border. One glance at the Mexicans beyond told me how poor they were; shabby houses that looked more like pigpens were packed together, and I could hear the cries of half-naked children. A bunch of Mexicans on the other side were peeping through at us. One of them called out to me in Spanish.

"What's he saying?"

"He says, 'I'm coming in tonight. Got any work for me?' The *Mexis* know that the Japanese have farms, so whenever they see us they ask for work."

An immigration official walked up to us, looking suspicious of my exchange with the man on the other side.

"Just try to come in, and I'll break open your head," he said, brandishing his stick at the Mexicans. The Mexicans responded in kind.

"What did they say?"

" 'Think you could catch us.' "

Just then four or five men leapt over the 6½-foot chain-link fence right in front of the officer and ran off. The officer followed in hot pursuit.

"They come in that way even during the day?"

"*Yuu,* at night hundreds, even thousands, of them leap over the fence the same way. Might as well not have a border. But, if the *Mexis* stop coming, we farmers are in big trouble. The American government knows this, so they go easy on border patrol."

As I listened to Ted's words, I touched the border. An ordinary chain-link fence was all that divided the two countries. America had big houses, kitchens with hot water, televisions, and all the comforts of modern life, while on the other side (as far as I could tell) people lived in houses that looked like pigsties without television, radio, or even work. It was strange that a single fence could make such a difference. This was the first border I had ever seen, and I felt disappointed by its crudeness. And I got butterflies in my stomach looking at it.

Charlie seemed to sense my confusion. "Young man," he said, "do you know why there are two different countries on either side of this fence, even though they share the same continent? I'll tell you why. Spain came to Mexico looking for gold. Get it? Gold. But our ancestors came here searching for God. Do you understand me, young man? This is important. The letter *L* is the only thing that separates *God* from *gold,* but the Spaniards were greedy for *L.* The letter *L* makes a big difference. That's why Mexico turned out so differently from America. The people who were looking for gold got poor, and the people looking for God got rich. People must worship God."

Charlie, a fundamentalist Christian, fixed me with his blue eyes and enunciated each word slowly. At the time, I didn't have the knowledge or the English ability to rebut him, so I merely nodded my head. Now, whenever I cross a border I remember Charlie's simple, self-serving American logic.

Night had come to Tijuana. We went into a Mexican restaurant and filled up on tacos, tortillas, and burritos. Spanish was the only language we could hear. The town was dirty, but it hummed with energy.

"*Yuu*, your brother's not around, so you can *puray* with a *garu* here before we go back to San Diego," suggested Ted. There were lots of whorehouses in Tijuana. "We'll have González take us," said Ted, turning to address González in Spanish.

After dinner, González led us to a big house. Inside about ten Mexican girls, in low-cut long or backless dresses, were sitting on a sofa, obviously with time on their hands. One glance betrayed their profession. Would I do it tonight, finally? My knees went weak.

"*Yuu*, which one do you want? It costs five dollars, and a two-dollar tip will make her happy," instructed Ted.

González and Ramón seemed quite at home in the place, and they started joking around. With a wink at me, they took the hands of the girls they had chosen and started up the stairs. Charlie had decided instead to drink at a bar at the edge of town.

76

Swirls of cigarette smoke and the scent of strong cologne gave the place an air of decadence.

"*Yuu,* how about that girl? She's small and pretty," Ted recommended.

Taking a deep breath, I approached the girl. She wasn't as pretty as María, but her skin was golden and her eyes sparkled.

As I was about to lead her by the hand up the stairs, Ted leaned close to me and said worriedly, "*Yuu,* you know how to *maku rabu?*"

"Don't worry," I lied.

"Good luck," Ted said, drawing his girl upstairs with him.

The woman took my hand and pushed open the door to her room. Next door I thought I could hear González's voice.

When we got inside, the woman spoke to me in Spanish, and though I couldn't understand a word, I could see doubt lurking in her eyes. How was I to begin?

At that moment I remembered reading articles in the magazines *Wife's Helper, Wife's Club,* and *Heibon Punch* on how to make love to a woman. With these as my guide, I put my hands on her shoulders without a word and drew her to me. The woman responded and pressed her lips lightly against mine. Then she pushed my hands away and went off to the shower.

The sensation of my first kiss lingered, and, touching my fingers to my lips, I sniffed them; I could see faint traces of lipstick. When the woman emerged from the shower, she was wrapped only in a towel. The sight of her made me tremble, and I had to go take a shower to calm myself down. When I came back, she was lying in bed. I knew we couldn't speak to each other, but if I didn't say something, I knew that it wouldn't go any further. I racked my brains for something to say. Finally I decided on her name.

"*¿Como se llama?*"

"María."

"María!"

Her name was María too. I felt relieved, for at least now I knew the name of the woman I was going to sleep with. I lifted the sheet and climbed into bed next to her. Her naked body was very firm. It was hard to believe that she was a prostitute.

In the next room González seemed to be having a great time.

Memories of the other night's mingled voices through the wall came back, and my excitement rose. Every muscle in my body tensed. I climbed on top of the woman and began to caress her hungrily. Though I couldn't ask her where she was born, how many men she had slept with, or what her life was like, I had entrusted my body to her. As I rubbed the prostitute's breasts, a vision of María's white breasts in the office rose up behind my closed eyes. This woman's body, like María's, gave off a sweet scent. In the next room González and his woman were coming to a climax. Their savage cries tore at my insides. I no longer cared about anything—the loneliness, the hard work, the inability to communicate, the frustration—all was forgotten as I fumbled to find the opening in her body and felt her mound against me.

The next morning I was drinking coffee by myself in the hotel in San Diego when Ted, the early riser, found me.

"*Goodo moningu. Yuu,* up early as usual. Farmers get in the habit. Even on a holiday, *weiku upu suru.* You're looking more and more like a California farmer. You know, before the war, Japanese farmers all came to Tijuana for women. If you made money in the field, you got a woman in Tijuana. There was even a brothel run by a Japanese man. *Butto yuu, lasto nighto maku rabu wa?* Were you good?"

The question I had feared had come. If he had to ask me if I had been good, the only thing to say was yes. Before running into Ted, I had been mulling over the very same question. I knew about prostitution from the *onlys* who had lived on our island. I remembered one of the ones I liked best laughing and talking with her friends one day. "Oh . . . it's that time already? My *darulingu* will be home from the base soon. Let me tell you, last night we did it so much I hurt all over. My *darulingu* is a horny one. If it's like that tonight—oh no, I can't stand it!"

In those days in California I was pretty confident about the knowledge of sex I had gleaned from the erotic books we passed around and things I heard in the street. All my expectations were focused on the ritual of sex. The American women I saw at school, on the street, and at the beach were very beautiful, and they seemed the ideal choice to put my secondhand knowledge into practice.

At the same time, however, I knew that I could buy sex, and since I wanted to experience it as soon as possible, I had taken the easy way out. My morals told me that I should have waited to meet a girl I loved, and grown close to her before making love to her. In the end, my first partner had not been the María who set my heart pounding but a woman who would sleep with anyone for five dollars. My only consolation was that I had finally gone the whole way. Still, I was overwhelmed by emptiness for having come to it that way.

To top it all off, the prostitute had gotten dressed when we were finished and left the room abruptly. I felt awful. As we walked back to our hotel, the others bragged about how wonderful their women had been, but I felt no urge to join in the conversation.

Under these circumstances, I didn't feel like answering Ted's question. I thought he wouldn't understand how upset I was, so I avoided responding directly. "Japanese girls and Mexican girls are both women," I said. "But, Ted, do the Japanese farmers always come to Mexico when they want a woman? White women are *betta*, don't you think? Why do you come all this way? If you're going to *puray*, why not pay a white woman?" I, too, had started talking like the farmers. Sometimes I hated myself for doing it, but it was even stranger to speak normal Japanese in the fields; without realizing it I was becoming more like one of the men.

"No American girl's going to *puray* with Japanese. No matter how much money we have, white girls won't touch us. Before the war *nebaa;* now *meibee* a few would. . . . *Mee* don't know. That's why we come all the way to Tijuana. Mexican girls are *alrigh yo*."

I had in fact seen a number of Japanese men who looked like farmers as I wandered around Tijuana the night before. Maybe they had come looking for fun, too. I asked Ted.

"*Meibee soo*. You know, everybody's talking about *furee sexu* in America, but it has nothing to do with the Japanese or the Mexicans."

According to Ted, free sex only happened in one segment of American society; it would never reach our community. My friends in Japan who were going to college or getting jobs wrote me letters: "I envy you. With all this free sex in America, how many girls have you slept with?" To me, however, free sex was an elusive dream.

I also began to get letters from my friends in college, who had joined the student movement. "I want to fight against the imperialist American invasion of Vietnam" was a typical sentiment. My friends would ask whether I was fighting American imperialism and racial discrimination, but on the farm, where we made our money off the sweat of illegal aliens, you could turn over many a stone and never find such bright words. It was hot on the farm and language broke down and we could barely protect ourselves from roasting alive. Although I looked forward to my friends' letters, I also began to dread them.

Anchan got back from his wife's parents' house around noon. I didn't want him to know about the night before, so I pretended that nothing had happened. I might have bragged about my sexual exploits to friends, but not in front of my own flesh and blood.

"I found out where my wife is, but she has a boyfriend. Maybe it's my fault because I was late coming back here. . . . There's nothing to be done about it now. . . . I left a message for her with her parents. One of these days she'll show up with divorce papers. Well, it's about time I started a new life."

When Frank got back to the hotel, we all went and had fun at the horse races in Del Mar, a resort town about twenty miles north of San Diego. That night we stayed at a motel in town, and the next day we spent the whole day driving through the Imperial Valley, on the Mexican border. The sky was blue and clear, not a cloud in sight, and we were swallowed up by the wilderness. Every now and then we stopped at a small coffee shop, had a cold drink, then climbed back into the car. Was this what my brother had meant in his letters when he described America?

America in 1965, the year I turned eighteen, meant being unable to understand the language, picking strawberries, living in a shack with my brother, and struggling with the sharp sexual desires that often plagued me. America was the farm. But there was another America out there, and it was rushing headlong into turbulent times.

On June 3, *Gemini 4* took off. Over the next four days, it

successfully circled the earth sixty-two times. Though I couldn't understand what people were saying, I was duly awed. At the same time, I felt ashamed for not celebrating as loudly as the American kids.

The Vietnam War was escalating in 1965, and the kids who were old enough for the draft began to whisper about it among themselves. That February, America had started bombing North Vietnam, and by July Secretary of State Rusk had declared, "There is no sacred ground in Vietnam."

As the war escalated, so did the antiwar movement. In March, three hundred Americans had sent a letter to the *New York Times* demanding that the government immediately cease military intervention in Vietnam. At the same time, various minority groups rallied and the civil rights movement gained momentum. On February 21, Malcolm X, the black Muslim leader, was assassinated.

America wasn't, however, all antiwar movements and riots in those days. Hippies appeared around 1963, looking for a new life, love, and peace. With them came the drug culture centering on marijuana and LSD. By the time I arrived, the subculture was spreading across the nation. The Beatles had started a revolution in music, and, as their music crossed the Atlantic, the frenzy became more and more extreme. In my high school, one band played frenetic hard rock during lunchtime. The students, clapping their hands and shaking their hips in time to the music, were in ecstasy.

The words *freedom, love,* and *peace* were on every young person's lips. Freedom, love, and peace. Can anyone say these words now with the same enthusiasm people had in those days? People then believed utterly in the power of these three words, and chanted them deliriously. LOVE AND PEACE stickers were pasted on cars, and T-shirts had hearts printed on them: it was everywhere.

On Sunset Boulevard in Los Angeles, hundreds, even thousands of young people gathered each night to sit in, hug, debate, play guitar, recite antiwar poetry, and create their own "zone of liberation." The first flower children—pretty young girls in long dresses with flowers in their hair—walked the streets of southern California.

Antiwar demos, drugs, hippies, identity, antiestablishment, rock, African-American riots, flowers . . . The America of 1965 was rumbling, about to explode, and it continued this way until the early seventies, when people began to talk about the "end of the American century." During the years I spent on the farm, the country went through some of its biggest changes. But the waves created by those changes never reached our Japanese immigrant community.

Change came to our community in different forms. By about 1965, the traditional Japanese blanket men—the migrant workers—were disappearing. At the same time, Japanese enterprises began to prosper in Japantown, and businessmen began to outnumber the old immigrants. But this wasn't true only of Japantown. California as a whole began to change from an agricultural state into a commercial one. Even Japan had been stimulated by demands for goods during the Vietnam War and had started on its crazy upward economic spiral. Upon my return in 1969, I was awestruck by how much Tokyo had changed.

I had lived on a farm in California in the midst of great changes, but I never felt the direct effects; it was as if I was living on the margins of a country, an age, and a people.

That summer something else happened to me that in some ways eclipsed sleeping with a woman. In late August, I was invited to a party, where I met a person who would become very important to me.

Pomona was the largest town near the farm. In Los Angeles County, Pasadena is famous for the Rose Parade, which is held there every January 1. But Pomona, the shipping center for all southern California citrus before the war, is also well-known. The fair held every September in LA county originated in this town.

In the 1920s, nearly two thousand Japanese blanket men lived in Pomona. Although now there isn't much left of the thriving Japanese community, in 1965, there were still fifty Japanese households in the center of town.

Every year the Pomona Japanese-American Society would celebrate their children's high school graduations with presents and a huge party. Parents who had been victims of anti-Japanese sentiment before the war had only been able to do manual labor, and a good education for their children made life worth living. First-generation Japanese parents threw themselves wholeheartedly into the party. Today, second- and third-generation families continue to throw parties to encourage their children and pay homage to those who came before them.

Pete, my boss's younger brother, invited me to one of these parties. *"Yuu,* want to go to a Japanese high school graduation party? *Me no furendo* is chairman *yo.* There'll be a lot of food. My friend can get you in."

Pete didn't understand the nature of the problem, and his plan worked without a hitch. It was decided that I would attend the party in spite of the fact that I had just arrived from Japan and, more importantly, hadn't been able to graduate from high school. I didn't feel much like going.

The party was held in a shabby church hall. A long banner in Japanese hung over the entrance—THE POMONA JAPANESE-AMERICAN SOCIETY CONGRATULATES OUR HIGH SCHOOL GRADU-ATES.

"I'm going to watch a movie downtown. I'll pick you up at the end," Pete said, leaving me there.

As usual, Pete had abandoned me. I felt terrible.

I entered the room timidly. About a dozen students and forty parents were mingling in loud conversation.

"Kathy, congratulations." "Bill, Frank, George, how are you?"

Listening to the flat-faced, short-legged nisei and sansei calling each other by their American names, I burned with shame. Kathy, I thought to myself, if you were in Japan a name like Hanako or Momoko would be good enough for you, wouldn't it? And Bill, you jerk, I'd give you a name that would suit you, like Yotaro or Kinhachi. I couldn't stand the way the nisei kids kissed and hugged as they congratulated each other.

When white Americans embraced they looked happy and natural. The nisei kids—with their yellow faces, snub noses, and flat chests—might have acted just as easygoing and unself-conscious as the white kids, but underneath their "white" gestures, I caught glimpses of an inferiority complex. It drove me crazy. They could say they were Americans all they wanted, but they wore their insecurities on their sleeves. I had begun to wrestle with my own deep-seated prejudices.

I was in search of a seat when a voice called to me from behind, "Are you the student from Japan? There's a seat here." It was a pleasant-looking man with a thin face. He did not speak Japanese English with all its *yuu*'s and *mee*'s, and there was an air about him that distinguished him from the farmers. I finally sat down next to him and his wife.

"What part of Japan are you from?"

"Tokyo—no, actually Ōshima Island in the Izu chain. Do you know it? It's the one with the dormant volcano, Mihara."

"Eh?" the old man interrupted. "I'm from Shimoda in Izu. Isn't that surprising, dear? He's from Izu Ōshima." He turned to his wife. She had white hair and looked very intelligent.

"When did you come to America?" I asked.

"Let's see. About forty-five years ago."

"Are you a farmer?"

"No, I'm the minister of a church."

I felt disappointed. All the other Japanese in America sweated blood to make a living while this couple read the Bible, so I dismissed them. Before long the party began. The president of the Japanese-American association gave a speech: "On this wonderful night, we are proud of our fine students who, like the students before them, will be attending first-rank American colleges." Then he pointed a finger in my direction and added, "Tonight we would also like to welcome a student from Japan. Let us pray that our organization will continue to grow and flourish."

The moderator then read aloud the names of the students, their grades, and the colleges they would be attending. When the names of the best universities in California—UCLA or Berkeley—were read, you could hear comments around the room: "Their kid studied hard" or "That's impressive."

The boy who had looked the most put out when I had spoken to him at school was going to UCLA on a scholarship from the society and went around shaking hands with everyone. He smiled at me, and I managed to stammer, "Congratulations."

The minister, whom I would come to call Sensei, or "teacher," said, "It must be confusing for you. But you'll understand better soon. You must come visit us. I'd like to hear about Izu." He lived less than a thirty-minute walk from our house.

"If only we'd met earlier, Sensei, I could have brought you strawberries, but now the season's over."

"Don't worry about it." The minister laughed softly.

Soon it was time to eat, and the tables were piled high with barbecued chicken and sushi and other dishes brought from home. The focus of the party slowly switched from the children to their parents, and soon the singing began. We heard Hanakasa Ondo, "Geisha Waltz," and the military song "Soldier Gods of the Sky." As the atmosphere grew more and more Japanese, the children made their thank-you's all around and left. Parents who had acted very American earlier mysteriously began to behave more like Japanese once their children had left.

Americans wouldn't accept the nisei children as Americans, and they weren't Japanese by my standards. There was even a language barrier between these kids and their parents: "Bill, *yuu* go to UCLA? *Goodo na unibāshite yo na. Yuu,* what you going to *meja* in? *Whatto? Kemisutori?* Hey, Missus Yamada-san, what is *kemisutori?* Oh, chemistry. I don't know anything about it, but it sounds like *hardo sutadei. Zattso goodo. Biru, wa-ku hardo.*"

This was the way Japanese parents talked to the children. Children who knew Japanese only by hearing it at home would make a guess at what was being asked and respond in English. When they used an English word like *chemistry,* the Japanese parents had to turn to their neighbors for help. How tiring it must be for parents to converse this way with their children.

Now I understood the reason Americans always use high-sounding words like *communication, conversation, media,* and *debate:* because of the many barriers that have arisen among so many different groups. To an American who lives in a heterogeneous society, the "barrier" is a reality of everyday life. Today America is engaged in aggressively trying to knock down Japanese trade and market barriers. The reason Americans are so eager to remove the barriers set up by other people or countries is that Americans have to confront so many of them in their daily lives.

The children were eager to get back and enjoy themselves in the "America" that lay beyond the door. Their parents, on the other

85

hand, were relieved that their "American" children had left and they could enjoy themselves in true Japanese style. Someone cranked up the volume on the record player, and out came one Japanese hit after another. Surrounded by drunk, singing Japanese, I retreated to the corner with a handful of potato chips.

A few days later I went to visit the minister and his wife. They had an old, well-kept house, with calligraphy by Shimazaki Toson on the wall. The thing that most surprised me was their extensive library: they had the prewar editions of Natsume Sōseki and Akutagawa Ryūnosuke's *Collected Works,* and first editions of Nagai Kafū's early work.

"Have you read them all?" I asked.

Sensei laughed softly and didn't answer. He had gone to Aoyama University and received a Ph.D. from Boston University. At one time he had taught in Japan, but he had returned to America to dedicate himself to his Japanese-American ministry here. His wife had graduated from Tohoku University with a degree in English literature. Her grandfather, she said, was a samurai under the shogunate who had gone into hiding with Enomoto Takeaki in Hakone during the Boshin War, and she showed me his short sword.

I was amazed by the names of writers and intellectuals that flowed freely in that house—Sōseki, Uchimura. To me they were merely historic figures. But they had been close to this old couple in Japan and had inspired them in their studies.

Sensei had lived near Hongo, where the great writer Sōseki spent his last years, and he had often seen him. Although I had never read most of these writers and scholars, I began to feel familiar with them through my talks with Sensei.

"It was Sōseki," he said.

"No, it's Mushakōji, I tell you," his wife argued.

It was the first time in my life that I had been in an intellectual environment. It made me long for Japan. I got up and searched the bookcase and before I knew it had picked up two books—*Texas Rambling* and *American Japs on the Go.* Perhaps I had a presentiment that I would end up like the people in these books.

"Hasegawa's book? That's interesting."

"It's actually by Tani Joji. That's a pen name. When he wrote

*Tange Sazen* he called himself Hayashi Fubō. I lived with him for a while when he was young and wandering around America. He's dead now. He was a nice man."

I was starting to like this couple, and was ashamed of myself for having brushed them off at the party.

"Sensei, umm, could I come visit you once a week? I have to go to classes in English for a while, but I would like to learn from you. I feel very weird because all my friends in Japan are going to college and I'm repeating high school in a place where I can't speak the language. Otherwise all I do is work in the fields with the Mexicans. I don't know if I'm doing the right thing."

They listened quietly to my words.

"Come anytime. It's just the two of us here. Our children have gone off and made their own lives. Oh, wait a minute. I want to show you something."

He left and came back with a letter from the library. "This is a letter from President Kennedy."

"He was a friend of yours, too?"

"No. When Kennedy was campaigning for president, I thought he might be the one to ban nuclear weapons, and I wrote to him as a follower of Christ. He wrote me back a letter filled with hope; it's one of my greatest treasures."

The minister and his wife had lived in America for forty-five years but had never become American citizens. He had taught at an American university, was well-known in the Christian community, and a man of standing among the best American scholars. Offers to help them become citizens had come many times. Most would have given their eyeteeth for this right. But this couple refused to become citizens to protest America's use of the ultimate weapon—the atomic bomb.

"That's why we refuse to become Americans. People laugh at us but nuclear weapons go against our beliefs. Kennedy wrote in this letter that if he became president, he would try to do away with them. I don't know if he could have, but at least he had the desire to. His hopes were mine. I value that a great deal."

On the huge American continent, the community of Japanese immigrants was small. And smaller still was the world of these two Japanese who were born in the early 1900s and now lived all alone in the countryside. Perhaps hope, like God, finds its natural place among the small people. I was moved to tears by this couple, whose dreams far surpassed my own. My first visit to them marked one of my brightest moments in America.

The Japanese who lived in America were actually a diverse group. Laborers like my brother who worked themselves to the bone; Frank, the boss; Jiisan, the old man on the hill who had stolen over the border from Mexico; and all these people's second-generation Japanese children. These people might live on the same patch of farmland but not know the others existed, let alone know of one another's joys and sorrows. Perhaps that was the nature of America. When I told the old couple about the people on the farm, Sensei said, "Are there so many Japanese living in this area? We didn't know—we hardly ever go out. And somebody from Izu Ōshima that close. . . . When I was a student, I stayed in an inn at Habu Port. Now what was its name?" The old man closed his eyes as he summoned up the past. His face looked just like that of a man from the Meiji Era that I had seen in a photograph.

I told my brother about the evening when I got home, but his mind was elsewhere. He had his reasons. Frank had made a lot of money that year and had become my brother's financial guarantor; there was a chance that Anchan might be able to rent land in time for next year's season. It was all he could think about. Anchan had started going with Frank to the bank, the fertilizer store, and the gathering places for illegal Mexicans. If he was going to rent his land, he had to be on good terms with the fertilizer man and the coyotes.

"I've been here for almost seven years now. It goes fast. If I get my own field, I can send lots of money to Mom and Dad. They would love it—what with two of us here, that's the least we can do."

My brother didn't show any interest in what I was learning from the minister and his wife; all he could focus on was getting his field.

America's long summer comes to an end the day after Labor Day, but in California, Indian summer comes and it's still so hot you can fry an egg on a rock. Around mid-September, a hot wind begins to blow through southern California. It's called the Santa Ana, and it blows up from the Santa Ana mountains and the desert before spending itself over the farmland. This is the time that fires inevitably break out in the mountains. Since it hasn't rained for half a year, the vegetation is dry and withered. All it takes is one spark, and a sea of flames erupts in a field. I saw one of those fires that year. A strong wind had been blowing over the mountain behind the school, and, when fire broke out, the wind swept the flames before it. The only plants growing on the mountain were bushes about three feet high. When they burned, the flames weren't tall, but they fanned out far and wide. Over the course of a few days, the fire ravaged several mountains. When the wind changed, it blew ashy and hot into our fields, and we couldn't open our eyes.

From an ecological point of view, the fires in southern California are desirable. As the ash mixes with earth and rain, it enriches the nutrient-poor soil in the mountains. When spring comes, the mountains—saturated—turn green again.

I had made a white friend over that summer; his name was Bob and he was a second-generation Italian. Toward the end of summer vacation, Frankie Noda had brought Bob to the field. "This guy likes Japan. He comes to my house and eats sashimi. Strange American." As if Frankie weren't one himself! Bob was heavyset. He knew a few Japanese words from hanging out at Frankie's house.

What really surprised me was when the three of us went on a drive one day and Bob started singing a popular Japanese song called "Walk with Your Head Up High." But Bob called it "Suki-yaki."

"*Sukiyaki, sukiyaki,*" Bob sang.

I still haven't discovered why the title of the song was changed to "Sukiyaki," but this record eventually sold a million copies in America, and I began to notice it everywhere. One day I was in a supermarket where they usually played canned Beach Boys music, and I heard "Sukiyaki" with a samisen accompaniment. Immediately I assumed that the clerk had put it on just to call attention to me. Such was my inferiority complex in those days that I made up new words to the song: "Walk with your head high, so you won't see any Americans. . . ."

The song was so popular that I eventually became "Sukiyaki Boy" to my white friends. Though they only meant it in fun, it stung me.

One day in September I came home from school, and as I was going out to the field, my brother came running toward me. "Hey! We got it. We can rent the field!"

# 6

## "Revere the Emperor, Banish the Barbarian" Comes to the Farm

My brother's land lay across the road from Frank's: a 20-acre plot that was the fruit of six long years of dreams invested in America.

"Hey, Jiisan, we're going to be neighbors," said Anchan the day we signed the contract and went to look at our land. "If you need help, just let me know and I'll bring some people over."

"*Yuu-tachi* getting your own land to grow strawberries, eh? Congratulations. Took me forty years to get a field. You're young, you'll make it," the old man replied, getting down from his tractor. Barely five feet tall, Jiisan was dwarfed by his tractor. He had to stand up and press with all his might to put on the brake because his legs didn't reach the pedals. An ordinary American would have jumped right up into the seat, but Jiisan had to find a foothold midway or he wouldn't make it. Little Jiisan had to expend twice the energy of an American farmer just to operate his machine.

Jiisan wasn't the only one who had trouble with the size of American farm equipment; we all did. The handle of a shovel was taller than I, and after a day of shoveling my shoulders throbbed and I couldn't straighten out my fingers. Then there were the trash cans—seven feet around, made of heavy metal; a Japanese couldn't budge them even if they had wheels.

I was always taught that language is the most difficult thing about living in a foreign country, but I soon realized how traumatic it is to have to use tools and equipment that weren't built for you. Chances for accidents skyrocket.

"We all made money *thisu yea,* so it'll be rough *nexto yea—* everyone's gonna grow strawberries. If we don't have a really good crop, the price'll come down. *Farma is a gamburu,* and I'm always on the losing side," said Jiisan, pulling a handkerchief from his belt and blotting his forehead.

"That's why I'm planning to put in five acres of cauliflower," my brother replied. "I can pick the cauliflower in February, just about the time strawberries start, so I won't waste any time."

"That's a good idea. It's smart to have a safety net." Anchan had borrowed almost twenty thousand dollars for his first venture. There was no margin for failure.

"If *yuu* and me work together, we can make it," my brother had told me the night before. "Save your money for college; you don't need it for high school."

I was attending American high school simply to improve my English for college, and I chose courses accordingly. Some days I only took two or three classes, which left plenty of time to work. In fact, it was much easier for me to work in the field than sit in classes where I couldn't understand what was going on. I half-worried that if my English improved and I got used to American life, I might turn out like Frankie Noda or the other nisei. Part of me wanted to become American as quickly as possible; the other part of me wanted to run back home.

Little by little I learned how pleasurable it was to cool off by lounging naked in the evening air after a day of hard work in the field. Physical satisfaction is usually linked with sex, but I definitely felt it after working too. Human beings are built not only with a desire to reproduce, but to work, and we can do any task if we push ourselves hard enough.

We had risen in the world, but we were still mere laborers. In Japan it's easy to predict how much you will make in a year of hard work. But on an American farm you can make a huge amount of money on a single harvest if the competition slips up. The few thousand yen a man gets for simple physical work in Japan can turn into hundreds of thousands of yen here.

Frank Machida had come back to America as a nisei speaking little English at the age of eighteen, leased an 800-acre field for five years, bought land, and made hundreds of thousands of dollars. But Frank had paid for his prosperity: although wealth had been the fruit of his labors, you had only to look at his leathery face and his swollen, dirt-stained fingers to see that it had taken its toll on his body. And then there were subtle disturbances of his spirit.

I have no doubt that cruel physical labor can inflict brain damage on people. The damage that preys on farm workers does not destroy them; rather it turns them back into children. When the body is maltreated, one is cleansed of a sense of shame and a regard for custom. The civilized obsession to assign "meaning" to things breaks down; man pushed to the limits of his endurance reverts to his most basic form.

Once, soon after arriving in America, I had seen my brother watering the rows in the field. Saying he was thirsty, he bent down, drank some of the muddy water, wiped his mouth with his hand, and exclaimed, "Delicious!" It startled me, but when I think back on it, my brother's life *was* the farm, and he had simply adapted to it.

Six months later I, too, found that I could drink the muddy water in the fields, and consider it delicious. A farmer can't mold the land to suit himself; rather, it transforms and creates him anew. We were the ones who had to change.

The day I discovered that Anchan was really a farmer we stood talking about our hopes for our patch of land.

"Frank has made so much on his land—we should be able to do the same," I said.

"*Yuu*, it's not that simple. We still don't know if this soil is right for strawberries."

"But they're doing fine next door, and we're just across the road."

"But, this land has never been farmed. I don't know if we can grow strawberries. The only way to find out is to try. That's the way farming is in America." Anchan sounded different from usual. He scooped up some soil from the field and popped it in his mouth, his face crinkling at the taste.

"What are you doing? Are you drunk?"

"Umm, this here . . . this is OK."

My brother walked around tasting soil in every section of the field while I followed mutely. Suddenly his eyes narrowed.

"Do you know what I'm doing? I'm testing for salt. It doesn't

93

rain much here, and the sun's very strong, so the salt never gets washed out of the soil—it just hardens on top. This spot is a little salty, so it will only produce small strawberries."

I don't know where he learned it, but my brother could test the soil just by tasting it. Next he examined some rocks and turned over the earth in different places with a shovel.

"Too many rocks, too. It's never been farmed, and it isn't flat either."

Anchan knew what he was doing. Somewhere along the way my carpenter brother had become an accomplished farmer. The land had taught him. Often I heard him say, "Learn by doing." I was impressed.

Anchan then lay down on his stomach to measure the angle of the ground. If the ground was uneven, pools would form when water was piped in and the strawberries would end up different sizes. So, my brother said, we had to till the land many times with a tractor to make it as flat as possible. This was especially important because we were completely dependent on underground water. On many of the farms around us there were ponds to hold water that was siphoned off below ground. In order to draw water from these reservoirs to irrigate, we first had to put down pipes 3 feet below ground.

So how did we convert our field?

First we used a tractor fitted with a big rake that dug effortlessly through 2 feet of soil and unearthed all the rocks. This tractor was followed by another, slowly dragging a cart. Farm workers walked on either side, picking up the rocks and throwing them into the cart; the large ones were the size of a man's head and the smaller ones the size of a fist.

After the rocks were gone, we watered the field again and again. This was done not only to wash the salt from the soil but also to make the seeds of any weeds sprout. The wind had scattered all kinds of seeds over our vacant plot. After the seeds had sprouted, we turned them over with the tractor and left them to wither and die in the sun.

When we watered the dry earth, however, all kinds of bacteria and insects flourished, so next we had to exterminate. We covered the soil with plastic and sprayed the pesticide underneath. The gas sank two feet into the earth as it blended with the water, killing off pests and their eggs.

Next we put down fertilizer a number of times. Southern California soil is not of the highest quality (even weeds don't flourish here). After that, we watered the whole field again and turned the soil with the tractor. Finally, we used a bulldozer to get the earth as flat as possible, to ensure that water would spread evenly.

When all this was done, a piece of scrubby land had been transformed into a fertile field before our eyes. The black soil looked saturated with moisture. If we had planted flowers, you can bet that blossoms would have appeared in no time.

Now, we began to farm. First we made rows and planted two-inch strawberry seedlings four inches apart. To do this, we needed a lot of temporary help. Strawberries in a field of hundreds of acres must be planted in no longer than two to three days if you want the fruit to ripen at the same time. This autumn we would need as many illegal Mexican workers as we had last harvesttime. The farm workers tied bags that held fifty strawberry plants in a bundle around their waists and moved silently down the rows, setting each plant in the ground.

When the planting was done, we turned on the sprinklers connected to the underground pipes. It takes hundreds of pipes to run the sprinklers, each of which covers an area about fifteen feet square. When all the sprinklers were running, a little rainbow appeared over the field. After about two months of sprinkling, the strawberry plants had taken root. Then we started to pipe water directly into the rows.

Farming means different things in Japan and America. In Japan farming means planting land that has been used before, putting down fertilizer, and eventually harvesting a crop. The outcome is fairly easy to predict. But in America you have to begin by making the land arable. No one can guess what will happen if you plant a crop in land that is being farmed for the very first time.

"Things look good so far. As long as it keeps going like this into next year. I don't see any salt deposits and the strawberry plants are one hundred percent rooted," my brother said with relief in his voice, two months after we had gotten the field ready.

Early every morning my brother went out by himself and checked the roots of the strawberry plants one by one. By the time I woke up, he had finished this task and was sipping coffee. Having his own field had lifted his spirits—he nearly glowed. Every day I was back from school by three o'clock to help him.

One morning in October, when the days and evenings were much cooler, I came home to find my brother gone. I went to the adjoining field, where I found Frank, Pete, Ted, Charlie, Anchan, and the secretary in a huddle. Everyone looked tense.

"What is it?" I asked.

"*Yuu*, it's bad. The Mexicans are on strike. They didn't show up today, and González and Antonio have been missing since this morning," said my bewildered brother.

"Goddam Chicanos," swore Ted. "This is why I don't like them. Son of a bitch. This is going to screw up our schedule."

"*Yuu*, listen, if this were picking time, we'd be in hot water. The strawberries would rot. But it's not so bad now—we're just watering and weeding," Frank answered.

Frank's uniform was muddy. I wondered if he had been weeding since the morning. With the Mexicans protesting, the well-oiled machine of farm life had gone haywire.

"I wonder how long it's been since I weeded," Frank mused, not sounding altogether upset. All the supervisors that morning had returned to the simple tasks of the old days. In a field that held two hundred workers at harvesttime, it was a rare sight to see only four or five Japanese talking together spiritedly.

For a while anyway, all we had to do was to take care of the strawberry plants, so the farm didn't need too many hands. Frank had only hired about twenty Mexicans that month. But who would pick all the strawberries if they didn't show up next year? Our farm wasn't the only one. Bob Yamada's onion field in the next town and Imanishi-san's cauliflower field would be hit equally hard. The survival of California agriculture depended on the mood of the many Mexicans who came from all over to work for us.

"*Don worri*, it's OK. They'll be back. They're pigeons, the *Mexitachi*," said Frank typically.

"Why are they striking now?" I asked.

"There's a Mexican leader named Cesar Chavez in central

California. The strike started out on the grape farms, but for some reason it's spread this far," explained Frank.

According to him, on Mexican Independence Day of that year, September 16, the Mexicans, led by Cesar Chavez, had boycotted the grape fields of Delano, a town in central California. They were demanding a wage increase and a formal guarantee that the Immigration Bureau would grant them visas. We heard from the Japanese Americans who dropped by and the white representatives of the fertilizer company that many farms paid below minimum wage and that the worst ones would report the illegal workers on their farms to the authorities the day before payday and pocket their wages. In the face of such injustice, the pickers could do nothing. The Mexicans wanted special visas, because it was their cheap labor that kept the farms going. Their demands seemed perfectly reasonable to me, but I wondered why it had happened so suddenly. Then I remembered that the Mexican farm workers had been on the news frequently for the past month or so. Perhaps I just hadn't noticed what was obviously a big social problem, but I wasn't the only one in the dark. The supervisors themselves who had lived and worked with the Mexicans for years didn't seem to understand why they were striking.

"I didn't think the strike would get this big," said Frank.

"Frank, this is different from Chavez's strike. *I thinku jisu yea too muchi hotto weza,* so maybe the *Mexis* don't feel like working." Frank's younger brother Pete was spouting nonsense, and Frank interrupted him. "*Yuu,* shut up, Pete. *Whato aru yuu talkingu?* If hot weather's the reason, the *Mexi-tachi neba* . . . never come to *Californi* farms," he yelled.

"Easy, Frank, easy," said Charlie, trying to calm him down. "It's hard on the Mexicans since the bracero program ended. Still, I can't believe they've all joined this strike. It's never happened before. Maybe it's going to be a hot year, you know."

The bracero program, founded by the Mexican and American governments in 1951 to send seasonal farm workers to America, had ended in 1964. After the war, America had industrialized quickly, and people had gravitated toward the cities, which resulted in a shortage of farm labor. The bracero program had been created to fill this gap, and it had succeeded, particularly in the

Southwest. Its goal had been to send approximately 300,000 workers to various harvests on American farms every year.

Braceros worked hard, but in the end their low wages froze those of American farm workers, and the agricultural unions put pressure on the government to cancel the program. When it was halted, 250,000 to 350,000 Mexican workers were suddenly sent home. Panic spread through the Mexican border towns and a tidal wave of illegal immigration began. The Mexicans had returned home having tasted the riches of America; they would set out again to pursue their dreams to the north. Many of the workers on our farm had come into the country on the bracero program and stayed on when it ended.

Of course, illegal immigration had always been a problem for the two neighbors. But it was only in the mid-sixties that the numbers of illegals started climbing into the hundreds of thousands. The situation along the border was very tense. After years of working on American farms, they had connections there and they could expect to get work from their former employers.

Because of the tense situation, the American and Mexican governments had put their heads together and come up with the Border Industrialization Program, which was an attempt to stabilize the area. Under this program, American raw goods and capital were brought into Mexico, Mexican labor assembled a product, then it was shipped back to the States. The program had other names: "twin plants" or "maquiladora." Nowadays the phrase "borderless economy" is commonly used, but in 1965 "maquiladora" seemed ground-breaking. The "borderless age" between Mexico and America dates back to 1965. One can't deny that this program really suited American interests. American capital built workplaces in Mexico, and Americans profited on cheap labor. In addition, the program had a different outcome than was intended. It blurred the jurisdictions of the two governments, and a free zone emerged along the border.

Cesar Estrada Chavez was a second-generation Mexican from Arizona. Born to migrant workers, he moved from farm to farm as a child, having attended thirty schools by the time he dropped out in seventh grade. Chavez established the first union for farm workers in Delano, a town of grape farms in central California.

98

His eloquence enthralled both the farm workers and Christian groups, and his union grew very powerful. He became even more active in 1964 after the bracero program ended, and in 1965 the pickers went on strike. One should note, however, that the Mexicans went on strike because they sympathized with the Filipino grape pickers who were demanding better working conditions.

Japanese immigrants were an important presence in California agriculture before the war. Japanese farmers produced 11 percent of California's fruit and 40 percent of its vegetables. When World War II broke out, Japanese Americans were sent to the camps and the Japanese farmer all but disappeared from California. Filipinos took their places.

After the war, the Japanese returned to their farms after a four-year hiatus, but they had lost too much and only a handful managed to become big farmers again. Most had to start over as blanket men. Men like Frank, who left the camps and rebuilt their businesses in less than five years, were rare exceptions.

The plight of the Filipinos, however, was also horrendous. As more recent immigrants, they, too, had been terribly exploited by white farmers. Cesar Chavez had stood up in solidarity with the Filipinos.

"It's a Mexican strike, but even Ramón the Filipino didn't come to work today. What's going on?" grumbled Frank.

Chavez's movement reached its peak in 1966. Nearly 300,000 Mexican and Filipino workers walked 300 miles from Delano to Sacramento, the state capital, during almost a month of protest. The damage to the fruit and vegetable crops of 1966 (especially lettuce and grapes) was tremendous. The farm workers had simply disappeared from central California, the largest farming belt of the state, and thrown California agriculture into the greatest crisis it had ever known. But there was one man who helped to resolve the situation—a second-generation Japanese American named Harry Kubota. His story will come later.

That day the discussion on the farm went on and on.

"America's getting all stirred up," Frank commented. "First the blacks got restless and now the Mexicans."

"*Zatso raito.* So I say don't give civil rights to the blacks and the Mexicans. Or the students. *Looku whatso happeningu to zisu kan-*

99

*tori. Studento tachi neba studee.* All they talk about is free speech and marijuana. Remember when we were young. They always called us Japs but we never *gibu uppu.* But young people these days—*no goodo yo. Justo crazy.* Next time the Mexicans show up, we should work them harder and pay them less so they won't get even lazier," Ted ranted.

Ted's son was in Vietnam. Soon we were on that subject. "We were put in camps in the last war. No matter how much we say we're Americans, the government *neba* believe us. Even when we say we'll fight for America they don't let us out right away. So I say to my son, when America goes to war, you go too. What's this all about, these students at Berkeley draft dodging and making speeches. What about my poor son? *Rasto weeku,* I get a letter. It's a horrible war, he says, but at least we're fighting the commies. I'm telling you."

Just when I thought that the conversation had moved from the Mexican strike to the Vietnam War, Pete chimed in.

"*My garu,* she's always talking about *woman ribu,*" Pete chimed in. "*Garu* should stay at *homu.* But now she comes home late at night and fights with my wife."

In my experience, all immigrant groups in America—Chinese, Italian, Irish, and Mexican—shared this belligerent conversational style. As everyone knows, Americans love to express their own opinions. Raising their voices, they pound on a table to make their point. Their behavior at the negotiating table or in the conference room comes from growing up in a jostling immigrant society where everyone is a talker.

When immigrants come to this country they survive by talking at other people, not by listening to what they have to say. Everyone they meet at work or school is a stranger, and they must make others understand who they are, by force if necessary. Otherwise, they will be doomed to live here eternally as invisible people. This is why it is so important to "sell yourself" in America. Later generations have inherited this tradition even if they were born in this country.

Moreover, when Americans enter into diplomatic or economic negotiations with other nations, they hope to find good listeners. With a good listener, an American may take his most natural role—that of the talker—and the meeting will be fruitful. The reason that economic negotiations between Japan and America have gone askew is due to the fact that Japan doesn't know how to listen correctly, and wavers in the face of an opinionated and forceful America. A nation must be mature to be a good listener, and Japan has had to take on this role too soon after a period of rapid economic growth.

Just then Jiisan drove slowly up the road in a '49 Ford that looked like an armadillo. "*Yuu-tachi*, what's with the Mexicans? They didn't come to my field today," he called out.

"Jiisan, they're on strike," my brother explained.

"Oh, really. I thought they just weren't coming. Well, it's *alrigh* if they take a break sometimes. They'll be there tomorrow. But, Frank, I wanted to ask you how your roots are doing. Some of my plants look sick; maybe I didn't water them right."

"Maybe the field wasn't flat enough so the water didn't spread evenly," said Frank sympathetically.

"Hmm. Maybe I just got some bad plants."

The old man was more talkative than usual.

"Hmm, these plants have good roots," he said, walking into our field and examining the rows.

Two days later, the strike ended and everything went back to normal.

As the year progressed there were subtle signs of change: the temperature dropped and the light became much clearer. Most Japanese on the farms said that there weren't any seasons in California, while the Americans insisted that there were. In Japan the environment changes dramatically every month of the year. Even my brother, who thought of nothing but work, once said, "Well, America's a good country, but one thing bothers me. There aren't any seasons. It feel like time has stopped 'cause I can't see things changing. All year I have the illusion that I'm living the same thing over and over again. It would be so different if it rained even a little here, but we don't get any rain from spring to fall. And it's later than usual this year. I wish it would rain." My brother still appreciated the seasons, in spite of his deteriorating Japanese and his American mannerisms.

At that time I had been in America for six months, and it hadn't rained once. Soon after, on the third Saturday of October, I experienced rain on the farm for the first time. Having almost forgotten that there was such a thing, I watched it transform the dusty, hot land before my eyes. The rain washed down the leaves of the trees and revived the grasses by the road, as well as our spirits. The expressions of the men who put all their energy into work grew more gentle.

A few of the men who worked like machines, however, couldn't sit still. In the morning, they moved about restlessly, their muscles longing for physical labor. Some put on work clothes as usual and went out to check on their neighbor's crop or exchange news about the market. Others walked out into their own fields getting soaked by the rain.

"Listen. If you fall down in your field, you don't just stand up. Look around and pull up a few weeds first. That's what makes a good farmer," advised Frank.

All the field supervisors eventually gathered in Frank's office with time on their hands.

"We can't work in this rain. Let's play poker," Pete suggested.

Anchan, Ted, and Charlie gathered around a card table in the next room. Rain lashed at the roof. We could still see the field, but everything up to the mountains in the distance looked hazy. An unfamiliar car drove up the narrow road in the field toward the office. It pulled up by the window, and a small, elderly Japanese man got out. He wasn't from around these parts. With a knock on the door, the man came in.

"Is the boss here?" The man directed his question to me. Hearing the voice, Pete came in from the room next door.

"You're really early this year. What happened down in Imperial Valley?"

"Farmers no good this year. There wasn't much work, so I left. Wonder if you got anything."

"Hmm. It's still a long time till strawberries, but you could do some weeding."

"Can you believe this rain? I've been driving since this morning, and some of the roads are flooded."

"Look, you can use a room in the house over there."

102

The man took the key and drove to a shack in a corner of the field that was used by Mexicans during harvesttime.

"Pete, do you know that guy? He isn't very friendly."

"Oh that's Taoka, a blanket man. He didn't come this season, so you wouldn't know him."

Frank emerged from his office after his phone treatment. "Who was that?"

"Taoka, the blanket man. We're going to get busy soon, so I let him use the Mexicans' house. He just came from Imperial Valley, and he says that they didn't plant many cantaloupes, so picking won't be any good. That's why he came here earlier than usual," Pete answered.

"Taoka, eh? He's always going to be a blanket man, and there aren't too many Japanese blanket men left these days."

"Tell me more," I asked.

"*Yuu* probably know this already, but it's the Mexicans who keep *Californi* farming alive. The year begins with the cantaloupe and honeydew melon harvest down in Imperial Valley, near the border. It's warm there even in winter, so the growing season starts early. By February you can pick great fruit. After that it's strawberry season around San Diego and Orange County, from about April. Then, north for more strawberries, until June; then they head for central *Californi*, where they pick grapes through the summer, before heading for northern *Californi* to pick apples. By the new year they head back to Imperial Valley and start all over again. They never stop moving—that's why we call 'em pigeons. Before the war, let's see, there were three or four thousand Japanese blanket men. They were pigeons, too. A man would pile up all his blankets and clothes in a car, go to the places he felt like, work a little, make some money, and then move on."

The seasonal progression of harvests in California made the state sound like one big farm. Once I had been overwhelmed by the size of our farm, but now I tried to imagine the vast number of harvests scattered across a state larger than all of Japan. It was not unlike the way Japan's cherry trees blossomed—in a line moving ever northward.

It wasn't until two weeks later that I actually got to have a conversation with Taoka. One day, when I was on my way home

103

after watering the rows, Taoka called out to me as I passed his little shack.

"Come in for a minute. How about some coffee?"

I had seen him in the field a number of times since the rainy day, but we had only exchanged greetings. Like that of a true blanket man, Taoka's room was nearly empty, except for some pictures and art supplies scattered over the table. "Do you paint?" I asked.

"A little. People like me don't have much to do with the world. It's how I pass the time when I'm alone." Taoka also did calligraphy; sheets of heavy brushstrokes were pinned above the sofa.

Taoka never said much—maybe because he had never settled down and had a family—and he never mentioned his past. Though only a laborer, he seemed more sophisticated than the other Japanese Americans on the farm.

"Do you know if there are any swap meets around here?" he asked me. Swap meets were markets held during the day at drive-in theaters where people would buy and sell used goods—lots of American towns had them. Anchan and I had gone a few times to buy used work clothes.

"Yes, every Sunday at the drive-in not far from here. What do you need? We have lots of old tools in the house if they'll do. Just let me know."

"Thanks. I don't want to buy anything; I want to sell," he said, pointing at the calligraphy over the couch. "The paintings are hard to sell, but if I frame the calligraphy, it will sell. It's something Americans can't make themselves."

Nonchalantly, I glanced at the calligraphy. The slogans were very old-fashioned: "The Way of the Sword," "Karate," "Eight Corners of the World Under One Roof," "Kamikaze," "Revere the Emperor, Banish the Barbarian." Along with these expressions were pieces of calligraphy that looked like poems.

"Are you going to sell these too?" I asked.

"Yes, this one is the words to a song, and these are Japanese poems."

When I took a close look, I recognized poems from *Chikuma River* by Shimazaki Tōson, and poems Takamura Kōtarō had written for his mad wife, Chieko—works that I knew well from

104

high school. Then Taoka showed me one that he had just written: Sakamoto Kyū's "Walk with Your Head Up High."

"This song is popular now, but it's called 'Sukiyaki.' You know that, right?" He began to hum the song.

"How much can you get for these?" I asked.

"Between three dollars and twenty dollars. They look pretty good framed."

It was true that most pictures looked better in frames. But how would Americans feel if they knew they were hanging framed calligraphy that read "Kamikaze" or "Revere the Emperor, Banish the Barbarian" in their own living rooms?

"Want to come with me to the next swap meet? If you look hard, you can pick up a sword or old books for a song," Taoka offered.

Agreeing to go, I started home. When I got there, it was pitch dark.

"*Yuu*, where have you been? You're late," my brother grumbled moodily: I'd forgotten that it was my turn to cook.

"I'm sorry. Taoka invited me in for a cup of coffee on my way home."

"He's a strange one. He shows up when the mood strikes him. I think it was the year before you came, on his way here in that old station wagon he picked up a Mexican family and brought them along. The four of them worked together all summer. But while they were here the husband got arrested. Next thing you know, Taoka's acting more and more like the woman's husband, living in that small house with her and the two children. She was very pretty; all the men envied him."

"What's his background?"

"I don't know much about him, but his father was a famous right-wing leader. When he was growing up, he spent a lot of time with the renegades who fought in Manchuria."

"You mean there are right-wing Japanese Americans too?"

"What are you talking about? You can find anything in America. Look at the Ku Klux Klan."

"But why would a Japanese person like that still want to live in America."

"I have no idea. The old man on the hill, the minister you're always talking about—none of them would have an answer to that question. But if you asked them why this country is the way it is, they could tell you. Sometimes this country doesn't feel real to me—being a farmer so far from where I was born. I always dream about the island. The big pine tree in front of our house, the shrine at Habu Port, our field. Sometimes I feel I got here because a long thread reeled me in. But I can't tell you what kind of thread it was. What connection is there between our island and America? But here we are living on a farm in *Californi*. I wonder what kind of thread is holding Taoka."

He drifted off into thought.

After a while, Anchan announced, "Dinner's ready. Eat up."

The next day Taoka and I went to the swap meet together. People from the town were unloading lots of junk from their trucks, lining it up close together, and attaching random prices to it.

"Let's stop here." Taoka took the paintings and the framed calligraphy out of a box and began to set them out. The paintings were landscapes with simply drawn mountains, rivers, and a few trees. Before long, a small, fat man with a mustache and his wife stopped in front of the paintings and began to examine them closely. The wife picked one up curiously.

"Honey, I like this. This is gorgeous," she said to her husband.

She asked the price. Twenty dollars. Next the man picked up a piece of calligraphy and asked what it meant; if it was a great poem, he might buy it, he said. But twenty dollars was a little high, so could they get a discount? The calligraphy in his hand looked like "Revere the Emperor, Banish the Barbarian." Taoka couldn't possibly explain this to an American. Wouldn't the man explode if he knew what it meant? I tensed.

Taoka first picked up the picture slowly and read out in Japanese "*Sonno—jōi.*" Then he made up a translation: "Yankee go home," he said in a normal voice.

I was impressed by his apt translation but shivered in anticipation of the American man's anger. To my astonishment, the man merely replied happily, "That's right, Yankee go home. Yankee go home."

Then he shook Taoka's hand and embarked on his life story—

106

his passage from Italy to America as a child; the terrible discrimination he had suffered here. Taoka listened, a gentle smile playing about his lips, nodding slightly.

That day Taoka gave me ten dollars for helping him. On the way home I found myself worrying about his slogans. Unable to restrain myself, I asked, "Mr. Taoka, are you right wing?"

" 'Revere the Emperor, Banish the Barbarian'—that's all we Japanese need to know," he answered.

Although I showered him with questions, he didn't say much, just smiled in his personable way. Less than two weeks later, Taoka moved on.

"Where are you going?" I asked him. "The strawberry season hasn't even started yet."

"Hmm. I'll be back soon enough. We'll meet again some day."

I never did see him again. But during my four years on the farm I often heard rumors about Taoka living just the way he always did.

# 7

# The Search for America

One Sunday in November, Sensei and his wife invited me to attend their church in northeastern Los Angeles. "Our congregation is all first-generation Japanese," Sensei explained on the way there. "The nisei have another service in English with their own minister. After our service, the Japanese Christians of southern California are giving a picnic, and I thought we'd go."

Our car was being driven by a Japanese member of the church; Sensei hadn't driven for quite a few years.

"How many Japanese churches are there in southern California?" I asked, quite uneasy about going to a church for the first time.

"Oh, there are many. And not only churches. We have branches of some of the older temples, including Zen, and some of the newer sects, too. Actually, religious freedom is a basic tenet of this country, so religious groups get preferential treatment when it comes to visas and taxes. Some people disguise themselves as priests or ministers when they come into this country, call themselves religious men, and preach. You have to watch out for fakes."

"Like the minister of you know what church—he's terrible," his wife confirmed.

"Why?" I asked.

"He says he graduated from the religious studies department at Waseda University and got a Ph.D. from a famous university. But Waseda doesn't have a religious studies department. Since most of the Japanese here don't know it, his church has a good name *and* a big congregation." The wife laughed.

"Don't get us wrong," Sensei added. "It's not just the Japanese. You find the same kind of people in any group of immigrants."

"Making up family trees, faking school records, changing your name—it's all run of the mill here," his wife added.

"But how did it get this way?"

"Well, it may sound ridiculous," Sensei said, "but it's because so many political refugees and outlaws came to this country. Then there were also some people—like the Jews—who changed their names to avoid discrimination." He named several famous movie stars.

"The Japanese community is made up of people from all over Japan, so people don't know anything about each other when they first meet. At parties on the farms or at Japanese clubs, they introduce themselves in the most extraordinary ways. Dear, what's that man's name, the one with the round face who comes to our church?"

"You mean Mr. Suzuki?"

"Yes, that's the one. Mr. Suzuki goes around Japantown pretending that he's related to the imperial family. Someone who visited him told me that his house is full of furniture with the imperial chrysanthemum crest on it. Suzuki says that circumstances are making him live in America now, but one of these days he'll go back to Japan and be the heir of a noble family. Our church members get invitations to visit him there. They're so honest, you know, and some of them have been giving him a lot of money. It's a real problem," said the minister with a painful smile.

"Then there was that man who said he was a descendant of Fukuzawa Yukichi," said Sensei's wife.

"Now he might have been the real thing," her husband answered. "What he said about the people closest to Fukuzawa sounded pretty accurate."

"I wonder. Maybe it's because of that terrible thing that happened to me with the *Shinsengumi,* but people like that make me nervous," replied his wife, not altogether convinced.

"Did you say Shinsengumi, the group led by Kondō Isami? Are any of their descendants in America?" I spoke up in surprise that Fukuzawa Yukichi, the Imperial family and Shinsengumi would be mentioned one after another in a conversation in California.

The Shinsengumi were a group of swordsmen who protected the shogunate in the 1860s, and their exploits are legendary.

"It happened a long time ago," Sensei's wife began, "around the end of the Taishō period, when I came here with my husband. We got to know this blanket man in Fresno, and he told us that he was descended from one of the members of the Shinsengumi. Remember I told you that my grandfather had gone into hiding with Enomoto Takeaki under the old shogunate? Even as a small child I knew that I came from samurai stock. So when I came to this country and heard the name *Shinsengumi*, well, I was beside myself—I was young, you know. Anyway, we gave that blanket man a room in our church, and he made off with all the church valuables. Some Shinsengumi! More like a descendant of the famous thief Ishikawa Goemon, I'd say."

"You know, dear, lots of failed political activists emigrated here during and after the Meiji period. Maybe that man really was related to someone in the Shinsengumi. Quite a few descendants of the shogunate came here, too," said her husband, trying to console her. "In this country it's hard to tell if someone's a fake or not. Sometimes honest people go bad here, and, sometimes, dishonest people go straight. I could live here forever and I still wouldn't understand America. When people throw away their old selves and conjure up new ones, I guess it's too tempting to resist. Living here makes it easy to change. Look at Mr. Suzuki, the relative of the imperial family. If he had said those things in the village where he was born, he'd have been thrown out.

"Before the war the Japanese here were completely ostracized. You'd think they'd have gotten fed up and gone home. But most of them stayed in the end. Of course, it was partly because their children were born here; it would have been hard to take them back to Japanese schools. Still, they made their choices. Maybe they felt they could find what they were searching for in spite of the awful prejudice.

"And lying about your lineage is even more common in other communities. White men are claiming all the time that they're descendants of European nobility. To claim that you're Fukuzawa Yukichi's descendant or that you have Shinsengumi blood in your veins is child's play next to that. No, in the Japanese community the biggest lies aren't about family background; they're about education. Like inventing a religious studies department at Waseda.

"A little while ago I was visiting Mr. Hayashi, a member of our church. There on his wall was a framed diploma from the Military Lower School. We've known each other over twenty years, but he never mentioned to me that he went there. I must have been staring at it with a puzzled look on my face, because Mr. Hayashi said, 'Oh, Sensei, you've found me out. I bought that recently.'

"The reasons he gave were comical: his son and daughter are very bright; one is going to UCLA and the other to Stanford. Both of them have joined the student movement and are passionate about the cause of Asian Americans. They kept criticizing their father for going into the detention camps meekly without putting up a fight. And they kept pestering him about his Japanese past: where were you born, when did you emigrate, what kind of education did you have? Mr. Hayaski is very pro-education, and he wanted to make his children feel proud of him; he was dying to tell them that their father was well educated and had only become a manual laborer in this country because of the language barrier and discrimination. So he decided to get a diploma from a Japanese school."

"Do they sell them here?" I asked.

"He says they do. Mr. Hayashi called a man who had this kind of business, and the man said that he could make him a diploma from Tokyo University, Keio University, the Naval Academy, or any primary or secondary school. He was also selling tea ceremony and flower-arranging certificates. Anyway, Mr. Hayashi thought it would be ridiculous to buy a diploma from Tokyo University—if he had graduated from Tokyo Imperial University he would never have ended up a blanket man in southern California, no matter what. So he chose the Military Lower School. None of his friends would find out, because everyone in Japan before the war had some connection to the military. Supposedly, his kids were thrilled, and now they tell people, 'Daddy graduated from the Japanese West Point.' "

"But what kind of people sell these certificates? I mean, they're handmade, right?" I asked.

"From what I hear, a blanket man around fifty who's good at calligraphy makes them."

"His name couldn't be Taoka, could it?" I told them about "Revere the Emperor, Banish the Barbarian."

"Well, it takes all kinds," Sensei replied. "Maybe he's making them under a different name."

I felt sure that it was Taoka. The day I'd visited his room, he had been furiously writing something that he wouldn't show me. When I asked him what he was doing, he answered, "Doing somebody a favor." Certainly the diploma in question was keeping the peace in Mr. Hayashi's home.

All of America's immigrant communities are havens for swindlers, yet this fraudulence is the source of tremendous energy. Yet if living in America meant having to lie about your family, fake your academic record, and change your name, how did society survive? Perhaps people just plodded on through life even if they couldn't trust those people around them.

Eventually we arrived at the church—a rough-and-tumble affair furnished with nothing but twenty long benches and an altar. It fit in perfectly with the simple rural life-style of my hosts. When we arrived, about thirty Japanese were already gathered inside. Their average age was over sixty.

Sensei introduced me to the congregation and began the service. First we sang a hymn, then listened to his sermon. Sometimes he spoke quietly with closed eyes; at other times his voice boomed out over the congregation, and he spread his arms. The words poured persuasively from that frail body.

Finally, Sensei turned to his congregation and said, "I now conclude my sermon for this morning. Today we have a young man with us in our house of prayer. For him and all of us who trust in Christ, I would like to give thanks for our gathering today by reciting one of my favorite poems."

Sensei, whose degree from Boston University was in literature, began to recite:

> Grow old along with me!
> The best is yet to be,
> The last of life, for which the first was made:

Our times are in His hand
Who saith, 'A whole I planned,
Youth shows but half; trust God: See all, nor be afraid!"

Not that, amassing flowers,
Youth sighed, "Which rose make ours,
Which lily leave and then as best recall?"
Not that, admiring stars,
It yearned, "Nor Jove, nor Mars;
Mine be some figured flame which blends, transcends
   them all!"

As he recited each stanza, Sensei would close his eyes, then suddenly open them again and stare out at his audience. Although I couldn't understand a word of the poem, the beauty and power resonated through me.

When Sensei had finished he told us that it was a poem by Robert Browning entitled "Rabbi Ben Ezra"; then he translated it into Japanese.

After the service was over, we all drove off to the picnic, which was being held in Elysian Park, not far from Japantown in Los Angeles; a stage had been erected, which made me wonder if they were going to perform a play, and a Japanese song was on the record player. Little Japanese-American children scampered about underfoot. People had come from as far away as San Diego and Orange County. Little reunions were in progress everywhere.

"*Rongu taimu no shee.* How's the missus? What? She died last year? We didn't hear a thing about it. *Zatso too bado.*"

"I hear Mr. Yamamoto *meiku mahnay* this year. What are you going to do—somebody like that too *muchi meiku mahnay.* I'm cutting grass for white people as usual."

"*Haroo,* Missus. I heard about your boy-san, all-A *studento,* getting a scholarship for UCLA. *Zatso naisu.* My boy doesn't study a bit; he's out chasing white girls. *Lasto naito,* he brought one back to his room. Can you imagine?"

Everywhere conversations blossomed like flowers.

Eventually the emcee took the microphone, thanked God for letting them have a picnic on such a beautiful autumn day, and asked everyone to join him in a prayer. After this we all took out boxed lunches and began to eat. I ate the lunch prepared for us by church members with Sensei and his wife as a singing contest began on the hastily constructed stage.

"Sensei, do you always finish your sermon with a poem?"

"No. I just felt in the mood this morning. There was a time in my life when that poem was a great comfort to me. During the war, my wife, the Japanese singers over there, and the children were all put into detainment camps, but I was in the hospital with a lung disease. For four years, while my people were in the camps, I had an American nurse taking care of me as I fought for my life. It was Browning's poem that kept me going. I don't know how many times I whispered it to myself. After a while the nurse could recite it by heart, too. We often recited it out loud together. We talked a lot, too, about how men still went to war even though we have such a beautiful poem."

The voice of the emcee broke in. "Excuse me, everyone. Now we are going to hear a song by the branch manager of Sumitomo Bank, who very kindly donated three cases of beer and fifty dollars to our picnic. *Ando nau, radies ando gentoruman, Mista Yamada-san! Mista Yamada, purizu.*"

The branch manager was obviously a new arrival. Looking very puzzled, he took the mike and began to sing.

"That poor man," said Sensei's wife sympathetically, "to get accounts from the Japanese he has to come here and sing."

"I still recite that poem today, but it pains me every time," Sensei continued. "I was a disciple of the pacifist Uchimura Kanzo. What troubles me is the thought of what I might have done if I had been healthy enough to go to the camps with everyone else. Would I have had the courage to preach pacifism in the camps? I wonder what it meant—those four years I spent in the hospital. Maybe God was ordering me to rest." Sensei went on in an uncharacteristic anguished tone, but the PA system was so loud, there were moments I couldn't catch what he was saying.

"Now, everyone, it's time for the Picture Bride Game!" thundered the emcee.

"What's that?"

"In the old days, men had to send for their brides from home, and couples had to choose each other through photographs—that's

114

why the women who came to the States were called picture brides. Go take a look for yourself. This game's unique to Japanese picnics," Sensei's wife explained.

Just as the game was starting, my brother arrived. "Sorry, sorry. There was a big accident on the freeway. Is that you, Sensei? I'm Yoshimi's older brother. You've done so much for him." My brother acted nervous in the presence of such an educated man.

After the usual introductions, we returned to our meal. My brother, who had been watching the Picture Bride Game, suddenly stood up, saying, "Could it be? . . . maybe . . . it's been such a long time . . ." then walked off toward one of the players.

"Must be someone he knows," said Sensei as the game ended. We could see Anchan shaking hands with someone around his own age. Eventually the two men moved into the shade and sat down on a bench; though I couldn't hear their voices, I could tell by their gestures how happy they were to see each other. Watching them, I heard a voice behind me: "Sensei, is that you? I was a member of your church in Sacramento years ago."

Sensei turned around to face the owner of the voice, a man of about sixty who was with his wife.

"Oh! I can't believe it," he replied in great surprise. "Is that you, Mr. Okada? How are you? How many years has it been? Thirty years . . . yes, it must be about that."

"You both look wonderful. We caught sight of you from over there, and I thought it must be you."

Sensei stood up and drew me toward the Okadas. "Let me introduce you. This is Ishikawa Yoshimi, who came to California this spring. His older brother has a strawberry farm near us, and Yoshimi helps his brother while going to high school. This is *Mista ando Missus Okada-san*. They were our closest friends when we were in Sacramento."

I stood up and shook hands with the old couple.

"It brings back memories, doesn't it? We heard on the grapevine that you were doing very well in Los Angeles. We're living in Salinas now, but our son is in LA. He and his wife just had a child—so we came for our first visit in ages. It was just by chance that we came to this picnic, but I'm sure glad we did, because we got to see you!"

"Your son—you mean your eldest son, John?"

"No, Robert, our second son. John fought in the 224th Division in the war. He died in Germany."

"John . . . in the war . . ." Sensei's expression clouded.

"He volunteered while we were in the camps, and we never saw him again. We were in the Manzanar camp. Where were you, Sensei?"

"I wasn't in the camps; I was in the hospital. But my wife was in Heart Mountain in Wyoming."

The topic of the camps made Sensei's face darken. He obviously felt guilty because he hadn't been interned with everyone else.

The Okadas didn't mix English words like *yuu* or *mii* in with their Japanese, and they called Los Angeles *Rafu* instead of *Losu Angeros,* which was typical prewar Japanese. But they did call their sons John and Robert. How could people who were born in the Meiji period call their sons by English names?

Once on the farm Pete had said to me, "*Yuu,* it'd be *alrigh* to add John or Henry to your name. You'll get more American *furendo* that way." Later I practiced calling myself Robert Ishikawa and Clint Ishikawa when I was all alone in the field. Yet when I said aloud "My name is Clint Ishikawa," I felt terribly embarrassed.

My classmate Frankie had a proper Japanese name, Go, but he had given himself the name Frankie. In his case, Frank or Frankie fitted him much better than Go, especially because he rarely wrote his name in Chinese characters. But Clint Ishikawa?

As the two couples talked, I began to pack up our lunch, but soon Sensei and his wife tried to draw me into the conversation.

"Mr. Okada used to be a teacher in a Japanese school in Sacramento before the war," Sensei's wife was saying. "Nowadays most of our kids can't speak Japanese very well, but they could before the war. That's because people like Mr. Okada put a great deal of effort into it. The more recent immigrants were planning to make money and go home, so they really wanted their kids to learn Japanese. They were passionate about it. Mr. Okada even wrote his own textbook."

"Missus, that was a long time ago," Okada protested, looking embarrassed.

It seemed that the prewar nisei, like Ted and Pete, spoke good

Japanese; yet none of the nisei or sansei kids I had met at school came close to speaking it well. I asked why.

"I'm positive it's because Japan lost the war," Okada pronounced abruptly.

"The Japanese here planned to make money and go back home. They worried that their kids would end up speaking only English, so they built Japanese schools everywhere. I taught in one of them. In those days the nisei kids who felt like Americans were lumped together with us as 'Japs.' It was hard for us, but it must have been even harder for them, and it put quite a strain on our relationships. Parents and children had always been close, whether for good or for bad, but prewar Japanese parents and their American-born children . . . well, Sensei, it was unique, wasn't it?"

Okada looked toward Sensei for approval and continued, "Parents told their children that there isn't such terrible prejudice in Japan. People are kind, it's a beautiful country. Feeding them a lot of nonsense, if you ask me. You can't say there isn't any racism in Japan. But they were trying to cheer up their children because it was so bad here. The poor children were desperate. A lot of them thought that they would never be accepted in America. And, of course, a few of them couldn't stand Japan. So, parents and children painted Japan in rosy colors. The parents were always trying to give Japan to their children. I thought that if I could teach them the language, I could teach them about Japan. To me that's what teaching is all about.

"But then we lost the war. The nisei children felt less like learning Japanese. What was the point in learning the language of a defeated nation? If they spoke Japanese, it would only confirm that they were Japs. We parents mulled this over. When we got out of the camps, life was hard. There weren't any Japanese schools around. We felt we had lost the . . . um . . . how do I say it? . . . justification for teaching our children Japanese. Japan sounded like a very depressing place in the news; thousands of people were starving. How were we going to teach our children the language of such a Japan? The kids wouldn't buy it," said Okada in one breath.

117

"Oh, Mr. Okada, you're just as fiery as you always were," said Sensei's wife.

Sensei listened to him silently, nodding in places, his glance occasionally wandering to the festivities around us.

"Nowadays, more and more nisei and sansei children are getting interested in Japanese again, though still not as many as before the war. Japanese goods are making their way into the States; the wounds of the war are healing," Okada continued.

By 1988, the number of enthusiastic nisei and sansei students of Japanese was once again on the rise. I believe this was because Japan had developed into a great economic power. It takes a powerful country to export a language and a culture and increase the self-confidence of its emigrants.

"Sensei, the faces have changed, haven't they? I'm glad that there are now other ways to get green cards. New faces liven things up," Okada said, watching the people absorbed in their games.

Japanese immigration to America was initially prohibited in 1924; finally, however, in 1952 a new immigration law was passed. In addition to the agricultural trainee programs, the Displaced Persons Act of the 1950s—which was primarily meant to aid political refugees from Eastern Europe, also aided the Japanese. Many of the people playing games at the picnic acted as if they were newcomers.

The people participating in the picnic games gave the impression of not having lived long in America. One would have expected to see elderly people, considering the more traditional tone of the gathering, but instead there were vigorous young men like my brother, who, though looking quite puzzled, were playing the game of an earlier generation.

"Your brother looks very happy," said Sensei. "You run into all sorts of people at these things—like Mr. Okada today. That's why everyone comes."

"Sensei, won't you take part in the Picture Bride Game? I've been chosen to do it," Okada requested.

"If you don't mind, I . . ." The minister declined.

"That's fine. But it's my turn now, so I must go. If you ever come to Salinas, please . . ." said Okada, as he gave his address to Sensei and walked toward the game.

"Attention, everybody, team ten is next. Please get ready." The emcee's voice boomed over the grounds.

Men and women divided into groups of ten as the game began. A man had to run up and choose an envelope; inside was a written description of what his 'wife' looked like and where she was born. He had to find her in the group and run with her back to the goal.

This game is no longer played in the Japanese community. Even in the midsixties, it was disappearing. But whenever older Japanese people gathered, it was a popular pastime.

"The only way a man could get married here in the late eighteen hundreds and early nineteen hundreds was through the mail," Sensei began, keeping one eye on the game. "There were lots of funny mishaps, because it was all done overseas. But I have stories about these photo marriages that aren't so funny.

"When I first started to preach here, picture marriages were prohibited—people said it was barbaric to marry someone just because you liked their photograph. Supposedly this custom fueled hatred of the Japanese. But people still did it secretly, because they didn't have any choice. I was in a church in Sacramento in the twenties, and one young man sent photos to his girl to make himself look rich: first, he posed in the middle of a big farmer's field, then in front of a big house in formal dress smoking a cigar, and finally next to an expensive Ford."

A smile of recollection lit up his wife's face.

"He came to me one day and said, 'Please, Sensei, I can't write, so please write a letter for me.' His letter went like this: 'The farm and the car in this photo are mine. If you marry me, we can get a bigger house and farm.' He was nothing but a blanket man! Those letters did a real disservice to the women who received them. Especially in such hard times."

Chuckling at the memories, Sensei looked at his wife. "So, this sounds wonderful to the woman who gets the letter. She makes herself up, does her hair, and sends him a photograph. After they exchange a few letters, she gets on a boat. With only a photograph to go by, the man searches for his wife among the hundreds of brides who have arrived at the San Francisco pier. We used to call them pier marriages, too. But sometimes it's very difficult to find your mate. You can see why, can't you? In his photograph the man is in a formal suit, which he never wears. In hers, she looks her most beautiful. But after twenty days on a boat crossing the Pacific Ocean, she looks haggard. Both of them have ideal visions of the other, so it's impossible to see the real person. At least a couple dozen men and women start to argue and cry on the pier, saying, 'That couldn't be him,' or 'I've been tricked.' That's where the game came from."

Sensei paused to watch again.

"Then there are the ones—usually men—who spot their brides, but run away without announcing themselves because they don't like their looks. Isn't that terrible?"

"What would those women do?"

"From what I hear some of them gave up and went back to Japan, but some stayed on. Remember, these women were brave enough to cross an ocean to marry a man they had never seen; they weren't about to give up that easily. They put ads in the Japanese newspapers—like 'Mr. So-and-So, I am your wife. Please come claim me soon.' Some of them didn't even stop there. They'd travel all over the state looking for their man.

"Then there's the story about the man who couldn't find his bride. He called out to another woman and fell in love with her at first sight. The woman liked him, too. She had already seen the man she was supposed to marry, but he hadn't seen her. Gazing into each other's eyes, the first two knew they had fallen in love, so off they went to a nearby church and got married."

"What happened to the man and woman who were left behind?"

"They were the only two people left in the end, and they needed to get married, so they did. A few years later, by accident, the two couples ended up working on the same farm. When the first man asked the second man's wife where she was from, he discovered that she had come from Hiroshima to be his bride! Luckily, both of the couples were happy, so the man who'd stolen the other's bride confessed. The other man replied, 'Thanks to you, I have a wonderful wife.' From that time on the couples grew to be close friends."

"I wonder if we are the only ones with marriage stories like that."

"I doubt it. I don't think white people did picture marriages, but think about it—the men always immigrate first, and then they send for their women. They have to come up with good strategies. I bet other people have lots of stories to tell, too."

In the midseventies I returned to California and worked as a gardener. One day my assistant asked to borrow my truck and my tools. When I asked him why, he said that his girlfriend from Mexico wouldn't come live with him in America because she feared discrimination. To change her mind, he wanted to show her how well he was doing. If he told her that he had an expensive truck and a Japanese working for him, she might agree to immigrate.

I don't know if this story is a good analogy to the picture bride story, but I suspect that some of America's idealism grew out of the plaintive love calls that men made to entice women into this wilderness. The men who came here broadcast their dreams to the world, describing them as though they had already come true, and that idealism has never flagged. But those men weren't talking to people around them; they were calling out to women in faraway countries. By coming to this country alone and making impossible promises to women back home, they made the history of America.

The love calls of the Japanese are relatively modest. A man might call another's field his own and say to a woman, "If you come, the next field will be ours too." Or, if he has started a small business in America to avoid Japanese taxes he might say to a woman in Tokyo, "I bought a condo in Los Angeles, and I want you to live with me." A slightly more sophisticated European might say to his love back at home, "I am now in Texas. Mexico is next door. Come to this country, and we will conquer the west together." Or maybe, "I'm writing from Manhattan. There's plenty of work. Soon I will own two or three small companies. If you join me, we'll get a luxury apartment and start a new life. You can run one of my companies. We'll get a house in the Bahamas and go sailing every summer. Of course, if you'd prefer Santa Monica, that's fine with me." This is the kind of letter some men will dash off before breakfast.

Aren't such daring love games the key to America's excessive idealism?

After a long talk with his friend, Anchan returned. "*Yuu,* what a surprise. I ran into Takita, a buddy of mine from my trainee days. Now he's here on a tourist visa—it was the only way he could get back. He invited me to have dinner with him in Japantown so we can talk some more. You're invited, too. Some of his friends will be coming."

Anchan apologized to Sensei and his wife, and made a date to visit them in the future. At the end of the picnic, I got in my brother's car, and we headed toward Japantown to meet Takita. As we drove, Anchan told me, "When I got to the farm this morning, my wife was there with divorce papers for me to sign. I'm a bachelor again. And, believe me, next time I'm going to find someone good."

I couldn't believe my brother was divorced—probably because I had never seen the white woman he had married. They had never made a life together; it was a paper marriage only. Yet this piece of paper had given my brother permission to live in the land of his dreams.

Still, I wondered about those dreams. I had lived with Anchan for over half a year and still hadn't seen them bear fruit. Had his decision to live in America forced him to settle for something less than he wanted? My brother wasn't alone; the people in the marriage game at the picnic had probably also sacrificed some essential part of themselves to keep hold of the American dream. But maybe it gave them the strength to go on. At any rate, their furious attempts to pursue the American dream made them a little comical.

By the late sixties, we began to get letters from my mother saying that things were improving in Japan—Dad had steady work, wages had gone up, and Mr. Yamazaki had even built himself a new house. At the end of her letters she would add that there was lots of carpentry work on the island; if my brother couldn't find good work, he could come back to Japan anytime. My mother was probably bluffing when she said that life on the island was improving: just as we wrote to her about America's booming economy so that she wouldn't worry, she was shining a light out into the darkness to lure us back.

Our mother did not, however, know anything about my brother's marriage.

"I can't tell her now," he said. "I don't want her to worry. Next year we'll make money on the strawberries and send her some. That'll ease her mind, and then I'll tell her."

At that moment we were driving through a wealthy neighborhood.

"Look at that big house," my brother said, eyes darting from side to side. "Boy, I'd like to try living in a big house like that sometime. They've got a Thunderbird. Best car on the market. And over there, that house has four luxury cars parked in front."

My brother was lost in thought about our dream house. America might have been in an uproar over student demonstrations, black riots, and the Vietnam War—all of which were shown on television in grisly detail every day—but from here those events seemed to belong to another world. Just thirty minutes away by car was East Los Angeles, a gathering place for illegal immigrants; Sunset Strip, which had been taken over by the hippies; and Watts, where the riots had broken out. Heaven and hell couldn't have been more different than this wealthy section and those other areas of LA.

"*Yuu*, don't look so surprised. Beverly Hills would knock you off your feet. Anyway, things aren't so bad. I've got my own field, and the rest'll come naturally. Lucky for us the strawberries are doing good. We'll make a profit if this keeps up."

Before we went to meet Takita, we decided to shop for Japanese food in Little Tokyo. Pickles, dried mackerel, bean paste, bean cakes, sweets—I tossed whatever I could get my hands on into the shopping basket.

Once we had stocked up on Japanese food, we went to kill time at the bookstore and bought Japanese magazines. Now you can get a day-old Japanese newspaper in LA, and, by some trick of distribution, the magazine *Bungei Shunjā* arrives in LA bookstores a day before it hits the stands in Tokyo. News about Japan is broadcast almost simultaneously into the living rooms of Japanese Americans in California. In those days, however, both the weekly and the monthly magazines came by boat, so we were often reading news that was more than a month stale.

On the farm we shared magazines, sometimes tearing them in half; then the covers would get lost and we couldn't tell the date of an issue. This led to confusion on the sequence of events; a celebrity got married and then divorced, but we had mixed up the issues of the magazine: "*Yuu*, remember that actor? He only just got divorced, and now he's marrying the same woman again! Japan's getting just like America."

It might have been Sunday, but Little Tokyo was packed.

Pinned up in the entrances of Japanese restaurants were many long notices announcing different suppers:

The Hiroshima Prefecture Club Proudly Announces a
Celebratory Autumn Supper Picnic for Its Members

Autumn Bash for Citizens of Kumamoto Prefecture

Hiroshima Girls' School Alumni Gathering

Congratulations Party for So-and-So, Who Has Just Been Awarded
His Poetry Certificate by the Chinese Poetry Society

and

Folksingers Extraordinaire Supper Party

"It's hard to believe that Japanese who come all this way still make *shigin* and folksong clubs," I commented.

"Yeah," my brother answered, "but they do. They even have clubs for bonsai, go, and card games. I've heard there's even one for novelists."

That year a group of young writers who had put out a literary magazine when they were in the detainment camps reunited and published a mimeographed magazine called *Southern California Review*. This magazine has come out twice a year since. Among the original group were many well-known writers, such as Kometani Fumiko and Furuta Sōichi, who have won literary prizes. It is a testimony to the Japanese fascination with language that a literary magazine that had planned only about three issues is still published in the Japanese community in California.

> Waiting for you
> It rained
> I got wet . . .

As I stood at the entrance to the bar, the strains of a Frank Nagai tune from a jukebox floated past me, stirring up memories. I remembered my first night in America the previous April.

"*Yuu* ever been to a place like this before?" asked my brother.

Of course I hadn't. We didn't have bars like this on the island. The room was smoky. Seven or eight women showing lots of cleavage were busy snuggling up to their customers.

During the early 1980s, nearly twenty bars, looking very much like their Japanese cousins, opened within a six-mile radius of Japantown. Many of the hostesses in these bars were Japanese students or travelers, but among them were career hostesses who had come from clubs in Roppongi or Akasaka. Stories about men on business trips running into their favorite Roppongi hostesses in Little Tokyo abounded. Back then, the locals still ran all the bars, and most of the hostesses were war brides who had married Americans during the Occupation. Quite a few of them were divorced and had migrated to San Francisco or Los Angeles. They were in their last bloom.

When the photo brides had flooded into America in the twenties, the Japanese community had grown very lively. The same thing happened through the fifties and sixties when the divorcees rejoined the Japanese communities on the West Coast. We were going to meet Takita in a bar where many such women were working.

"There they are."

My brother's friend Takita was already drinking with friends at the back of the bar.

"Takita, this is my little brother," Anchan said, and I shook the man's hand.

"This is Sakaue from Kagoshima, and Tamashiro from Okinawa," said Takita. The three of them looked ready for anything. I guessed them to be in their early thirties.

"This is Takita, the fastest picker on the farm. Once when we were doing strawberries in San Diego, he picked fifty boxes in a day. That was a new record."

"You have a memory like an elephant." Takita laughed, bringing his beer to his lips.

"You remember what we were talking about before. . . . Which one is she?" My brother suddenly changed the topic.

Takita turned around, saying, "That's her. Sitting over there." Then he turned back. "It's been tough. I went back to Japan after the training program and did a few jobs. But all I really wanted to do was to get back here and try my luck. I tried everything, but I couldn't get a working visa. So I thought coming here as a tourist would be better than nothing; I got here about a year ago. With my old connections, I got work right away. But then my luck went bad. The Immigration Bureau thought I was a Mexican, and they investigated me. I was on a tourist visa, right? So it was forced repatriation; I got sent back."

Takita's being mistaken for a Mexican made sense; his features looked it.

"It just made me more determined. I kept on trying, and finally I got back here this spring on another tourist visa. But it's already expired."

"Then you got in good with this hostess. You're going to marry her and get a green card, right?" said my brother.

"She got divorced from her black husband in North Carolina five years ago. She's been working here since, and has residence status. But I'm only thirty-three. She's forty. It's a problem."

Takita glanced at the woman, and she waved back. "Anyway, I wanted a green card. I probably shouldn't tell you this, but she's a war bride, and, well, I have to admit I lied to her a little. I planned to marry her, get my green card, and divorce her sometime. And at first it looked like she wasn't serious about me either. . . . But now she's changed her mind. I don't want that kind of burden. I was thinking of breaking it off before I got in too deep. Then I met Tamashiro here. He told me about a Japanese woman who does fake marriages. Another war bride. I met her yesterday. She charges three hundred dollars for a Vegas wedding. I can't figure out what to do."

Takita pulled a cigarette out of his pocket and lit up.

"Sakaue, here, who was with me in the training program, he also came back on a tourist visa. He paid a woman in a club like this for a fake marriage, got his green card, and then wanted to divorce her. But wouldn't you know it, she had fallen in love with him and wouldn't keep up her end of the bargain. I can understand her problem. She marries an American guy during the Occupation; he takes her to the sticks, where she's the only Japanese person for miles around, then he dumps her. Here she is almost forty and she meets this young Japanese guy. She doesn't want to let go. Who can blame her? It's a big mess. Finally she gives him the divorce, but he has to pay: two hundred dollars a month till she gets married again. Which is never. So he'll be paying till she dies."

I looked at Sakaue, who was staring into his drink.

"So now Sakaue is miserable wondering why he came back to America in the first place and thinking maybe he should go back to Japan even though he's got his green card."

Takita turned to my brother. "When I think about it, I wish I was in your shoes. You married a white woman, got your green card, and divorced her. You never even had to live together."

My brother was silent; Takita had touched a raw nerve. Pity for my brother welled up in my heart. All these young Japanese men, including my brother, would do anything to live in America. Takita would marry a woman he didn't love. Sakaue had gotten his green card, but now his life was in a shambles. Anchan had married an American, gotten his green card, and his wife had deserted him. To keep his visa, he hadn't been able to see other women for over four years.

I had heard the ups and downs of the Japanese picture brides. Now I was hearing about the various sacrifices the men were making in order to become Americans. I felt very depressed, and ordered my first drink.

The American Dream . . . what kind of sordid dramas did people have to enact for the sake of the American dream?

"Drink up, everybody, it's on me. I hit it big at the Santa Anita horse races today!" A loud voice sounded at the table behind us. At the booth next to that table, a man of about forty was in a tête-à-tête with a hostess. Was he after a green card, or was the woman pressuring the man to return her lost youth, which she had never enjoyed with her American husband? Two "Japanese" men who had just come into the bar passed our table speaking crudely: "All the women here are divorced war brides. They're starving for men; just give them a little money, and they'll *meku rabu* with *yuu*."

"*Longu taimu no shee*," said the hostess, grasping one of the men by the shoulders. Turning around, he kissed the woman on her neck. Ted had once told me white girls would never flirt with Japanese men.

"Exams comin' up. I worked part-time all term. I'm worried that my grades will suffer."

"Yeah, me too. That's why I'm taking Japanese. No problem getting an A. My GPA should be the same."

I could hear two college students talking quietly. To keep up their averages, they had come all the way to America and studied Japanese!

"Anchan, I'm getting drunk. I'm going to go take a walk to clear my head." I was fed up with the conversation around me and felt like escaping.

"Don't go far. It's dangerous. Stay in Japantown," my brother ordered.

As I walked, I eventually left Japantown, passed Third Street and then Fourth Street. It was nine o'clock on a Sunday night; the shops were closed, and I couldn't see a soul. I found myself in front of a shelter. Five or six bums were wrapped in blankets, sleeping in the street. One of them yelled, "Hey, Bill, how's your business?" From across the street another homeless man yelled back, "Not bad, not bad at all."

I kept on walking, and a group of Hell's Angels roared by. A young woman on the back of a big man's bike screamed to me, "Love and peace!"

"I wish I could go to America too." "If we had connections, we'd go to America too." The voices of my friends on the island and the man bound for Paraguay on the *Africa-maru* sounded in my ears.

"What a country," I whispered to myself, kicking an empty can along the street. The can hit a lamppost with a bang.

128

# 8

# New Year's Greetings from an Old Friend

Since the summer, my life had definitely improved; my acquaintance with Sensei and his wife had broadened my horizons considerably, and I had made inroads into the invisible world of the Japanese in America. When I had first arrived, I had felt anger and even shame at things of which I was not a part, but eventually I noticed that my whole life was becoming the immigrant community. My hunch was that I would never escape from the world of picture marriages, fake marriages, and shabby Japantown as long as I lived in this country. Yet when I lost myself in the landscape of the farm, it fed my senses. I began to love the land.

I loved the process of making a field out of virgin land: first, planting seeds and watering them; a few days later watching the shoots push up through the soil; then the mouth-watering scent of strawberries growing in the field. The brown, muscular limbs picking strawberries quickly under the hot sun. The stalwart farmers who won't give up no matter how hard the work. The sunset over the quiet field at day's end. The stars and the moon illuminating the fields at night.

And then there were the wild beauties, like María, popping red, ripe strawberries into their mouths, their firm breasts visible through the gaps in their work shirts. Our eyes followed their every move, and they shot back looks to inflame us. Lustful stares, coquettish looks, melting together among the strawberry plants. We'd rest our hands awhile and sigh, warmth spreading through our bodies. The air tingled.

\* \* \*

On Frankie's recommendation, I had joined the baseball team when school started again in September.

"*Yuu*, to get American *furendo*, you should play either *basuboru* or *footoboru*. *Footoboru's* not so good for Japanese 'cause *yuu* need *pawa*. But you should do OK at *basuboru*. This high school ain't too good. If you get good, you'll be popular. Plus, you'll get lots of girlfriends."

The harvest was over, so, after consulting with my brother, I decided to join the team.

My brother, the worrier, said, "*Yuu*, it's a good idea, but you probably won't be able to keep up with those white boys. They're built differently. You won't make Japan look bad, will you?"

But Pete jumped at the idea. "*Yuu, goodo idea.* Try for the major leagues."

Pete, who knew I had played baseball during my high school days in Japan, took me to see the Dodgers play the San Francisco Giants. With the pitchers Sandy Koufax and Don Drysdale playing for the Dodgers and Willie Mays, Willie McCovey, and Juan Marichal the pitcher on the Giants' side, both teams put up a good fight.

It must have been around this time that Dodgers Stadium designated certain days as "Japan Day" and kept a section of the stands for Japanese fans only. I saw my first major league game on one of these special days.

The following year the Japanese community in California went into a frenzy over Murakami, who had been transferred from the Pacific Hawks to the San Francisco Giants, and was the first Japanese pitcher to debut in the major leagues. In the midsixties, when Japan was barely mentioned in the American media, Murakami's story would go down in sports history.

Frankie had told me that our team wasn't very strong, and a week after joining I could see that he was right. Soon I had made the regulars and was chosen as top batter. Every Friday through November, we played different high school teams, sometimes driving as long as three hours for an away game. There were no national championships, as there were in Japan, and practice was loosely structured. After a game, our team did whatever we felt like—played basketball, or even football, or swam—and this troubled me, since I had been told as a child that a baseball player's arm will freeze up in water. Even when we played games at rival schools nearby, it was rare for our school to cheer us on; there might be thirty people gathered in one corner of the stands. It was football that really drew the students.

I couldn't communicate very well with my teammates, but they were overjoyed when I made an aggressive play and would run over to grab me and shake my hand. One day, as I stole into home from third, I collided head-on with an incredibly beefy catcher and suffered a light concussion. My teammates carried me to the bench and fussed over me, wiping the sweat from my face and murmuring, "You're a great kamikaze." "You're Vietcong."

That day my story was featured in the school newspaper, and the shameful name *samurai* from the previous spring was wiped away forever. When I took the newspaper back to the farm, Pete shook my hand. "*Yuu*, this is great. I'm so happy!" Pete had suffered from polio as a child, and his legs were weak. Later I learned that he had dreamed of becoming a baseball player.

Frank commented, "See, whatever we Japanese do, we're *alrigh*. Look at me, I'm a big farmer. Whites still make fun of us, but we're the best. We try hard even when they knock us down. Do a good job so we can be proud of *yuu*."

So, I thought to myself, maybe I have done something good for morale on the farm.

After I joined the baseball team, my life at school changed. My friends on the team would invite me over and take me along on drives with their girlfriends. At first they seemed like typical young Americans—always smiling and saying, "It's no problem, no problem"—but after I got to know them better, I found out that they did have problems with their families and their girlfriends, and worried about when they would be drafted.

After practice every day in the shower, we would discuss our next game. One day, however, we were talking about the blackouts on the East Coast. On November 9, there had been a power failure in seven eastern states for the first time in America's history. All the skyscrapers in New York City—the city that never stops—went out, and much of the East Coast was plunged into darkness.

It was as though a darkness had fallen over America to quiet those turbulent times. People returned home quickly and spent the evening by candlelight looking into the faces of their spouses and their children for the first time in a long while. One journalist predicted that many "blackout babies" would be born the next summer, and he was proved right. People in the big cities hit by the power failure feared that there would be an increase in violence and crime, but in fact it seemed that just the opposite happened. The darkness made people kinder to each other for a little while.

Just as we were discussing how such an accident could happen in America, our coach came in and gave us some sad news: a graduate of the school who had played on the baseball team two years earlier had just died in Vietnam. People had said this boy of Mexican descent was destined for the major leagues, and he had been the star of our team. Some of our team members had played with him. Jim, our pitcher, put his head in his hands and began to cry, while others clasped their hands together in prayer. I found myself doing the same, for a boy I had never known.

The day would come when many of the young men my age would have to go to war. The death of someone they knew had brought the truth home to them, and they looked frightened. At a loss for words, especially in this kind of situation, I returned to the shower alone and washed myself down with cold water. As far as the war was concerned, I would remain an outsider. Yet from that day on, the topic of Vietnam often came up on the farm.

"*Yuu*, know that *babashoppu* near the *supa maketo*, right? It's run by a Mexican. He just lost both of his sons in Vietnam," Anchan announced at dinner one night. "The father had a green card, but the sons didn't. They came here illegally when they were twelve and thirteen. Both of them were real smart and wanted to go to college, but they had no money, and, what's worse, they were illegal, so there wasn't anything they could do. But in America, you know, they'll give you a green card if you volunteer to fight, even if you're an illegal or just a traveler. And with a green card, you have a shot at becoming a citizen. So the two of them volunteered for the marines."

"And they died in the war? How old were they?"

" 'Bout the same as *yuu*."

"Could anyone want a green card that bad?"

"Sure. Look at the Mexicans on the farm. They get paid a dollar an hour. But just try taking that dollar to Mexico. You can get about ten times what you get here."

"So that means people with green cards have to go to war, too. Anchan, you have a green card."

"Yeah, I do, but I'm still a Japanese citizen. Still, if we got into a big war, like the Pacific War, I'd probably be called up. You'd probably have to register for the draft, too, since you came on a student visa."

"You're joking." I turned pale at my brother's words.

"No, it's true. It probably won't get that big, but there's a chance."

"Well, if it happened, would you go? To that kind of war . . ."

"I'd probably have to. I chose to live here. But let's drop it. We don't want to ruin dinner." Anchan started brewing coffee on the gas range.

All through the end of that year, my brother's words weighed heavily on my mind. Over the next three or four years, a number of Japanese boys my age whom I had met on the farm would go to the war.

I went back to Japan in 1969 and entered a Japanese university in 1970. It was during my first autumn term that Frankie Noda called me from a Tokyo hotel: "Hi, I'm here on leave. I got five days, so I decided to visit my homeland. I really want to see you."

I met him right away. But after only six months in the war, Frankie was no longer his happy-go-lucky self; he was callous.

"Since I'm gonna die in Vietnam anyway, I wanted to see Japan one more time. Y'know, I lived in Yokohama till I was ten—I want to see what it looks like now. *Yuu,* where can I meet some Japanese girls? I'm loaded; I've got three thousand bucks. It's *alrigh* if we use it all. I'll buy a girl for you, too, but we gotta find them tonight."

Frankie was dead serious. We spent three thousand dollars on women before he went back to Vietnam.

A Japanese guy I knew fought in the fierce battle at Danang; he got shrapnel wounds all over his body and spent a long time in the military hospital. I also heard a story about a man I'll call Watanabe, who was drafted and did his military training in

Arizona. Just before leaving for Vietnam, he went back to visit his parents on their farm. All the neighboring farmers threw him a big farewell party, during which one of the guests held up a Japanese flag and said: "Watanabe is going to war tomorrow. Please, everyone, write something on this flag, so we can send him off with good luck."

Some people wrote "Great Success in Battle" and "Come back safe and sound" on the flag, but a number of others wrote imperialistic slogans like "One Asia" and "Revere the Emperor, Banish the Barbarian." Although this young man was going to fight an American war, the older people had gotten all stirred up and seemed to believe that he was off to fight for Japan.

Oblivious to all this, Watanabe took his flag with him. The day before he was to leave for Vietnam, it was found in a routine luggage check by a soldier who had fought the Japanese in the Pacific. Accused of taking a Japanese flag to an American war and of being disloyal, Watanabe was stripped of his military credentials.

Some of my young Japanese friends received notices from the Immigration Bureau asking if they would go to the war in an emergency. Luckily I never got anything like that.

On Christmas Eve of that year, President Johnson called a ceasefire. That night I was at a Christmas dance party in a restaurant at the invitation of my teammates. Frankie was with me. The news of the ceasefire had spread quickly that day, cheering up some of my teammates who knew they were going to war once they graduated.

Most of the guys were with their girlfriends. A number of girls danced with me, probably because they had been asked to do so. One of my teammates introduced me to a girl. "This is Sukiyaki [my newest nickname]," he said, "the fastest guy on the team." Although I didn't know any of the steps, I danced with a white girl for the first time, pressing my chest against hers and wrapping my arms around her back. The music changed from slow music to rock and back again. Couples were necking in the corners. Overcome with envy, I squeezed my partner even tighter and moved my hands up and down her back. Finally, after the party ended, and we all agreed to meet there again next year, I left in Frankie's car.

"*Yuu*, that knockout Barbara, she's got the hots for you. She's got big tits too. You gotta take her out on a date. Japanese guys act like jerks 'cause they're so scared. *Don be shai*," Frankie said, egging me on as he drove. We had reached the farm; on Christmas Eve we were the only car on the road. I could faintly see the lights from Jiisan's house on the hill.

"Frankie, drive me over to the old man's place, will you? It's Christmas Eve, and I bet he's all alone."

"Can you get home by yourself? I'm tired. I wanna go home after I drop you off. OK?"

"OK."

I got out of the car and knocked on the old man's door. Going in, I found him weaving bits of rope together at his table.

"Jiisan, merry Christmas. It's not much of a present, but here's some cake." I put some leftover party cake on the table.

"*Ooy, sankyu yo na.* I'm making New Year's decorations. *Shimenawa.* One for *yuu-tachi*, too."

Here was the old man, spending Christmas alone making *shimenawa* for New Year's Day, a whole week away.

"Been in this country a long time, but I still care more about New Year's Day. Least I can do is make 'em somethin' for New Year's. Your cauliflower's doing good. Got a look at it this morning. Probably get some good strawberries next year too."

"You can see our field from here," I said, stepping outside. From where I stood, I could see the whole farm. The leaves of our cauliflower plants glowed green in the moonlight. After New Year's, we had to start picking them. Jiisan followed me out. As we gazed into the distance, we could see the lights in our house in the middle of the field come on.

"*Yuu, buraza's* home. *Yuu-tachi* been workin' hard. I wish you luck," Jiisan whispered, looking out over the fields.

"If this were Japan, we'd have lots of New Year's cards," said my brother on his way back from the mailbox.

Even so, our mailbox was much fuller than usual.

"Look how many there are for you." Anchan handed me four or five letters. This was my first New Year's in America. My high school friends and my friends on the island must have tried to mail

135

things so that I would get them by the first of January. The New Year's cards with the lottery numbers on them made me especially homesick.

"Japanese love to get New Year's cards wherever they are. This is my sixth New Year's in America, you know, and I still get homesick. Anyhow, here, it's business as usual on the second. Really, it's better not to work before the seventh if you're Japanese," my brother said, sorting out a few cards from the gas and electric bills. Even my workaholic brother wanted to enjoy himself during the first week of the new year.

Since we had just gotten our own farm, we decided to pray for success in the new year, so we waited for the sun to rise near the old man's house on top of the hill. After we got home, we ate some of the traditional delicacies my brother had made and went back to bed. When we woke a second time, Anchan, following the Japanese custom, kept checking the mailbox, even though we didn't expect any more mail.

"Hey, here's a Christmas card I wasn't expecting," Anchan had said earlier.

"A Christmas card now?"

"No, not really. Do you remember Akiko from the island? Akiko, who married Bob, the soldier, and went to New York? She says in her letter that she got our address from someone on the island. It brings back memories. It sounds like she and Bob are doing very well."

I certainly did remember Akiko. Right before Akiko went to America, she'd had a terrible argument with one of the men on the island, and I had witnessed the whole thing.

Akiko wasn't a native islander. She had come from the country to Tokyo and had met Bob when she was working in a club there. When Bob was transferred to the base on our island, she, like the other *onlys*, followed him there. Among the seven or eight *onlys*, however, Akiko was a little spitfire—and one woman I would never forget.

Once we saw a drunk Akiko chasing Bob down the street. Bob, an American soldier who needn't have apologized for anything while he was in Japan, sat down in the road and begged her forgiveness, a sight that delighted us.

136

The other incident occurred after she had gotten her marriage papers and was about to leave for America. She and Bob were drinking in a small neighborhood bar when a man from the island near them spoke up. "That slut. He's going to dump her even if he takes her to America. Poor thing."

Akiko had already had a few drinks, and this remark set her off. She took the man outside and started arguing angrily with him. Hearing loud voices in the street, I rushed out of my house.

"Whadda ya mean, slut? What's wrong with marrying an 'merican soldier? Japanese men—hah!—my darlin's much better than any of you. You lose the war, and you apologize a million times. You're spineless. My darlin's bringin' me flowers and chocolate every day and tellin' me, 'Ai rabu yuu.' But you, you jerk, have you ever told a woman you loved her? Huh? He fell in love with me, madly in love."

After this outburst, Akiko lay down in the street and sobbed. Bob picked her up very gently in his arms and carried her away. I will never forget the sight of the two of them comforting each other.

Over the twenty years after the war, hundreds of thousands of Japanese women married American men and emigrated to America. Many of the women were rudely dismissed by Japanese men the way Akiko had been and went off as lonely brides to their new home. Many years later I got to know quite a few war brides, and some of them told me stories like Akiko's.

"Yeah, in those days everyone was against women seeing American soldiers," one war bride told me. "But for those of us in the business, if you know what I mean, just try having someone bring you flowers and say 'Ai rabu yuu, ai rabu yuu.' You can't resist!"

I am sure they were telling the truth. The Japanese women who came to America were probably the first ones in Japanese history to be courted by men who brought flowers and said "I love you." Many of the women told me that, in spite of linguistic and racial barriers, American men had great bodies and were very sincere and open.

The women had chosen these men themselves. If this was true, they were behaving as real women should. Their marriages to strong, verbal men made them perhaps the most sensible people in postwar Japan. But it was a different story once they got to the U.S. To become American, they had to start from zero again. Sadly enough, many of these women were abandoned and came to live in the little Tokyos on the West Coast.

"She writes about *yuu* too," my brother went on. "She says come visit New York anytime. Actually she lives near Niagara Falls," he added, after finishing the letter. This letter would set a chain of events in motion, but of course my brother had no idea about it then.

"We should write back soon; she was on the island with us, and she's probably feeling homesick. *Yuu*, write something too."

"If she lives near Niagara Falls, I bet she doesn't have any Japanese books. Let's send her some of the magazines we've finished reading. Anchan, is this what New Year's is like in America? What should we do to celebrate?"

"Our vacation usually goes from Christmas to New Year's Day. I'd go with the boss and other guys to Las Vegas, or take a drive," Anchan replied. "But this year I'm in debt, and I decided to hold off. But Frank, Ted, Ramón, and some of the others should be in Vegas by now."

Our table was decorated with *kagamimochi*, special rice cakes for New Year's Day, that we had bought in Japantown. Usually one placed tangerines on top of the cakes, but we had to substitute large oranges. Over the doorway, we hung the twisted rope, the present from Jiisan. In place of the pine branches that usually lined the doorways in Japan, my handy brother had cut some scrubby branches that looked very similar.

Although it was nearly noon, we hadn't heard a peep from next door. What a dull New Year's it was going to be. How had my brother survived on his own here for over four years?

I went outside. Although it was winter, the temperature still hovered around 60 degrees. The air was clear, and I could see quite a long way off. There at the edge of the farmland were the snowy peaks of the San Bernardino mountain range, glittering against the blue sky. All around the house were strawberry plants, their tiny leaves spreading in lines as far as the eye could see. In three months' time the quiet field would come alive with the return of the pigeons. Maybe María would be with them . . .

I turned around and caught a glimpse of smoke rising from a shed in our corner of the field.

"Anchan! I see fire!" I yelled.

"Fire?" My brother came running out of the house.

"See that smoke over there."

"You're right. Get in the car."

We rode bumpily down through the field. The smoke came clearly into view, then so did some people.

"I should have known. They're at it again. *Godamu.*"

"I don't get it. You mean arsonists?"

"No, I mean González and Antonio. I thought they were too quiet this morning."

"They're building a bonfire on the edge of the field?"

"No, no. *Rabbito huntingu.*"

"Rabbit hunting?"

"Yeah. They don't have any money and they're hungry, so they're catching rabbits."

Our car stopped at the shed. As my brother had said, the two Mexicans were there. González was burning weeds and using his shirt to fan the smoke into one end of a sixty-foot irrigation pipe. Antonio stood stock-still, holding a shovel over the other end of the pipe.

"Anchan, what are those guys up to?"

"I told you, didn't I? Rabbit hunting."

"But are there rabbits in that pipe?"

About twenty pipes were stored in the lot by the shed.

"The rabbits hibernate in the pipes. So they smoke them out, bash them with a shovel, and roast 'em. Unbelievable. Still, roasted that way, the rabbits around here taste pretty good. I've had some before," my brother said happily.

Anchan's face brightened that way whenever he ran into something unexpected. He turned to the Mexicans. "How are you doing, fearless hunters? Catch any coyotes or lions, maybe some cows?"

My brother's foolish bantering was an expected part of dealing with the Mexicans.

"No cows, but rabbits, squirrels, and one bird," Antonio said, as he held up two rather hefty rabbits.

"Well, anyway, Happy New Year," my brother said, extending his hand.

González and Antonio looked a little mystified; they wiped their dirty hands on their trousers, shook his hand, and replied, "Happy New Year."

"I bet you're out of money. If you're hungry, why don't you come to my house? Listen, in Japan we say that if you kill a living thing on New Year's Day, you'll have a bad year. Don't risk it."

It was just like my brother to lecture about the way things were done in Japan when he was living on an American farm. Taking a five-dollar bill out of his pocket, he continued, "Go to the market, buy some food. Boss is coming back *mañana* from Vegas. Get an advance from him. I'll ask him for you if you want."

The two men thanked him. *"Señor, muchas gracias, muchas gracias."*

In that instant, a rabbit jumped out of the pipe. He looked at us for a second, then raced off into the field. Still holding the shovel, Antonio looked crestfallen at having missed such a splendid catch. We heard the sound of a car approaching; it was the old man.

"Look, it's Jiisan. He must have been worried about the fire, too," my brother said.

The little old man emerged shakily from his '49 Ford.

*"Whatso matta?* What happened? I was looking out of my house, and I saw this shed on fire. I brought some water just in case."

"Jiisan, it's just what it looks like. The *Mexi-tachi* were hunting."

"Oh, that's all. That's *alrigh.* But if the field burns on New Year's Day, we'll have a bad year, you know."

There were three half-empty buckets on Jiisan's backseat, much of their water having sloshed out on the rough ride over. The back of the car was awash. Anchan tried to stifle a laugh.

"Jiisan, since you brought the water, let's put out the fire anyway. It's about time. Antonio, González, put out the fire with Jiisan's water," my brother ordered, opening the door of Jiisan's car. For a moment, the two Mexicans looked disgruntled, but eventually they complied.

"Jiisan, it's a bit late, but Happy New Year."

I continued: "Yes, thank you for all your help last year. And for the coming year as well."

"*Oi, Happi Nyu Yea yo na.*"

"This morning we went up to pray on the hill near your house at sunrise. We were thinking about waking you but—"

"Oh, that was you, was it? The sound of a car woke me."

"Hey, Jiisan, have you eaten yet? Please come over, we have plenty of *osechi-ryōri* [New Year's food]."

"No, it's *alrigh yo.* Somebody from the Okinawa Club brought me some rice cakes, boiled fish, and vegetables yesterday, so I made my own. I ate already."

The Mexicans looked bored; the smell of burnt, water-soaked weeds and rags stung our nostrils. "Jiisan, what are you doing today? We're planning to go to Japantown to see a Japanese movie. Jiisan, it'd do you good to see a Japanese movie once in a while."

" 'Bout four years ago, I saw a Nakamura Kinosuke picture. That was the last time. I'm fine, you go. I have to weed the field."

This wasn't the only time the old man had turned down one of our invitations. Jiisan seemed to find other people very tiresome. During the war, when the Japanese were interned in the camps, he was mistaken for a Filipino and lived in hiding somewhere out on the farm, afraid of being discovered as an illegal alien. Perhaps this was why he found it difficult to socialize.

Jiisan didn't have citizenship or a green card, let alone a Japanese passport; his only ID was a driving license. He didn't have a bank account; the market paid him by check, which he had to cash at a check-cashing store for an outrageous 3 percent fee. Legally, psychologically, and socially, the old man was a shadow.

Once I went with the old man to the check-cashing store, which got most of its business from illegals. Originally, the farm bosses had paid their workers by check, and then offered to cash checks for a 3 percent fee, knowing that illegal aliens had no bank accounts and would have to get them cashed somewhere. Of course, the workers knew what was going on, but they were in no position to protest.

"He's a good man, but he doesn't like people," my brother commented. "A lot of the Japanese around here try to help him out, but he just won't listen to them. Even Frank said to him,

141

'Look, Jiisan, you're getting old. If you stop planting strawberries and come to my field, I'll pay you for not working.' But Jiisan said he wants to farm till he drops, so he keeps working that field and doesn't make a dime," my brother commented after the old man had gotten into his car and gone home. "It's still too early for the movie. Let's stop at the field. I want to take a look at the cauliflower."

We got back in the car and drove to our field. From the car window, we could see the old man on the ground, weeding. Why had he ever come to this country?

"Hey, look inside the leaves—this cauliflower looks great," my brother pointed out.

The cauliflower plants came up to my thigh, and, when I peeled away the leaves, I could see a gray-white cauliflower about the size of my fist.

"Hmm, looks pretty firm," he added. "Should be fine. We might be able to harvest them a week early. I wish we could show them to Mom and Dad."

"I wonder what everybody's doing this New Year's at home."

"There's a seventeen-hour time difference between here and Japan, so, let's see, that makes it already the second in Japan."

When I suddenly mentioned home, a vacant look came into my brother's eyes.

One day at the end of January, just after Anchan and I had decided to harvest our cauliflower crop, it rained. Since I had arrived in southern California, it had rained once in October, twice in December, and now in the new year, a total of four times.

I doubt anybody in Japan remembers how many times it rains in a year. But in southern California, we call it blessed rain. There's a saying, "To the Japanese, water and safety are free." Forget water being free here—the huge expanse of California farmland cannot depend on rainfall for a single drop of water. All water is brought hundreds of miles from the Colorado River or the Sierra Nevada mountains in pipelines that cost a huge amount of money.

Water is stored in tanks below ground, and, when it is used to irrigate a field, it barely penetrates to the roots of the plants. If you dig down a couple of feet after watering, you will see dry, dusty earth just beneath the moist surface.

When the precious "water of life" does fall, the earth drinks it up like a sponge. When the rain stops, the soaked land glistens darkly under the sun. Rain just before harvesttime cleanses the leaves and snaps them back to life. During their last surge of growth, the rain gives them an added boost. Farmers are all smiles.

"We needed this rain. They predicted rain yesterday, but listening to the weather report here is worse than being constipated. A couple of clouds and they tell you, "It's going to rain, it's going to rain," but it never does. Today they finally got it right," my brother grumbled, as he slogged through the rows.

We were discussing how we were going to harvest the cauliflower in three days' time. Like my brother, I was dressed head-to-toe in rain gear.

"This reminds me of being a fisherman back home," said Anchan, pointing at his thick rubber sleeve. It all came back to me: when there wasn't enough work as carpenters, he and Father would work as fishermen on a friend's boat, sailing off in search of flying fish and mackerel.

"Are you ready? *Yuu,* see you have to cut ones this big. Size is the problem. Look, like this one. Now . . . it's hard to say about this one, but if you have any doubts, don't cut it. On the fast-growing ones, see, the leaves are starting to open like flowers. Cut them, and shave off some of the leaves with this knife. Otherwise, the market won't take 'em."

Spreading open the leaves around each cauliflower, Anchan showed me the ones to pick. We walked down the rows, each holding a twenty-inch kitchen knife that we had bought in Japantown.

"Strawberry picking is hard enough, but this is more *hardo da zo.*"

"How do we do it?"

"OK. We gotta keep up with the tractor as it moves down the rows, so, we cut the cauliflower and throw it into the wagon. Cauliflower weighs a lot, and you have to work steadily all day. Your shoulders ache, you fall down because the ground's soft—it's tough work. With your pitching arm, you'll be great at this."

I didn't argue the differences between throwing a baseball and tossing a cauliflower.

The field was misty with rain as far as the eye could see. A few people were working in Frank's field, probably Mexicans who had come out to check that the rain was draining correctly. There were no holidays on the farm. A few moments later, we could see a white car emerging from the mist on the dirt road.

"It's the boss's car. What a show-off. Frank hit it big in Vegas, so he bought a car and still had enough left over for two tractors. That man . . ." My brother sounded a little bitter. Frank had made twenty thousand dollars in one week in Vegas. He bought a new car and two tractors in cash and returned triumphant to the farm.

"When he gets here, praise his gambling, tell him it's a nice car—even if you're just sucking up to him. People love to win alot of money at gambling. It's all he talks about from morning to night at the office. When I went there this morning, he was doing his thing with the telephone doctor and telling the doctor he's going to send him gambling telepathy, or some such bullshit."

The shiny Thunderbird, now covered with mud, stopped in front of us. Charlie and Frank got out.

"*Naisu. Goodo, bery goodo.* You've done a good job. Your cauliflower's going to ripen first. The white farmers in the next town, *jisu yea,* they aren't growing cauliflower. You've got a chance," Frank pronounced, marching down the rows.

"Beautiful, just gorgeous, Daiku," added Charlie, inspecting the leaves.

What's so gorgeous about ordinary old cauliflower, I thought to myself. Charlie says "beautiful" and "gorgeous" when he talks about strawberries, too. Everything is either "beautiful" or "gorgeous" to him. I was beginning to think that Americans were foolish to use grand words like that.

"Frank-san, that's a nice car. I heard you made it big in Vegas." I flattered Frank, under my brother's orders.

"*Zatso righto.* You got it. Blackjack, poker, slot machines, *yuu,* whatever I do, everything is money. I've been gambling for a long time, but this time, my luck was incredible. I won so much that the dealers were trying different tactics to beat me. But I never

144

lost. The waitresses never left my side. Total I musta paid over a hundred dollars in tips." Frank's breath became ragged. "Luck is with me, so *jisu yea, ai amu shur,* we're going to have a good strawberry crop."

A large truck approached us in the rain carrying Pete, Ted, and Ramón. If a few people gathered on the farm, others would gather, too, even if it was none of their business—no one wanted to miss anything. Everyone on the farm longed for company. The three men knew what Frank was bragging about. Behind Frank's back, Ramón was shrugging his shoulders and winking.

"Frank, *yuu* still talkin' 'bout Vegas? *Yuu* are *too muchi.*" Ted looked fed up. My brother told me that Ted had lost a lot of money there, had been in a foul temper ever since, and was taking it out on his Mexican workers.

"Frank," said Pete, stopping short.

"What?"

"That blanket man Matsumoto from Okinawa, he's here asking for work this year. What do you want to do?"

"Matsumoto? *Fhuu isu itto? Letto mi shinku.* Oh, that guy. *Rasto yea* he wasn't here. Where is he now?"

"In the office."

"It's a little early for strawberries and there isn't much work now . . ."

"He says he wouldn't mind weeding till picking season starts."

The blanket men were on the move; they knew that it was nearly time to pick the first fruits and vegetables. From time to time, Mexican migrant workers also stopped in to check up on the crops. Their footsteps sounded closer and closer to the farm. The agent José, who had visited us last year, would soon be on the border gathering workers. Maybe María was on her way. A warm feeling spread through my chest at the thought of her.

The cauliflower harvest went smoothly. As my brother had warned, cutting cauliflower was much harder than picking strawberries. With no one in the driver's seat, the tractor was set at its slowest speed; keeping in time, we had to hack off the cauliflower on either side of us, strip off the leaves, and throw the vegetables in the wagon. The tractor was still a machine, and we were only

145

human. Frequently, we found ourselves running after it, waving our knives in the air.

Anchan, two Mexicans, and I cut the cauliflower and threw it into the wagon until there was a white mountain of it. Then we took it to a shed, loaded it into cardboard boxes, and tied these up with rope. It was monotonous work. But when a week was up, the field reverted to its wild self.

"We got a decent price on those; it's a good start. If only I had planted ten acres instead of five . . . We have to see how the strawberries turn out," said Anchan, tidying up the receipts he had gotten at the market.

"*Yuu* should buy yourself a motorcycle with the money we made. You need wheels here. It'll be useful for getting to school or going into the fields. Yamaha would be a good one. You can make monthly payments. For three hundred yen, you should be able to do it. Let's see, with a down payment of maybe a hundred yen and then maybe twenty yen a month in payments. I can use it when I'm working. Let's get one."

I had been living with my brother for nearly a year. The two of us had worked hard. This was the first time we were going to buy anything new.

In the beginning of February, my brother and I went to a nearby dealer and bought a 90-cc Yamaha. It was easy to get a driver's license; that same day, I took a written test and a driver's test and got my license—my first American identification card.

In those days, Japan had just started importing cars to America, so you never saw Japanese cars on the freeway. Japanese motorcycles, however, were very popular among young people. The mood of the times helped. The Hell's Angels rode motorcycles around America, and the more curious youths were very interested in their equipment. Yamaha, Honda, Suzuki—the names of the latest models were on everyone's lips at school. Honda, in particular, had almost mythical status.

After I got my own two wheels and could drive around freely, my world widened considerably. On my way home from school or after I had finished work, I would take a spin through nearby towns, or drive around the farms. Without telling my brother, I also went to porno movies in downtown Los Angeles. It took me an hour and a half to get to the Pussycat Theatre, a first-rate porn theater in LA, on back roads, since I couldn't ride my small motorcycle on the freeway. For a nineteen-year-old living on a farm, without women or any sexual outlets, this place was paradise.

Porno films flourished in those days, as did porno theaters and peep shows. The Pussycat Theatre became the most famous theater of its kind in southern California. The high point of 1963 was when a decision was handed down that *Fanny Hill* was not pornography; it was also in the early sixties that the erotic novels of Henry Miller were being published. Aside from promoting sexual freedom, these events showed that the ways we described sex were changing dramatically.

The most striking example of this was the use of the word *fuck*, so popular among students at Berkeley. I'd learned the literal meaning of the word the previous year, but it wasn't until much later that I noticed how Americans used it in everyday conversation. On television the students at Berkeley cried out, "Fuck America. Fuck the Vietnam War. Fuck the racists." Fuck prefaced everything.

The age of porno also made waves on our remote farm. Although there aren't many bookstores in American towns, there were four or five bookstores in nearby Pomona, and one store's neon sign was changed from BOOKSTORE to FUCKSTORE. The townspeople who saw it nearly fainted from shock. For a while you heard of nothing else in the supermarket or at the gas station. Ramón and his friends, who loved dirty jokes, would often cry, "Let's go to the Fuckstore!"

The word *fuck* was on everyone's lips in those days, but what effect did it have on our lives? It seems likely to me that without this word the antiwar movement, the fight against racism, and even the student movement could never have gathered such momentum.

Blacks and whites, whites and Asians, upper-class kids and their blue-collar counterparts were able to join hands and demonstrate together even though what whites meant by freedom and what blacks meant by it may have been worlds apart. Why? I think that the answer lies in the word *fuck*.

147

No matter how lofty one's ideals or principles, people in this country cannot escape discrimination based on the color of one's skin. But the word *fuck* breaks down the barriers between black and white, man and woman. In front of such a word, the Harvard student and the black man from the slums are reduced to the same pathetic creature.

I do not know whether the times produced such language or whether the language produced the times. But that particular word inevitably levels and unites people. This is what I learned from the outrageous behavior and the angry voices of the hippies as I wandered around LA from the porn theaters to hippy-occupied Sunset Strip to Beverly Road.

I, too, breathed the air of those days, and I was to have an experience that made me a member of the "fuck" generation. One day in early March, as school was letting out, I ran into Frankie in the parking lot. *"Yuu,* remember that girl you danced with at the Christmas party? Barbara. She asked me to get her a date with you. I'm taking my girlfriend, Cathy, and we're all going to a drive-in this Friday. Double-o-seven's playing," he informed me. I had only exchanged a few words with Barbara at school since the night Frankie had told me on the way home that she "had the hots" for me.

"But I only have a motorcycle."

"Barbara's got a car. She'll *picku yuu upu, okei? Nexto Furiday, yo."* Frankie started his car.

A date with a white girl? Maybe . . . With a rush of exhilaration, I accelerated fast. On the back of the motorcycle, riding toward the farm, fantasies bubbled up in my brain. The strawberry field was bathed in spring sunlight, and there were little white flowers blooming here and there.

# 9

# A Discussion with Henry Miller

I waited impatiently for my first date with an American girl; meanwhile, my brother had his own reasons for growing impatient. Anchan and I had sent Japanese magazines and sweets to Akiko in New York. About ten days later, we received a photograph and a note from a white girl, a neighbor of Akiko's, enclosed in a thank-you letter.

"*Yuu,* she's pretty good looking, don't you think? In her letter she says that she's twenty-five, she's been to junior college, and now she's working in a bank. I guess we should write back soon, but it's so hard to write a letter in English," my brother said one day after work.

It was my turn to cook dinner that night. I had left work early but didn't feel like bothering much, so dinner was just some sliced cabbage fried up with pork. Still holding the photo in one hand, my brother took one look at the meal and started to grumble. "*Yuu,* what do you call this? You never put any heart into your cooking."

"Heart?"

"Yeah, no *harto.* You just threw some meat and cabbage into a pan. *Yuu,* it ain't enough for *hardo waku* people. We need *pawa.*"

I couldn't altogether disagree with my brother. But I was tired. No way was I going to put "heart" into my cooking every day. If he had to be so critical, why didn't he get married again, I nearly blurted out, but stopped myself just in time.

"Next time I'll make something better. Let me see that photograph."

The girl, who was six years older than I was, had clear eyes, blond hair, and a faint smile playing about her lips.

"Maybe we'll frame it and put it on the wall. Let's write back to her after dinner. *Yuu* help me," Anchan ordered.

"Me?" I said. "I can't write a letter in English."

"Yeah, I can talk all right, but I can't write. Damn. What a waste."

"Hold on. How about getting Sensei to write it for you? He writes perfect English," I suggested.

Although neither of us could express ourselves fully in English, we started to correspond with Akiko's neighbor with Sensei's help. Actually, Anchan wrote the letters; I just took them to Sensei's house to have them translated. After a number of them, Sensei said, laughingly, "These letters are getting more risqué. And it's not just your brother. It's the young lady, too."

Although Akiko's neighbor wrote in ink, her letters were curiously twisted, as though she were left-handed, and we couldn't decipher them. We had to ask Sensei to read them for us, too.

"The more of these letters I write, the more I feel like I'm writing them myself. Makes me feel young," he chuckled.

"Now these are other people's love letters. Don't start getting ideas," his wife retorted.

The two Mexican guys next door often came over to drink beer with us; when they saw the photo on the table, they teased my brother, saying, *"Ai, Ichikuwawa, bonita."* In a place without women, even a photo caused a stir, and made our lives richer.

The day before my big double date with Frankie, Akiko's neighbor asked for my brother's photo.

*"Yuu,* listen, she wants a picture of me. Tomorrow, maybe I should put on a suit and get a photo taken at a studio. The other guys on the farm want photos, too," my brother declared happily.

All I could think of were the photo brides. "Listen, Anchan, how about getting your photo taken in Frank's field—it's much bigger than ours," I suggested half jokingly.

*"Yuu,* what are you saying? It's better to be honest in these things," Anchan scolded. He seemed to be getting serious. When I told him about my date with Barbara, he responded gravely.

"Look at the two of us, chasing women. What would Mom and Dad say if they could see us?"

The next afternoon, while I was having lunch with Frankie and two other girls in the high school parking lot, we planned our date for that night. Frankie's father was using the family car, so his girlfriend had to pick him up. My date, Barbara, would get me at my house at six o'clock. The plan was that the two cars would meet at a restaurant near the drive-in; then we'd have supper and go to the movie. My main worry was that I wouldn't be able to say much while Barbara and I were alone in the car together.

As we were parting, Frankie lisped some advice to me. "*Yuu*, big *chansu yo*. American *garu*, it's *alrigh* to kiss them on the first date. But remember, Barbara's a *naisu garu*."

I rode my motorcycle home and stopped in at the field to tell my brother once again that I was going out that night. The green leaves of the strawberry plants shone brilliantly, reflecting the bright light of the early spring sun, and flowers were now sprouting on the stalks. Bees buzzed around the plants, looking for honey in the flowers. The shiny plants in the field, the weeds by the roadside, and the wild grasses sprouting on the little hill behind the field were all a pale, new green. The "green front" of California was moving slowly northward and would soon reach our field. I took a shower, put on a clean white shirt, and waited for Barbara.

At the sound of a car horn, I went outside and saw Barbara beckoning me from her car. Finally, I was having a date with a young American girl! I got in the car, and Barbara started talking immediately. She went on and on about how exciting she found Sean Connery's movies.

I had seen the second James Bond movie, *From Russia with Love*, at the American base before it had been released in Japan. In faltering English, I started bragging that I was the first person in Japan to see *From Russia with Love*. Barbara, who was eighteen years old, said that she did not know that American movies were shown in Japan. I was shocked. Even worse—she didn't know that there were American military bases in Japan! All she knew about Japan was the song "Sukiyaki," the emperor, Tojo, Fujiyama, and a Mifune Toshiro film that Frankie had taken her to see in Japantown.

Having done well in high school, Barbara was going to a state university in September. The fact that she knew so little about Japan made me a bit angry. I could recite the names of at least ten American presidents cold. And when it came to novels, I had read quite a few English ones, even if in Japanese translation. My spirits sank; I wished I had the vocabulary to tell this girl a thing or two.

Barbara didn't seem concerned with my silence and kept up a steady stream of conversation. She even mentioned my baseball steal, which had been reported in the school newspaper. She had a cute way of talking. Still, I didn't much care whether she liked me or not, as long as we could make out in the car. I only understood one-tenth of what she was saying, but I bluffed my way through, saying "yes," "no," or "that's right," all the while scheming about how things would develop at the drive-in.

After a light supper at the restaurant, the four of us went to the movie. About a hundred cars were parked in front of a gigantic outdoor screen. Barbara and I parked toward the back, and she left to get us Cokes and popcorn. Sound came from the little speaker that hung on the car window, and soon the silhouette of Bond was walking across a blue screen.

Through the front window of our car, I could see inside a number of other cars; women were leaning on men's shoulders. Barely aware of the movie, I focused on Barbara, finding it difficult to breathe as her scent filled the cramped car. When I looked at her, she smiled. I reached out a number of times in attempts to hold her hand, but always lost my nerve at the last minute.

"She likes you," Frank had said. But what if I make a move and get turned down? *"Don be shai."* Frankie's words echoed through my brain. My left hand inched toward her right hand and pulled back a moment too soon. This was no place to be watching a movie. I wondered what Frankie and Cathy were doing at that moment. Barbara gave me a long, hard look. Flustered, I jumped out of the car, saying, "I'm thirsty. I'm going to get a Coke. Do you want one too?"

Why are you acting like such a wimp? She's only a year younger than you, I whispered to myself while waiting in line at the refreshment stand. On my way back to the car, with two large

152

Cokes in hand, I saw many couples embracing furiously. Like a Peeping Tom, I stopped to steal furtive looks. Take courage! I told myself, she's just a girl. I returned to the car. The film was nearing its climax—James Bond was busy running all over the place.

Sipping on my second large Coke, I steeled myself and tried placing my left hand on the back of Barbara's right hand. She didn't pull away but kept her eyes glued to the screen. A damp spot formed where our hands met. I tried pressing down a little harder. Barbara flipped her hand over, and now her fingers were firmly encircled in mine. Her eyes were fixed on me.

The interior of the car was dark, but sometimes, when the picture brightened, we could see each other clearly. In one such instant, I could tell that Barbara wanted it, too, and turning toward her, I pulled her strongly to me. She looked serious. I closed my eyes and leaned over. We kissed. In the narrow interior of the car, it was hard to embrace her as I wanted to. When I opened my eyes a little, still kissing her, I saw her face clearly in the light from the screen as she leaned back into the seat.

After a long kiss, we pulled apart and took sips of our Cokes. I felt completely different than before, maybe because I had kissed her. She was about to say something when I cut her off. Emboldened by the touch of her lips, I gently stroked her neck, her breasts, and her waist through her clothes. Just as I'd unbuttoned her blouse and was about to touch her breasts, she opened her eyes and asked, "Do you want me physically?"

Still locked in an embrace, I tried to translate her question in my head. *Physically?* What does she mean? I knew the word *physics* in English, but did this have to do with that? Is she asking me if I want her in a permanent sense, I wondered. Wait a minute, maybe she's asking me to marry her. But that's impossible. Not even an American girl would ask that after one kiss. A debate raged inside me. I had fallen into the bad habit of literal translation, and, feeling frustrated over not being able to understand what she meant, I blurted out, "You want me 'fuck you'?"

Barbara didn't seem to like this—she gave me an angry look and pushed me away.

"Shame on you! Shame. I mean, shame on you! You are really

dirty. You're just a dirty Japanese," she scolded, completely red-faced. "You're not supposed to say that. I am not that kind of girl. You are . . ."

She wouldn't calm down. Even though I couldn't explain, Barbara kept on. "Get outta my car. Right now." She pushed me out of the car and sped off.

Left behind in the drive-in, without any idea of what had happened, my only choice was to search for Frankie and Cathy's car. A white car. I had to find that one car out of a hundred. And I had to find it before the movie ended—what would I do if I didn't find it? I couldn't call my brother, since we didn't have a phone. I would have to walk all the way home.

I was growing more desperate. In one white car, a couple was necking passionately. But it was the wrong car. I was in trouble now. Maybe they'd parked closer to the front. I started walking through the drive-in, a pathetic sight. I felt like crying.

After thirty minutes, I finally found Cathy's car. When I peeped in the window, she and Frankie were wrapped in a hot embrace; Frankie was on top, and I could just catch a glimpse of Cathy's contorted features. Her eyes opened a little and met mine on the opposite side of the glass. Abruptly, she pushed Frankie away and let out a yell: "Frank! Look!"

A loud discussion broke out in the car, and eventually Frankie stepped out. Just as he did, Cathy raced the engine and sped off.

"*Yuu*, idiot! *Whatso za matta?* What are you doing? American girls can't stand peeping. Shame on you. What are we goin' to do? We don't have a car!"

"No, it's not like that. The truth is that I . . ." I started explaining to Frankie why I was there.

"*Goddamu. Yuu*, what are you doing? Neither one of us has a car. How're we going to get home?"

"Let's walk."

"*Walku suru? Yuu curazy.* How far you think it is? Maybe four miles?"

The sound of Japanese seemed to irritate people. A couple of young guys got out of their cars, and shouted, "Shut up!"

"Frankie, let's get out of here. What else can we do?" We started to walk out of the drive-in theater.

"*Yuu*, what did you do to Barbara to get her like that?"

"I said, 'You want me fuck you?' Is that weird?"

"You idiot. Are you *curazy ka*? To a high school girl *yuu neba* say wanna *fucku*," Frankie said wearily.

"But *fuck you* means I wanna do it, right?"

"*Yuu*, *rissun*. It can mean that, but in these situations you have to say *maku rabu* or you'll get in big trouble. Would *yuu* say that in Japan on a date with a high school *garu—omechoko shiyoo?* You never say that."

So that was it. I had used a four-letter word with Barbara. Frankie was right, I would never say such a thing to a girl in Japanese. It had just slipped out because I was speaking a foreign language.

"But everybody's always saying *fuck*," I said to Frankie as we left the drive-in.

"That *fuck* and making-love *fuck* are different. *Eniway, yuu neba* say that to a *garu*. You'll make us Japanese look bad. *Yuu, undastando?*" Frankie added, halting in his tracks. "*Yuu*, if we walk all the way home, it might take more than two hours. What are we gonna do?"

"American girls are short-tempered."

"Yeah, they're stubborn."

"But, Frankie, do you go out on dates with different girls every weekend?"

"*Yuu*, in America if you don't stand out—in class or some-where—they forget people like us. Until you came to this school, I was the only Japanese. People made fun of me. So I did certain things to make people notice me."

The usually funny Frankie turned serious. He had only lived in Japan for the first ten years of his life, but here he was considered Japanese beyond a shadow of a doubt. Sympathy for him welled up in my heart. We kept walking along the dark road.

"*Yuu*, we're graduatin' soon. What are you gonna do? Are you gonna grow strawberries with your brother? I'm short on credits, so first I have to go to a junior college. Then I wanna go to Berkeley to be in the *studento riotsu*. By the way, do you wanna go to San Francisco with me this summer vacation? I got a half brother who lives there."

155

Frankie was right—graduation was in three months. It was time to think about the future. "Come with me to junior college," Frankie suggested.

After the incident at the drive-in, I saw Barbara at school, but she always stuck her nose in the air, so I never got a chance to talk to her. When I told Frankie about it, he said comfortingly, "*Yuu*, there are plenty of other *garu* around."

Another memory that fits into the "fuck" generation is the time I met the writer Henry Miller.

Every day we got a day-old Japanese newspaper, the *Rafu News*, delivered to our house. It was my main source of information. But toward the beginning of the year, my brother said, "*Yuu* came all the way to America, and you're not learning English by reading a Japanese newspaper. Let's take the *LA Times*."

So we took out a subscription to the *Times*. Every Sunday we got a newspaper thick enough to be a telephone book, and by the end of the week, we barely had room for it and all the daily papers.

"What a waste. So many pages, I don't know how much of it you're reading. Just like this country to have such big newspapers," my brother complained one day as he was throwing a bunch of them into the garbage.

Maybe the answer was that America is wealthy. When I arrived in this country, I was taken aback by the size of the trash cans, and shocked to see that much of the "trash" was still quite usable from a Japanese person's point of view at the time. In those days, a newspaper cost ten cents, and even though they printed a newspaper the size of a phone book every Sunday, three-quarters of the space used was advertisements. This was a sign of how much production and marketing was going on in this country.

The size of the trash cans, too, was symptomatic of a consumer society: the consumers' desire to buy was stimulated by TV and newspaper ads, but often the product was useless and ended up in the trash. The amount of advertising in a society seems to be in direct proportion to the size of its trash bins.

Although I couldn't possibly read the newspaper, just looking over its color comics, editorials, travel pages, business news, and other sections made me feel more in touch with America. The

156

section that I checked most religiously was the entertainment calendar, my guide to porno films and other kinds of dubious entertainment. About a week after the drive-in disaster, I was scanning the calendar section when I saw that Henry Miller was having his first watercolor show in a gallery in downtown LA.

During my days on the high school baseball team in Japan, I would go to Tokyo a few times every year to play away games. On one such trip, I'd bought a novel by Henry Miller, who was being advertised as the "pioneer of erotic literature." But instead of the bedroom scenes I had been hoping for, it read more like a treatise on logic, and I threw it away before I had read even a quarter of it. So, although I only knew Miller's name, I wanted to go to his show because I was curious about him and his watercolors.

The gallery was on La Cienega Boulevard, not far from Sensei's church. The day of the opening I asked Frankie, Bob, and some of my friends on the baseball team at school about Henry Miller's books, but no one knew his name let alone his books. On the way home from school, I stopped at Sensei's and asked him.

"Ho, ho, you know Henry Miller? Now that's really something," he reacted, and then told me about Miller's work and what he was trying to do as a writer. The Americans I knew might not know about Miller, but this old Japanese man certainly did.

I went on my motorcycle, using my map as a guide. My precious bike couldn't hack the freeway, so I had to take the old highway, Route 66, to LA, going through the small towns of San Dimas, Glendora, Azusa, Pasadena, and then down past Dodgers Stadium until I emerged in Little Tokyo. Then I headed west on First Street, which runs through the center of Japantown, until I hit La Cienega, a street known for its galleries. Driving slowly to see the numbers, I finally found the gallery.

The gallery was small. A poster announcing the watercolor show hung in the window, but when I peered through, I couldn't see a soul. As I was worrying that I had gotten the time wrong, an old man appeared inside, and I pushed open the door and went in. The old man, in a gray sweater, turned around to stare at me.

No, it couldn't be Henry Miller? The old man started speaking to me, but I couldn't understand him because he kept swallowing his words. Finally, he said something I could catch: "Where are you from?"

"Japan."

"Oh, Japanese, are you? I'm very interested in Japan. Would you like some coffee? I'll get you some."

With these words, Miller disappeared into the gallery office. I had a few moments by myself to look at the watercolors. They were just the opposite of what I had expected from the master of erotic literature; their childish colors and compositions made them look more like illustrations from a fairy tale.

Miller came back with two coffees. I must say something about the pictures, I thought to myself, but I had run out of English. Finally I flattered him falteringly. "Your pictures are great. I like this flower picture."

Miller smiled and told me to sit down at a table in the middle of the room. As we sipped our coffee, he started in to talk again. "How do you know about me?"

"When I was in high school I read *Tropic of Cancer*."

"High school students read my books in Japan?" Miller grew even more chatty, but perhaps he was excited that students in Japan who didn't speak English were reading his books, whereas in this country he was only known by a segment of radical youth. But I couldn't understand what he was saying, nor could I answer him.

"What other authors have you read? Japanese writers are fine. I like Japanese literature a lot."

By now he must have realized that he was putting me on the spot with his questions and that I couldn't speak English well. But maybe he was talking to me out of boredom, since no one had come to his opening.

"My favorite authors are Ishizaka Yōjirō and Matsumoto Seichō, and Minakami Tsutomu. Oh yes, and Shibata Renzaburō."

"Wait a sec. Ishizaka Yōjirō? Who's that? What kind of books does he write?" Miller looked taken aback.

"He wrote *Young Man* and *Blue Mountain*. He's very popular with young people."

"Never heard of him. *Young Man* and *Blue Mountain*, are these his major works? What else has he written?

"*Teacher Ishikawa* and . . ." I couldn't figure out how to translate *The Sunny Slope,* and merely said, "Lots of others."

"Well, what has Matsumoto Seichō written?"

"Umm . . ." I was trying to translate the titles of his books. "*Point and Line.*"

"*Point and Line?* Never heard of it. And Minakami, what's his name? Oh, yes, Tsutomu, what has he written?"

It was a difficult question. I couldn't think of the English word for *geese* to translate *The Temple of the Geese.* "*Badozu* Temple," I answered.

Miller was looking more confused at all the names he didn't know. He sipped his coffee more slowly. I kept answering his questions.

"And Shibata Renzaburō wrote *The Dozing Samurai.*"

Miller, out of his element, said, "If you're going to read Japanese literature, you have to read Tanizaki and Mishima. I have a high opinion of both of them."

What did he mean by "literature"? He had asked me what books I had read, and I'd given him the names of mysteries I liked in high school.

Miller, perhaps deciding that there was no point in talking to me anymore, stood up, picked up the empty coffee cups from the table, and said politely, "Well, thank you for coming to see my show."

I was free, and I decided to have another look at the watercolors. Although an hour had gone by, nobody had come in. I couldn't leave him here all alone. Our eyes met again. Although he had nothing left to say to me, Miller walked over. "Do you really like my pictures that much?"

"Yes, very much."

"Well then, I'm going to give you this sketch." He picked up a watercolor the size of a postcard from the desk and brought it over to me.

"What's your name?"

"Yoshimi Ishikawa."

Miller wrote in the margin of the drawing: "Yoshimi Ishikawa *Banzai Omanko.* Henry Miller."

Thus ended my meeting with Henry Miller, but twenty years

later I can still recall every detail of that day. And there is a short sequel to the story.

Soon after this, Miller was to marry Hoki Tokuda, a forty-year-old Japanese singer who worked in a club in Los Angeles. Hoki Tokuda had come to Los Angeles the same year I did. In the seventies I became friendly with her and told her about the incident.

"What?" she stopped short. "That was you? I remember that story. Mr. Miller, he started coming to see me at the club just about the time of his first show on La Cienega. We were just getting to know each other, so I remember it well. That day after the opening, he came to the club. He looked down, and, when I asked him what had happened, he said, 'Nobody came to my opening except one Japanese boy.' I can't believe it—that was you!"

A lot of things seemed to be happening in my small life: the silly drive-in incident, the meeting with the god of sex. In fact, the farm was a more important part of my life than either porno or my attempts at "fucking." Day by day the strawberries in the field were growing redder, and the harvest would soon begin. Then my brother made the unexpected move of planning a date in New York with the white girl who lived near Niagara Falls.

# 10

# Farmer Know-How

"The first strawberries are always big, but they don't look so good. The next bunch'll be about the same size but they'll look better. Timing is crucial—it all depends on how many good strawberries you can pick early, when the price is up. Then you know how much you're going to make that year," Anchan explained, the night before our strawberry harvest began.

Over the last few days, a handful of Mexicans had begun to arrive at Frank's office, asking when work would start. Within a couple of weeks, a hundred of them would appear out of the blue, like last year. A few days earlier I had tasted one of the red, ripe strawberries; it was so sweet and so moist it had nearly exploded in my mouth.

"*Yuu-tachi,* crop's lookin' pretty good," Frank had said, picking a strawberry.

"If only we make a profit," my brother had said when he rented the land.

"After we make some money, maybe I'll get married in New York," my brother mused happily, as we were discussing the next day's work. Here was Anchan planning to marry a girl he had never seen—Anchan did everything in a rush. I had a premonition that when he met this woman, he would propose to her almost immediately.

One weekend in April, he flew to New York, at her request. Akiko accompanied them on their first date.

"Don't you agree? It's better to have someone you know along on a blind date," Anchan declared, characteristically.

Not everyone on the farm agreed with my brother's impulsive trip. Frank had been vociferous: "*Yuu* might live in America, but that's no reason to marry a white girl you've never seen. There are so many Japanese women. Ishikawa-kun, I use a white girl as my secretary, and I had fun with white girls for money when I was young, but in the end you'll do better if you marry a Japanese girl."

"But I'm just gonna meet her. I'm not gonna make any big decisions," my brother had begged off.

People on the farm usually discussed how many Mexicans had been arrested, how So-and-So's field was doing, or how hot it had been that day. So when one of the guys decided to get married, nobody talked about anything else. Anchan was man of the hour.

By the first day of the strawberry harvest, a number of familiar Mexican faces had gathered on the farm. The big old buses driven by the coyotes had also arrived. Before school, I stopped in at Frank's office hoping to find María, but there was no sign of her. When harvest was in full swing, María and her family were sure to come. As I watched the Mexicans heading for the rows, boxes in tow, a faint hope rose in my heart.

Frank came over to me holding two big, shiny strawberries in each hand. "*Yuu, goodo morningu. Ima kara* high school *ka?* Look, *naisu na* strawberry *yo nō.* Sweet *taisto,* too." He offered me a strawberry. The first day of the harvest is still a thrill for people who raise strawberries year after year.

I left Frank's field and headed toward Jiisan's, trying hard just to stay on my motorcycle as I bounced over the road.

"Jiisan, good morning."

"*Oi . . . yuu ka?* On your way to high school? Get off your *autobai* and taste one of my strawberries."

He was proud, too.

"You're right. These are better than Frank's," I said to make him happy.

"*Yuu* think so, too? This crop's better than *lasto yea,*" Jiisan said, his face smooth as a Buddha's.

"This year, *meibee,* the crop's ready five days earlier than last year. Price'll be good," Jiisan commented. "*Yuu* goin' to graduate, right? What are you goin' to do? *Collegi ni iku no ka?*"

It was time for me to make up my mind. I had already made an appointment with a high school counselor to discuss it.

"Umm, I want to go to college, but I don't speak English, and I don't have any money. . . ."

"If you're worried about money, I've got plenty."

"Eh?"

I looked at Jiisan, but his usual smile was gone. He looked dead serious. "Come to my house when school is over," he told me.

That day basic English came first thing in the morning, and phys ed first thing in the afternoon, which meant that I had three hours to kill in between. Usually I would take a ride on my motorcycle, but that day I stretched out on the huge sports field and stared up at the sky. Jiisan's words, "If you're worried about money, I've got plenty," echoed through my brain.

It had been almost a year since I'd arrived in this country. Staring up at the sky, I was gripped by a feeling of unease. What was I doing here? The faces of my friends and family as I left the island came into focus. The events of the previous year ran through my mind like a film playing backward. My friends in Japan were beginning their second year of college this April. And here I was still in high school, having to decide my future in just a few months. According to my friends, the student movement in Japan was gaining momentum. One acquaintance from high school was sending me fanatical letters about the universities, the failings of the teachers, and the anti-Vietnam movement. In every letter he enclosed the radical newspaper of his group. Starved for news of Japan, I read the enclosed newspapers and pamphlets in his letters or pored over books by important Japanese critics, which the same friends had recommended to me. I felt the gap between my life on the farm and my friends' lives back home widening.

"One must break down the ego," one of my friends wrote. I felt left out by this kind of rhetoric and would whisper to myself a little ashamedly: What do you mean "break down the ego"? I'm just trying to hold myself together. I was deeply moved whenever a little bit of news about the Japanese demonstrators flickered across our TV screen. When a friend wrote to me, "There's going to be a revolution in Japan and I'm fighting for it," my agitation grew worse. How could such a thing happen, and was it all right for me to keep working as a farmer here? I still hadn't grasped America, but the Japan described by my friends involved in the student movement confused me even more.

One day while having lunch with Frankie, I asked him about junior college.

"Junior college, JC for short. Not the same as *foa yea kareji.* You only go there for two years. If your *averegi pointo*'s around a B, you can transfer to a *stato kareji* for your third year. Tuition's *cheepu.* All the kids who do bad in high school start there. But to transfer to a four-year college, you have to fill *rikuaiamento.* How do you say it, you know what I mean. How do you say *rikuaiamento* in real Japanese?"

"*Hissukamoku?*"

"Oh, *hissukamoku. Eniway,* you have to take *hissukamoku.* But it's *alrigh* if you take easy subjects and study English first, then take the *rikuaiamento* later. What's your *averegi pointo?*"

"Putting together my grades from high school in Japan and high school here, it comes out to about a B."

"That's *alrigh yo.* You can get into the JC here without taking an exam. JC's just like high school. You should come with me." Frankie probably wanted someone to keep him company.

After afternoon classes, I rode home. By that time of day strawberry picking was over, and nobody was around. Jiisan wasn't in his field either, and I accelerated up the hill toward his house.

When I knocked on the door and entered, Jiisan was reclining on his couch in a yellowed bathrobe, looking as though he had just emerged from the shower.

"Want somethin' cold to drink? Cola in the icebox."

"No, thank you. Jiisan, how many boxes did you pick today?"

"Ten boxes. *Wan boxu*'s goin' for five dollars. Eighty cents more than same time last year," Jiisan said, getting up from the couch. "Remember what we were talkin' about before. Come'n."

He beckoned me toward his shabby bedroom. Clothes lay scattered where he had taken them off. Jiisan leaned over and grabbed a corner of the mattress.

"Lift up that end, will you? Can't do it alone," he said.

As we lifted up the mattress, hundreds of one-, five- and twenty-dollar bills came into view.

"Where did you get this, Jiisan?"

"*Me no savingsu yo.* Can't open a bank account, so I save it here," he explained nonchalantly. "*Yuu* can use it for college. *Meibee,* two thousand dollars here."

Dumbfounded, I stared at the money. Finally I said, "But that won't do. If I want to go to college, I can work my way through. These are your life savings. I—"

"No, *alrigh yo.* I don't have kids. I won't need it when I die. Been savin' up for my funeral. If you ever need it, you just ask," he added softly.

In the bedroom was a photo of what looked like his parents.

"Your parents?" I asked.

"Yeah. Left Okinawa when I was eighteen—last time I ever saw them. After the war, I had relatives in Okinawa send me the photo," he answered. His expression never changed.

Jiisan had lived in America for forty years. In all that time, he had only managed to save two thousand dollars. Now he was telling me to use his money. I couldn't do it. Thanking him politely, I left the house.

That night I spoke to my brother, and we decided that I would go to junior college. Then I told him about Jiisan.

"That old man. . . . Work your way through. You can't take his money," Anchan responded curtly.

My brother returned from his date in New York on a Monday night in late April.

"Sylvana's much prettier in real life than her photo. *Puroposu?* Yup, I did it. She seems to feel the same way, but she wants me to wait for a month for an answer. We'll probably get married next summer if she says yes. This year we have to build a good base for the strawberry field, 'cause next year's crucial. Then I can get married. Sounds good to me."

"But it happened so fast. How could you talk about such complicated things?"

I knew how much English my brother could speak—the discussion couldn't have gone smoothly. I also couldn't believe Akiko had translated every word of the lovers' talk, but neither could Anchan have done it himself.

"She took Spanish in college and can speak it a little. Her mother's parents were Italian—seems they spoke some Italian around the house, and Spanish is close enough to Italian. So we talked a little Spanish mixed with English," said my brother, as if to quell my doubts.

I could trust my brother's ability in Spanish and pictured him proposing to a white woman in Italian, Spanish, and broken English. "Incredible," I said.

Probably I should have been more impressed by the woman herself. A woman who is approached by a stranger and who agrees to marry him without knowing where he comes from or much about him certainly has nerve. If there's anything wonderful about America, it's the spirit this woman had. The American soldiers had it too: young, healthy men in their twenties marrying not very good looking, usually older Japanese women. Fresh-faced, shapely young girls at home were a dime a dozen, and these men brought back strange women from Japan, Korea, and Vietnam to be their wives.

It seems to me that Americans are the only ones who treat marriage this way. Perhaps people from this kind of society have something to tell the outside world. Americans might have racial prejudices, but they don't seem to be prejudiced against individuals. This was the conclusion I came to after looking at the white woman who would marry my brother and the American men who married Japanese women. It wasn't until later, after a good deal more experience, that I began to suspect that I might be mistaken.

"If I marry a white woman, she can help you learn English," my brother announced practically. "By the way, Akiko is doing great. She was reminiscing about you when you were small. If it works out, we'll get married in New York, and I want you to come. New York's just amazing."

All that night my brother told me about Manhattan, the setting for his date.

A little while after my brother got back from New York, we had a phone installed.

"If she doesn't hear my voice once in a while, she'll forget me," Anchan declared passionately.

He had also suggested that we buy a new television to replace the old black-and-white TV we had gotten at a swap meet.

"We're doing great. *Yuu* got a motorcycle, and now we got a phone and a color TV. America's great. If I was still working as a carpenter in Japan, I'd never be able to get so many things in a year," my brother said, after we had bought the color television of our dreams at the famous store, Sears & Roebuck, as he sat flipping the channels.

Little by little life was improving. But something seemed to be lacking. Would a wife fill the gap? "*Yuu*, I feel like somethin's missing. Even though we keep getting new things, and I might be getting married," my brother mumbled from time to time, still managing to look thrilled at every new purchase we made.

May came, the sun grew stronger. We moved from the day-work system to the piecework system, and more than a hundred Mexicans were busily at work to meet the demands of the harvest. The air was sharp with the smell of men working. I asked the men I recognized from the year before about María, but no one knew her whereabouts. My beautiful pigeon had disappeared from the strawberry circuit.

The cauliflower and strawberries had been right on schedule, but most of the money we made would have to go to repay the loan my brother had taken out to get started. Painstakingly we picked every strawberry we could to build up our capital for next year—the crucial one. On our 20-acre field, strawberries only took up 15 acres, the other 5 had been used for cauliflower. For this, my brother and I and two or three Mexicans would suffice for the harvest.

And if we wanted to hire hardworking Mexicans, my brother said, it was better to choose them ourselves rather than rely on the coyotes.

At the end of May, when the harvest was at its busiest, Anchan and I decided to go "buy people" in a place where Mexicans hung out. "We'll go somewhere new. If we go to the *Mexi* boardinghouse, we have to pay commission. But if we find guys who are just floatin' around, we can *seibu mane*," said my brother, ever the business-man. We had to cut costs as much as possible.

"Let's go to a disco. They love popular music. I bet there are plenty of unemployed *Mexis* we can get for cheap there."

The Mexican disco was about thirty minutes from our house. Nearly a hundred cars were parked chaotically in the parking lot: hoodless cars with their engines visible, cars with spiderweb cracks spreading over front windows, dented ones without head-lights, painted in crazy colors—it was a museum of junkers. A gaudy neon sign ran the length of the disco outside, and from the inside we could hear loud music and Spanish voices.

" 'Bout half those guys are illegal. If we were immigration, we could get them all at once," Anchan said.

"I can understand why they're reckless enough to come here and dance, but why doesn't immigration raid this place?"

"*Yuu*, think about it. How're they going to pick up over a hundred *Mexis* at once? They aren't going to fit in the *imigure* car. The *imigure*'s got its own limits. No matter how many they catch, more come back in. Mostly they just pick up one or two at a time. What if three or four *imigure* came to arrest a hundred Mexi."

People were spilling out of the bar, its air heavy with tobacco, alcohol, and sweat. In the middle was a dance floor surrounded by tables where everyone's attention was held by a young man with a fine profile and a beautiful girl with long, flowing hair dancing together. The eyes she made at the rough crowd and the way she moved her body were incredibly sexy. "Lots of Mexican girls are beauties," my brother said to me as I admired her.

After looking around, Anchan started talking to some Mexicans who looked as though they might be good workers. In everyday life, my brother was an impractical dreamer and tried to put ideas into practice hastily; but here he acted differently—cautious and brave at the same time. After searching the room, he eventually returned with three men.

"*Meibee*, these guys are OK. They should work hard. The short guy's from Sonora. Fernández. Sonorans usually work pretty hard."

"You can tell they're good workers by where they come from?"

"*Yuu*, it's the same in Japan. Northerners work hard. *Yuu* think

168

Tokyo people could grow strawberries like us? It's the same in any country: people work hard in some regions, in others they don't."

The three Mexicans promised to be at our field the next morning at seven. The one with a beard worried me. He wasn't cheerful, like most Mexicans I knew.

The next morning, we were picking strawberries when they drove up.

"Look, *hora,* see all three of them came. They're eager. Gotta eat, I guess."

"*Buenos días.*" My brother greeted them and explained what needed to be done. The three men picked up strawberry boxes, went into the field, and bent down to work.

"*Yuu,* look at that. The little guy's pretty fast."

Watching the little man's hands dart in and out of the strawberries, I had to admire my brother's "horse trader's sense." But the bearded man was chewing on cigarettes, not doing a thing.

"Anchan, that other *Mexi,* he isn't working."

"Yeah, he's got a bad attitude. He's pulling unripe strawberries and hurting the plants."

My brother was losing patience; he walked over to the man and gave him a warning in Spanish. The man's expression showed he understood.

"I probably made a mistake with that guy."

"Well, you can't only choose good ones. You only just met him," I said comfortingly.

A little while later, Pete's truck came down the narrow road in the field. Two Mexicans were riding in back. They were on their way to Jiisan's field, to take his strawberries back to the office and then on to the market in Los Angeles in a big truck, Pete explained. The two Mexicans got down off the truck and were checking out our strawberries when both of them gasped and took off.

"What's with them?" Pete asked.

"*Ai don nō.* But they got upset when they saw my *Mexi.*" My brother followed them while I stood there baffled. A hundred yards away, Anchan caught up with them and the three began to talk. Meanwhile, the man with the beard had taken out another cigarette and lit it. On his way back my brother called to me, "Hey, come over here a minute."

"What happened?"

"You won't believe it. That *Mexi* is a murderer. They just told me he shot a bunch of people in Tijuana. The Mexican police were after him when he slipped over the border. He's famous around here."

"That's not funny, Anchan. I don't want to be murdered in our field."

"Daiku, *whato yuu say?* That Mexican, *kira ka?*" Pete's face went white.

"Pete, don't talk so loud. I'll speak to him tonight, and fire him as of today. It's lucky, because if those two guys hadn't told us, I could have been killed for bossing him around. Now, get back to work like nothing has happened. I'll deal with him when we're done."

We went back into the rows, placing the man between us. He glared, challenging me with his eyes. I avoided his gaze and kept on picking.

In the field behind us, about a hundred Mexicans were working for Frank; any one of them could have been a murderer or a thief. People who hadn't made it at home swarmed to America to make money. In high school I had learned that "America was built by people in search of religious freedom"; that sounded pretty hollow to me now.

I kept working, day after day. After a good night's sleep, my eyes now opened naturally at five in the morning. I never got sunstroke, even though the sun was painfully strong, and my fingers had grown so hard that I could weed thorny patches of grass without gloves. No matter how many miles I had to haul bags of fertilizer, my legs never failed me. I now had a farmer's body, just as Frank had predicted. When I got up in the morning and took my first gulp of fresh morning air, I felt like a farmer down to the soles of my feet.

The price of strawberries stabilized, and things went smoothly on the farm. The pickers arrived every morning at the same time, ate their homemade lunches together, even pissed at the same time—I'd see them lining up in front of the portable toilet. And every Friday, the men would slake their sexual thirst with Mexican prostitutes in their little huts on the farm.

The sun rose every day and sank behind the mountains at the same time. Every afternoon from two to three the wind blew sluggishly before dying down. By June, the strawberries were ripening quickly, and one could get seven or eight fat strawberries at once from a single plant. But then, at the peak of the strawberry harvest, southern California was hit by unseasonable rains. "What's up? Rain now? I've been a farmer for a *rongu taimu,* and I've never seen rain in June," Frank said as he gazed up at the sky on the second day of the downpour.

The rain reminded me of spring. The moist air felt pleasant on my skin. Not one Mexican had come to work, and the supervisors were gathered in Frank's office.

"Frank," said Pete, "*Weza reporto* says it'll end tomorrow. I *shinku* it's *alrigh yo.*"

"No, I don't know. If it rains tomorrow, the strawberries'll get *ōba-raipu,* and there'll be a lot of damage. What a disaster." Frank looked worriedly over his field.

The rain had lessened, and we stood talking outside. Strawberries have very soft skins, and when it rains for three days just as they are ripening, their skin turns puffy and white, and any parts touching the ground start to rot. When I went into the rows to check on the plants, many of the berries were already turning white.

"This is bad," my brother murmured, looking up at the sky. We could just see a small figure in the old man's field. Jiisan was checking on his strawberries.

The next day the rain had lifted, but the sky was still overcast. There were puddles all over the field, and the ground was soft underfoot. Anchan and I went into the field with the Mexicans.

"If the sun doesn't come out by noon and dry off them off, they're goin' to rot," said Anchan, hard at work. Drops of water lingered on the fruit and on the leaves.

"If these rot, we won't have a thing. These were going to make us a profit. Frank must be in shock—he didn't show up at the office this morning. I wonder how much he'll lose at the end of this." My brother's face showed that he wasn't about to give up yet. It wasn't in his nature to give up until the game was really over.

"Rain in June—it's really *goddamu yo na,*" he added gloomily.

Then we heard a sound—*buruburuburun*—a group of large helicopters was descending from the clouds.

"Look! What's that?" my brother yelled.

One, two, three . . . six helicopters started to circle the field.

"An air force drill?"

"Couldn't be . . ."

Startled by the sudden appearance of the helicopters, the Mexicans in Frank's field were yelling, one voice rising above the others: *"La migrá! La migrá!"*

When the Mexicans in our field heard, they flew into a panic and scattered in all directions. At this the six helicopters descended and, lining up in a row just above the ground, began to fly forward slowly. When they got to one corner of the field, they turned around and came back again, still in formation.

"Somehow they don't look like immigration helicopters," my brother said, transfixed. Mexicans who had been running toward the office now stopped dead in their tracks, turned, and watched the unusual proceedings. Frank's white Thunderbird charged up the road toward us, spewing mud on all sides.

"Frank, what's going on?" my brother called out.

*"Goodo aidea,* don't you think? Last night I came up with it 'cause I couldn't sleep. Wind's the best thing to dry a field, so this morning I go to a helicopter company downtown and charter some helicopters to blow away the water around the plants. *Goodo aidea,* right?" Frank was beaming.

The artificial wind reached down into the leaves of the strawberry plants, scattered all the water, and dried the fruit.

"Daiku, when the field's done, I'll send them over to yours. It'll be *alrigh.* Then I'll send them to Jiisan's."

Frank got back in his car and sped off to his office.

"He comes up with some crazy ideas," Anchan said. "A long time ago, I heard that he was growing eight hundred acres of lettuce in Salinas. For some reason the Mexicans stopped coming. So the boss charters an airplane, goes to the Virgin Islands, and

172

brings back about a hundred local people to work for him. In the meantime, the lettuce has grown too big to be harvested. He can't use the workers anymore. But the boss, he thinks that a farmer should harvest everything he grows; so he harvests this lettuce even though he almost has to give it away. He lost tens of thousands on that deal."

"I'm Japanese *yo*. Japanese can do anything," Frank had boasted. But I didn't believe him. No matter how much Frank insisted that he was Japanese, I knew that someone who dried strawberries with a helicopter could only be an aspiring American.

"Without ideas like his, you'll probably never get rich in this country," my brother said, stunned by Frank's resourcefulness.

By the afternoon, the clouds had vanished without a trace, and the sun was pouring down from a blue sky. Frank came over again.

"*Goddamu, sanaba bitchi, fucku, ai gotto heddoaiku yo.* Each of those machines cost me fifty yen. Seemed like a good idea at the time. I'm going to cool down at the horse races," he said, and left.

"Heaven isn't always kind to people. At least it could have stayed cloudy all day, out of respect for Frank's good idea." My brother bent down again and began to pick.

One night near graduation, Hirata—a new friend—dropped in, though he lived nearly an hour away. I had met him purely by accident. Hirata was from Kagoshima Prefecture in Kyushu, the southern island of Japan, and had emigrated under the Displaced Persons Act. He worked as a gardener. His skilled, thick fingers and the wrinkles in his face gave him a very distinguished, masculine look.

"Instead of just selling the strawberries in the market, why don't we build a stand and sell them to passing cars as well? It'll bring in cash," I'd suggested one day.

Anchan had agreed, and used his carpentry skills to construct a stand, and we opened for business. Since we were facing Route 66, there were plenty of cars passing by.

We piled strawberries in small baskets and put up a sign in big red letters that said "FRESH STRAWBERRY 4 BOX $1.00." When sales were brisk, we sometimes made as much as a hundred dollars in a day.

"Anchan, listen. If we wrote Japanese characters on the sign, too, we'd attract more customers. Japanese people would stop out of curiosity," I suggested, and he agreed.

"[Strawberries, real cheap, homemade strawberries warm from the field]," I wrote in Japanese. Beneath these characters, I drew a picture of two or three strawberries. Soon after this, Hirata drove by in a truck and, drawn by the sign, stopped. The sign was successful in attracting people's attention; Ted, however, gave me a hard time about it.

"*Yuu*, what are ya doin'? Me, I speak Japanese, but I *neba reado*. What does this mean?"

When I read it out loud, he continued, "Whadda ya mean by *hokahoka* strawberries? *Hokahoka* means hot, right? *Yuu-tachi* selling hot strawberries?"

"Umm, no . . . *hokahoka* means . . ." I stifled a laugh.

"I don't get it. . . . If you write in Japanese, the Americans will never understand."

Ted's head was cocked to one side. But Hirata had a different reaction when he spied our stand.

"*Yuu, Japanesu?* I thought this stand was run by *Mexis*. Then suddenly I see *hokahoka no ichigo*. Had to stop. Whenever I see a sign written in Japanese, I automatically pull over," he said on our first meeting.

We became friends, and Hirata would often stop by the stand, or even come to the field for a chat. A big fan of *shigin*, he attended a club in Los Angeles every Monday evening.

"If we don't get some young blood, our club is going to die out. Do you know any *shigin*? It's a good thing for Japanese to do."

This reasoning seemed a little off to me. "The tonal changes are real important. Listen. *Senkaku-uu, Kitarianobu-uuu, Ungai no-ooo-ooo, Itagakii-iii-ii.* . . . Those bits are the hardest. Now you try."

Who did he think he was? I had barely met him and now he was ordering me to sing *shigin*. He seemed to think of no one but himself, and he wasn't the only one. From my viewpoint, Frank and Pete lived only for themselves, too. Usually selfish people are a burden on others, but these guys were spared by their sense of humor.

"No way," I said.

"*Soo ka nō* . . . Well, *yuu* should learn folksinging. A friend of mine is a teacher. He's got a license," Hirata answered.

A folksinging license for a Japanese immigrant? I wondered where that had come from.

That day Hirata had come to our house with a preposterous proposal. "*Yuu-tachi* have grown some really delicious strawberries. When I first came to America, I wanted to be a big farmer, but things didn't go too well. So I ended up moving from Denver to Salt Lake City to Sacramento to Fresno, then finally here. My only piece of luck is that my children studied real hard and got scholarships. I have two kids, and both of 'em are in college. That's really all I have to say for myself."

Hirata paused for a breath, took a sip of my brother's coffee, and filled his mouth with strawberries. Then he got to the point. "*Yuu-tachi*, want to buy a grave?"

"Grave?" My brother's eyebrows shot up.

"*Soo yo*. A grave. The truth is, about a month ago, this salesman from a cemetery developer came to *me-tachi*'s house. I'd been thinking that I won't ever be going back to Kagoshima. And since my kids were born and bred in America, we're going to need graves. Obviously, my ancestors' tomb isn't here, so I thought it would be smart to get prepared. Just then this salesman dropped in, and I took the bait."

"So? You don't need the grave anymore? And now you're offering it to us," my brother guessed.

"No, not at all. There are four people in my family—my wife, two kids, and me. But I miscalculated and bought every person their own plot."

"So you bought graves for your kids as well?"

"Yeah. My kids got real mad at me. '*Daddei isu curazy,*' they say. They want to know if parents give their kids graves in Japan. And they keep saying that Japanese are barbarians; they're furious at me."

"I can see their point. Imagine saying to your child who is twenty, 'Here's a grave for you.' Really, Mr. Hirata, it's not just your kids. Anybody'd be mad if they were given a grave." Anchan looked aghast.

175

"Four? One plot would've been plenty."

"You're right. I noticed that after I had bought it. But it was cheap,"—I decided Hirata was crazy—"which would've been *alrigh,* but I just don't like the land they're on. It's new land, and I went to see it, and, how can I describe it? It's never been used, and there isn't a single tree on it. It gives me the shivers to think of being buried there. A graveyard should have a lot of trees where a ghost might pop out at any minute. I've been here fifty years, but I can't stand the idea of being buried in such a desolate spot. You don't have to buy it. There is a bond between us from the past that's brought us here together now, so it'll be my present. Please accept one." He was serious.

"I really want to thank you, but a grave just isn't the kind of present I could accept." My brother looked troubled. Then he looked over at me.

"*Yuu,* want a grave?"

I was about to say "Why the hell would I want a grave, I'm only nineteen years old," but I managed to contain myself and to suggest instead: "I don't need one, but wait a minute. What about Jiisan?"

"Umm, that's a good idea, but somebody'd have to tell him. Imagine saying to an old man, well, here's your grave. Mr. Hirata, listen, since you went to all the trouble of buying them, why don't you keep them? They're not going to go bad," Anchan said.

"Yeah, I guess you're right." Hirata looked resigned.

As I saw Hirata off, I went outside. This year wasn't as hot as last year, and the night air felt bracing. Last June it had been so hot that some Mexicans had collapsed from sunstroke. María had been one of them. A whole year had passed. Maybe my body had just gotten used to it.

The moon shone down brightly over the farm, bringing the leaves of the endless rows of strawberry plants into bold relief. When I looked up, I could see Jiisan's house on the hill, light leaking faintly from the windows.

"I'm savin' for my funeral," Jiisan had said, showing me the two thousand dollars. When he died, he'd be buried somewhere in this wild land. Jiisan had been born in a pretty little fishing village in Okinawa. Could somebody born in such a lovely place be content

176

to be buried in this sun-baked land? And it wasn't only Jiisan. Hirata was beginning to think that although he had come here to improve his lot, he wanted to die in his own country.

Maybe people who chose to live in this country should die here as well. If all the people who had come here had wanted to go to their final rest in their homelands, America would never have been become a nation. People always said that the Japanese didn't assimilate, and they were right—the Japanese were always wanting to go home.

"*Oi, yuu,* how long you gonna be outside? Got to get up early tomorrow," Anchan called, as I stood in the moonlight deep in thought.

# 11

# My Name Is Ishi

I never skipped school unless I had a good reason. As I had completed all my high school requirements in Japan, the school counselor had advised me to take easy subjects—Phys Ed, Art, and Basic English. I had fewer classes than anyone else, and, one day a week, I had only an hour of class. On that particular day, I attended first period, then went home. This meant that I was able to spend a lot of time on the farm.

Even though school was easy, some of the classes had final exams. My main problem was the final for Speech and Drama, a class that I had been taking since September. I had signed up for it on Pete's recommendation, assuming that it was an English conversation class. Later, of course, I realized that an English conversation class wouldn't be offered to Americans. How could a person who could barely murmur "good morning" possibly do well in a class devoted to the famous speeches of Shakespeare and other major writers? I sat through every class in a daze.

Our teacher was a black woman. Sometimes I could hear the other students snickering and calling her nigger in low voices. She seemed to hear it too. For some reason, she seemed to like me, even though I couldn't speak English. Perhaps she sympathized with me because the history of her own race in this country had been so tragic.

This teacher called me Ishi, a name that made the other students laugh. It wasn't until three years later, when I was more familiar with the English-speaking world, that I discovered that Ishi was the hero of a nonfiction book about the last wild Indian of the Northwest. Written in 1961 by Theodora Kroeber, an anthropologist at the University of California, *Ishi in Two Worlds* was an immensely popular book.

One day in 1911, an Indian man wandered into a suburb of Sacramento. His name was Ishi, and he was the last descendant of the extinct tribe of the Yahi. Through him, anthropologists were able to study the newly discovered Yahi and their language.

For this teacher, Ishi obviously was an abbreviation for my last name. Later, however, I realized that I also must have seemed very Ishi-like to her. When I think back over all the crazy things that I did at school—parading as a samurai through the campus, writing words like *existentialism* perfectly but mistaking "no way" for "there isn't a road," and the incident with Barbara—I begin to feel that I was very much like the primitive Ishi, who had emerged in the midst of a developed culture and struggled with new experiences. I, too, was a stranger with nothing to depend on but my wits.

Speech and Drama was my only final. The test consisted of reciting a dramatic passage or famous political speech. Talking for five minutes in front of an audience was no easy feat—especially in English. I wanted, however, to repay the kindness of my teacher, and I worked on my speech for days. I had chosen John F. Kennedy's inaugural address, but, no matter how hard I tried, I couldn't get past the third line. Whenever I tried to memorize a few more of the lines, I would forget what I had already learned. In spite of this, I prepared assiduously for the final, which would take place in the school auditorium.

Americans must be able to express themselves, so this class was good preparation for life. The basic philosophy seems simple enough—make sure others listen to you before you listen to them—but it is a key to how America was formed by people who spoke such different languages. Unity comes about much more speedily if you force your way of thinking on others and make them listen to you—something at which the Anglo-Saxons excel. The violent impression that America makes on foreigners is a result not just of its high crime rate but also of the one-sided nature of conversation here. The power to persuade and be

179

eloquent are weapons one needs to survive in America. Therefore, every American high school has facilities for public speaking.

The exam began. One by one the students got up onstage and recited speeches or soliloquies from famous plays. I felt bewitched by the power of English speech. When one of the less bright students recited a speech by Hamlet, he sounded superb, and exclamations rose from the audience. Our teacher was taking notes at the foot of the stage. Finally it was my turn.

"Ishi, you're next."

I got up onstage. My classmates knew just how much English I could speak, and I could tell by their expressions that they were wondering what I was going to do.

"We observe today not a victory of party but a celebration of freedom—symbolizing an end as well as a beginning—signifying renewal as well as change."

When I had gotten this far, whistles and applause broke out in the audience. This ruckus was my downfall. Distracted, I lost my train of thought. No matter how bad it got, I had thought, I could easily make it through fifteen or twenty lines. But after being thrown off balance I couldn't pick up the thread again, and the more agitated I got, the less I could remember. One minute passed. The teacher shot me a worried look.

Suddenly, in desperation, I charged toward a pillar at the side of the podium, wrapped both arms around it, and started chirping like a cicada—"Miin, miin, miin." What made me do such a thing? A scene from a Japanese film had popped into my mind. The film was *A Tale of Foot Soldiers,* with Ban Junzaburō and Hanabishi Achako. In it the commander yells at the soldiers, "Do you think you're imperial soldiers? Now, do the cicada!" whereupon the poor soldiers cling to a pillar singing, "Miin, miin, miin."

My classmates bent over double with laughter. Some students booed. At any rate, they must have been surprised. For a good three minutes I clung to the pillar thinking, You should change places with me, you damn Yankees.

After my cicada impersonation was over, my teacher said, "I don't understand what you just did. But I know that you were trying to express something." She shook my hand and then continued, "You really are Ishi. Yes, you are."

I have lived in America for a total of ten years now, but that incident was perhaps the most embarrassing thing that ever happened to me. It still makes me blush in the middle of the night when I'm all alone.

My teacher seemed to admire my efforts, for she gave me a B. Three years later, after I had returned to Japan, a classmate from those days called me when he visited while on leave from the Vietnam War. He invited me to his hotel in town and treated me to dinner. When we started talking about high school days, he spread his arms out against the wall saying, "Ishi, miin, miin."

Just before graduation, on the last day of Speech and Drama, we put on a final play. Our teacher had been involved in the student movement, and she was interested in contemporary social issues. She wanted to send us away thinking. The play, *MacBird*, by Barbara Garson, was a parody of Shakespeare's *Macbeth*, and based on the nickname of Lyndon Johnson's wife, Lady Bird. During the next year, it was performed by various casts all over America and caused a great sensation. It seemed a shame that after my debut on campus as a samurai, I could only play an extra in a parody of Macbeth before the curtain fell on my acting career. At any rate, I finally got my diploma.

"Hey, you're doing pretty good. Diplomas from a Japanese high school and an American one," said Anchan, who treated me to dinner at a nearby restaurant after graduation. His mouth was crammed with steak. "You know, this means somethin'. But I've got an interesting story about diplomas. Happened some time ago." Then Anchan told me about a forger who made diplomas in the Japanese community of Los Angeles, the same story I had heard from Sensei and his wife.

"But why do Japanese here need fake diplomas? They won't get work by showing them to an American employer," I asked.

"I don't know," he answered.

"Did he ever approach you? I bet if he got hold of Frank, he'd buy four different diplomas!"

Anchan laughed. "You're right. Boss likes those kind of things. If only we'd known, we could have got Taoka to make up two or three. What a shame, his would look real to anybody."

I had forgotten about Taoka. His calligraphy would make anything look authentic.

"Taoka couldn't have been doing it on the side, could he?" I asked.

"I don't think so. He had no business sense."

My brother was right. Living as we did in such limited circles, it seemed strange that Japanese diplomas could be so important. But to immigrants like my brother, documents in general—Social Security cards, driver's licenses, personal checks, credit cards—were directly related to one's participation in American society; the more credit cards you had, the more you fit in. In fact, the number of credit cards you had showed how American you were. One day Frank showed me his "documents."

"Lot of credit cards, eh?" he boasted. The cards were proof that he was an American, and he beamed with pride. In order to get a gasoline card or a Master Charge card, you had to pass a number of financial tests. The people who didn't pass were considered rejects.

In postwar America, especially in the latter half of the fifties, racial prejudice began to be dealt with more harshly. In its place, the credit card created new forms of discrimination. Although the ideal of America is equality, people don't give up the pleasure of stratifying each other easily. If cash were the criterion, then the people who were most liquid—the illegal aliens—would have been powerful. And in a country with approximately 4 to 5 million illegal aliens, their power would have been substantial. In a credit card society, it is possible to inquire into an individual's assets. You can find out through credit records whether a person came by his money legally. Illegal money does not easily translate into credit cards.

People who don't pass their credit checks become increasingly isolated in America and gravitate toward cash jobs on the outer fringe of society. Like on our farm. But when they work in such places, they suffer from low wages and required kickback payments, and escape is impossible. This is how America perpetuates its lowest classes.

"Well, even so, American diplomas look pretty neat. Printed in old English letters like that," offered Anchan.

I put my useless diploma on the table of this hick restaurant way out in the sticks. The two of us just stared at it.

"*Yuu*, San Francisco has hippies, student riots, and drugs. It's the most interestin' place in California. Berkeley is hard, but the student activities are radical. *Yuu* know what radical means?"

With a long summer vacation ahead of us, Frankie Noda told me all about San Francisco. We were deciding on a date to go there. Since the end of June, Frankie had been working at our strawberry stand to make money for the trip. For the first few days, he tried picking strawberries because he said he needed to make a lot of money, but the work was too hot for him, and in the end he chose the easier job of sales boy.

"*Boku*, me, even though I'm Japanese, I can't do such hard work. Maybe I just got lazy in America," he joked.

Frankie liked his work as a salesman—he had plenty of chances to chat up the girls who stopped in. He also yelled out to every passing car.

"*Yuu*, the girls are great in San Francisco: Telegram Avenue, Union Square, North Beach. . . . In Haight-Ashbury, the hippies are always *sitto in*. If we make the right move, we can *meku rabu* lots of times."

Frankie narrowed his already narrow eyes. Then he told me that he had a half brother in San Francisco. "My brother, he's from a different mother, but he's *very smarto yo*. Graduated from Berkeley, got his master's at a college in the East. Now he's back at Berkeley teaching. Last time I called him, he said he was going to an antiwar demonstration."

As we were talking by the stand on Route 66, a car of young people passed us, yelling at the top of their lungs. One guy gave us the finger.

Frankie knew why. "That's because *yuu* painted Japanese on the stand. That annoys them. Now listen, when we're in San Francisco, you can't call it that. It's cooler to call it Frisco." Frankie was infatuated. "Frisco. Just rolls off the tongue."

"Like it's better to call Los Angeles LA. We'll go by bus. Then you'll see how big California is. *Looku, naisu garu. Looku ato zatto.* Outta sight. Wow, boy, whew . . . Hey, you! Gorgeous!"

183

At the sound of his voice, a carload of girls wearing T-shirts stuck their thumbs down, telling him to "go to hell." Frankie yelled right back—"Hey, gorgeous. You want my dick?"

No matter how many years I lived here, I knew I could never talk like Frankie.

He said, "Ever try marijuana? We can do marijuana, drugs, and have free sex in Frisco."

"Marijuana? I've never tried it before."

"Me neither, but it sounds great. It's supposed to be really great when you *maku rabu*. Remember John, the football player? He was always high. There are plenty of things around like LSD."

It wasn't until later that the midsixties was named the Psychedelic Age, but rough-looking kids were already talking about drugs in corners of the school grounds. The ones who had taken them bragged in colorful language about the pleasures of marijuana and sex, and were the envy of the other students.

I, however, was more interested in "free sex" than in drugs. If drugs made sex better, then I was willing to give them a try. Having gotten lots of letters from friends back in Japan saying, "I'm jealous of you in America, the country of free sex. Give me the details," I was embarrassed because I had none.

"If you say 'let's fuck' to a girl sitting in Haight-Ashbury or Telegram Avenue, you get free sex just like that?"

"What're you talkin' about? No way it's so easy. The hippies do it because they have *firosofi*. *Yuu* got *firosofi*?"

"*Firosofi*? You mean *tetsugaku*?"

"Is that how you say it in Japanese? *Yuu* know hard Japanese. I really should learn some more."

Whenever the question of Frankie's Japanese came up, it put an end to the discussion. Frankie—always droll and popular at school, who never seemed to worry about anything—turned utterly serious when he spoke Japanese. He had only lived in Japan until the age of ten. But he liked to emphasize the fact that he was Japanese more than I did. Although Japan and the Japanese language were fading away inside him, he was resisting desperately. The farther one gets from one's birthplace, the more reverent one feels.

"*Yuu*, this Route 66, it goes *zutto oru za way easto*. Past Las Vegas and through Chicago. I hear your brother's goin' to marry a girl in

Niagara Falls. You should take the bus there for the wedding. I only went halfway, but the West is huge. There's the Grand Canyon . . ." Partly on Frankie's advice, I eventually did take a bus across the country on Route 66 to attend my brother's wedding—in Port Jervis, New York.

As our trip to San Francisco drew near, I got a letter from a man who had been on the *Africa-maru* with me. Ōta was thirty-five and single. After working as a farmer in Gumma Prefecture without much success, he had decided to go to a new land: Bolivia. We had become friends and talked about many things on our Pacific crossing.

I had given him my brother's address, but he wouldn't know his address until he got there. I hadn't heard from him for a year. When I had first arrived in America, the faces of the one hundred and sixty people going on to South America had stayed with me, but within the space of that first busy, adventurous year, they had dimmed. Then his letter arrived:

> The settlement that the Japanese government told us about is absolutely barren. You can't grow anything no matter how hard you try. We don't have enough food. Every day we barely survive on the bananas that grow here. I have failed in Bolivia. Many families have already pulled up stakes and gone back to Japan. I'd like to go to America if I can. I'll do anything. Could you give me work on your farm?

I told my brother about this over supper.

"It's really hard on them. I've heard there isn't enough food in some places. Maybe it was last year, some guys who had emigrated to Bolivia and Uruguay came all the way here to work on a vegetable farm in Orange County. They came in on a tourist visa and planned to stay if they could get green cards. One of the guys left his wife in Bolivia and came here to work. Imagine, going to Bolivia to work and that's no good, so you leave your family there and come by yourself to work here. . . . Can't imagine anything worse," Anchan said, cutting into a thick steak. "It's hard to understand fate. We got to America, so we're eating big steaks and buying a color TV, but we live in a dump. But the people who went to Bolivia, forget work, they're barely surviving on bananas. I

185

guess we're pretty lucky. We can even send Mom and Dad a little money."

"I feel sorry for them. Couldn't you ask Frank to give this guy a job?"

"I can ask Frank, but we can't take responsibility for him. Even if we make a casual invitation, it's not that easy. *Yuu* know how hard this work is. Still, I do sympathize. The truth is . . . I haven't told anyone in the family this, but, well, I . . . About two years before you came, I wasn't doing too well here, and I decided to go to Brazil."

"Brazil?"

"Yeah, I thought I'd work on the coffee plantations and see what I could do," he said. "*Yuu* mind getting me some ice water? It's hot tonight."

It had gone over 95 degrees that day for the first time in a long while; we were heading right into midsummer. Heat still clung to the house, and we were eating supper without shirts.

"So, I got as far as Mexico, but then I thought, it's probably going to be the same everywhere, so I decided to come back and try again."

"You had a hard time, didn't you?"

"That's the way it goes. Anybody who comes to a foreign country has a hard time. I have a hunch that even if we don't write back, he'll come here eventually. *Yuu* don't know this, but quite a few Japanese in California first went to Brazil and Peru, entered this country on tourist visas, and got their green cards by marrying war brides. Jiisan started out in Mexico. The port of LA isn't the only way in. People come in all over. Canada's a good route, I hear."

Just as my brother had predicted, Ōta arrived in California on a tourist visa. He spent one night at our house before going off to stay with a friend of a friend in Sacramento.

The countries of North and South America were primarily settled by immigrants. Yet between the Japanese who went to America and those who went to Bolivia, there was a gap: Japanese–North Americans and Japanese–South Americans are regarded very differently at home in Japan, with most Japanese prejudiced against those who went south.

That night the temperature was still high at nine o'clock, and, unable to bear the heat, I decided to cool down on my motorcycle. The wind felt great. Leaving the strawberry fields, I went down a road through an orange grove owned by a white farmer. The strong scent of oranges permeated the air, and insects rushed to meet my headlights. Lots of little creatures were resting under the shade of trees. Without a thought to where I was going, I realized that I was near Sensei's house and decided to drop in.

Stopping by the side of the road, I could see Sensei and his wife enjoying the coolness of their garden.

"Hello. It's me. It was so hot, I was taking a ride on my motorcycle, and I was passing by."

"We're hot, too, so we came outside. Come in."

The couple was sitting at a small table on the grass. I had been to see them once after my graduation to tell them about it. And once a month I went to hear Sensei's sermons at his church.

"This year seemed cooler than usual. But it looks like it's going to get seriously hot after today. Working on the farm in this heat must be very hard," Sensei said sympathetically.

His wife went in the house and brought out some cold juice. I told Sensei about the letter from Bolivia.

"I see. . . . I guess those people are still around. Before the war, there were a couple thousand Japanese who came in through Mexico. Since Japanese immigration to the States was cut off in 1924, first they'd go to Mexico or Peru and then slip into America."

"Now, now, the pot shouldn't go calling the kettle black. I'm one of those illegals," Sensei's wife said, draining her juice.

"What? You, an illegal alien?"

"Now, dear, no need to bring that up," Sensei rebuked her.

"It's all right, isn't it? It was so long ago. When I was going to marry him, Japanese weren't allowed into this country. So first I went to Mexico, and then he came down to fetch me. No one asked any questions because he was a man of the church, and he got a visa. We were married in Mexico, and I slipped into this country. But now I have a green card."

This elderly Japanese woman, who was proud of her samurai ancestry, had come into America as an illegal bride.

"This country has all kinds," I said.

"This country is a gold mine if you like to study people. Maybe that's why I ended up here." Sensei laughed.

Every immigrant to America seemed to have a dark secret. By listening, I had learned about the motives people had for moving here, and was gradually coming to understand them.

"There's a good side to it, too, but there's nothing to stop people who want to do stupid things in this country. Students might be infatuated with drugs now, but you wait, drugs will be a tragedy for this country in ten years," said Sensei, staring up at the stars.

"Dear, you remember Mr. Okamoto from our church at Yamaguchi who loves bonsai? He has an eldest son named Steve who's been drafted and is going to Vietnam soon. Last Sunday at church, he came to say good-bye to me. I've known that boy since he was a child."

As though in response to the escalating war, the student movement and the black movement had resorted to even more radical means. In July, the Student Nonviolent Coordinating Committee leader, Stokely Carmichael, preached black power, and riots broke out all over America: on the twelfth of July in Chicago, on the fifteenth in Brooklyn, on the eighteenth in Cleveland, and on the sixth of September in Atlanta.

One day I drove downtown and stopped in a bookstore. Promotional posters showing a knife dripping blood covered the walls. This image captured the uneasy, feverish mood of the time, and I remember being overcome with anxiety at the sight of it. *In Cold Blood,* by Truman Capote, was soon to become a best-seller. At the time I had no idea of the novel's content; yet every time I saw this chilling book advertised, I worried about whether I should stay on the farm.

Sensei stood up, proclaiming in Japanese, "We must do something to stop this war." Then he spat out in English, "Those fools!" I had never seen such a menacing expression on his face.

"Sensei, umm, I'm going to San Francisco with a friend soon. What should we see?"

Remembering that Sensei had been in intensive care during World War II, and that the current war wasn't the only thing irking him, I decided to change the subject.

\* \* \*

The harvest ended and the migrant workers headed to their next field. Free from the cries and the sweat of the laborers, the field returned to its natural quiet state.

"*Eburi yea, me-tachi*, we're always doin' the same thing. Well, this year went smoothly without too much drama," Frank summed up.

"One more week, and we're off to Tijuana," Pete added. Just like last year's trip. Only this year I couldn't go because I was going to San Francisco with Frankie Noda.

"It was weird. Helicopters aside, at least the price stabilized. *Eburithingu ga alrigh*. How did it go for you, Jiisan?"

Jiisan had come to Frank's office to take part in our yearly postmortem. Pete, Charlie, and the secretary were there finishing up the accounts.

"My crop was good. Gophers were digging up my field, and, thanks to them the water drained down the holes and didn't get to the plants. Had quite a few withered plants there."

At the height of the harvest, Anchan and I had stopped at Jiisan's field and seen him trying to fill in the gopher holes with a shovel.

"Jiisan," my brother called, "a shovel won't do it. I'm going to get some weasel traps in Japantown."

A few days later he set down five traps. The hardware store in Japantown didn't have enough weasel traps, so my brother had put down an odd assortment, including a mousetrap. The results were good, though; every day the traps easily snared more gophers.

"*Yuu*, American moles and mice are so stupid. You can fool them with a decoy. But not the moles in Japan. There isn't much leftover food, so the mice and moles have to fight to survive—their wits are much sharper. The ones here are stupid 'cause there's so much food in America," Anchan declared.

"In the end, they didn't do much damage," Jiisan said, looking at Anchan.

"*Yuu*, I hear you're goin' to San Francisco. You have to go to Benkei, a Japanese restaurant downtown. That's one of my places. Tell the manager my name, and you'll have a great meal," Frank offered. "Then you should stop in Fresno. There's a nisei named Muraoka there; he was my foreman when I was growing lettuce in

Salinas. Now he's in grapes." Frank was definitely entrenched in the circle of Japanese-American farmers.

"But," he continued, looking at my brother, "what about *yuu*? Are you goin' to raise strawberries again next year? If you marry a white girl, are you goin' to be *alrigh ka?*"

The previous evening we had finished doing our accounts for the year. On top of being able to pay back the $20,000 debt, we figured that we had also made enough to buy a truck and an old tractor. We had already planned to grow strawberries next year and hoped to try 10 more acres. If that worked, we agreed, we'd be on our way to becoming real farmers.

My brother's marriage plans were proceeding smoothly since the rendezvous in New York, and a tentative wedding date was set for the following summer. But even my optimistic brother wasn't without his doubts. He and his bride-to-be were ten years apart in age, not to mention the gaps in race, upbringing, culture, and language. Sometimes my brother let it slip that he thought all he was good for was work.

"Still, I've come this far. And since I don't know how it'll turn out, I just have to do it. Marriage is a gamble just like farming. When Akiko left the island, people were dead set against it, but it looks like she's doing fine. It's not going to go bad just because it's a mixed marriage. Frank is really against it, though. When I talked to him about it the other day, he made a nasty face. That guy has an incredible mistrust of white people. I guess I can understand it, since he's faced discrimination all his life."

My brother's feelings had been hurt when Frank and Pete acted put out by his marriage plans. One evening, my brother suddenly brought up the topic in front of everyone. "Boss, I'm getting married. She's going to help out with the weeding when she gets here."

"*Yuu*, what are you talkin' about? A white girl weeding? Your problem is, you're still young."

My brother looked offended, then Jiisan intervened. "Frank, it's *alrigh* to marry someone you like. When we were young, we couldn't even talk about marrying a white girl. But now it's time we produced young men who can marry white girls. I never

190

got married, but you do it with someone you like. Otherwise, forget it."

Frank softened. "Well, you still have a year. Think it over carefully. It's best if people don't do things they regret. I only warned you because you're a good farmer and I don't want you to lose your big chance because of a white woman," he said quietly.

At that moment, Ramón, González, and Antonio appeared with shovels, talking in loud voices.

"Hey, Ted, we're going to the *omanko* store next week?"

Ramón still seemed to remember the word that I had let slip on our way to San Diego last year.

"That's right, Ramón. We're goin' to Tijuana. Lots of girls waiting for us there," Ted answered jubilantly.

The secretary asked Ramón the meaning of *omanko*. But Ramón evaded her, replying, "I don't know, I don't know."

The short summer vacation was about to begin. To each his own, I thought.

# 12

# Flowers of San Francisco

The Greyhound bus terminal was on Sixth Street in downtown Los Angeles.

"They go all over America?" I asked Frankie.

"*Zatso raito.* You can go anywhere on one of these babies. Look at the board—Boston, Chicago, Albuquerque, Dallas, Miami, Minneapolis, Seattle. . . ."

Passengers bustled in and out of the gates around the large building. A young girl and a soldier wrapped themselves in a passionate embrace while a large black family with heavy suitcases went to board their bus, perhaps on their way home after visiting friends in California. Frankie and I took our place in line to board the bus to San Francisco. In my bag were the rice cakes wrapped in seaweed that my brother had made for me that morning.

In those days Greyhound was the best bet for long-distance travel. Ninety dollars bought you an open ticket that was valid for three months. Although airline routes crisscrossed the nation, plane tickets were expensive by comparison, so the young and the poor took the bus. During the midsixties many travel diaries were published in Japan: most described either their authors' experiences as Fulbright scholars or their travels on Greyhound. Any Japanese person who spent time in America in the sixties has vivid memories of Greyhound.

One of the reasons Greyhound flourished in that period was the student movement. Penniless students traversed America organizing huge antiwar demonstrations at major universities on their open tickets. Today Berkeley, tomorrow Columbia, and then on to a meeting in Georgia. You could get from Los Angeles to New York in three days of straight riding, and the demonstration attended by hundreds of thousands of students in Washington, DC, was made possible by Greyhound.

After the bus had filled up with passengers, we cut through downtown and were soon on the freeway. The speed limit might have been 65, but our hefty bus driver in sunglasses sped past one car after another.

"This guy really makes time," Frankie said.

A black guy in front of us turned on his radio and began swinging in time to the music. People were talking to their neighbors. We made a lively bus. When we passed through Hollywood and out into the San Fernando Valley, the sky turned a brighter shade of blue—we had outstripped the LA smog.

Two hours into the trip we climbed into the Tehachapi, a steep range of mountains that separates southern and central California. The bus pushed deeper into the mountains. It would take eight hours to get from Los Angeles to San Francisco. We stopped for a number of coffee breaks along the way—just like a full day's work.

"California's bigger than Japan, you know," Frankie explained. "Once we get through these mountains, we'll be in central California. San Joaquin Valley, famous for farming. Very *hotto yo*. In *summa-taimu*, you can fry an egg on the hood of your car."

"Is that why they call it 'Sun-walking Valley.' "

"No, no." Frankie laughed. "It sounds the same, but you spell it different. S-a-n J-o-a-q-u-i-n Valley."

Soon the immense plain of the San Joaquin Valley came into view through the bus windows. Our farm couldn't compare with this.

"Frankie, it's huge." I sighed.

"*Yuu*, see those mountains off in the distance? Those are the Sierra Nevada."

The bus made quick stops in typical central California towns like Bakersfield and Delano and finally arrived in Fresno. We took a coffee break there before heading out past immense grape fields straight for San Francisco; along the way groups of Hell's Angels zoomed past us.

Suddenly Frankie stood up and yelled, "Look! Frisco!"

193

As the bus started down a hill, the view opened before us, and we could see the ocean. The sky above was clear, but a thin mist floated over the sea, softening the outlines of the office towers.

"There's a lot of fog in Frisco," Frankie said. "Even in summer, it's much cooler than LA."

Other passengers were now standing up, trying to get a glimpse of the city.

"*Yuu*, now we're on Oakland Bridge. Don't confuse it with the Golden Gate Bridge." Frankie asked as we sped across the big bridge over San Francisco Bay.

This city looked completely different from LA. Finally I was seeing the American high-rise buildings and European residential streets that I had dreamed of in Japan. The bus bobbed up and down the hills and arrived at the terminal, in a grungy section of town. Seeing skyscrapers for the first time made my heart pound. When we got off the bus, Frankie's half-brother Jimmy and his wife were waiting for us.

"Hey, Frankie! Long time no see!" Jimmy called out, giving Frankie a hug.

Jimmy, quite tall for a Japanese American, was married to a white woman. Frankie introduced me. As a professor whose sympathies lay with the student movement, Jimmy had a forceful look about him, and I felt completely intimidated by his perfect English. His wife explained that she was a member of a research group on women's problems; she was also a fast talker. Although Jimmy barely spoke Japanese, he could understand a little, and he welcomed us falteringly, "*Yo kita ne . . .*"

We headed in Jimmy's car for the hotel where Frankie had booked rooms for us. Night was falling steadily over the city as our car meandered through the hills.

"Look, this is Chinatown." As we stopped at a light on a hill, we could see Chinese neon signs everywhere on a row of Asian-style buildings. Lots of people were milling about—perhaps because it was a weekend. I had lived in America for over a year, and this was the first time that I had seen so many people out on the streets. Even so, my own surprise at such an ordinary thing took me back a little. Our hotel, which was walking distance from Chinatown, had singles for six dollars, and we had each gotten our own room because Frankie thought we might meet girls. I had never stayed in a hotel before. This one was filled with transients.

"Frankie, is this hotel OK? It gives me the creeps," I complained as we rode up in an elevator that made a tremendous banging sound and looked as though it might grind to a halt at any second.

"I know. The ad said, 'Luxury hotel for six dollars a night,' what a joke." Frankie also looked worried.

Three black men in the elevator eyed us when we spoke Japanese. We left our luggage in the seedy rooms and went back to the lobby. That night we had dinner in Chinatown with Jimmy and his wife. At dinner Jimmy asked us why we had chosen a cheap hotel over his house. At first we had considered staying with him. But we couldn't pick up girls and bring them back to Jimmy's. We couldn't exactly confess this to Jimmy, though, so Frankie lied: "We didn't want to inconvenience you."

Chinatown was bustling: a jumble of gift stores, general stores, and restaurants. Chinese goods in the shop windows that I had never seen before. We never saw white people in Little Tokyo, but here there were plenty of them. I felt a pang of jealousy toward the world's most famous Chinatown.

But even here I did not see the Americans I had imagined back home, the Americans from "Father Knows Best," "Lassie," and "Rawhide." The America I had learned about in Japan did not include Chinese, blacks, or Mexicans.

Dish after dish of Chinese food was set down on our table. Frankie, Jimmy, and his wife were talking in rapid, heated tones, and I couldn't keep up. Jimmy was discussing how to oppose the war, his wife about how women could achieve equality, and both talked about racial prejudice. Jimmy's wife claimed that she didn't have a racist bone in her body; her Japanese husband was proof. She thought that more white women should marry men of different races. Were white people marrying people from other races because they were afraid of being called racists?

"Americans are broad-minded. That's why they don't hesitate to marry people of different nationalities. We should learn from them," Sensei and his wife had once said to me. But maybe people were becoming too zealous? Maybe marriage to a person from another race was becoming mandatory? I worried that Sylvana might marry my brother—a Japanese farmer who couldn't speak English—not because she loved him but because she wanted to make a statement.

We finished supper and agreed to meet again in three days. Since it was a waste to spend the rest of the evening in our seedy hotel, we decided to take a walk.

"Frankie, Frisco's pretty 'chilly.' " Feeling good, I puffed out my chest and tried the word that Frankie had taught me.

"*Zatso raito. Yuu rooku happi.* You really do. It gets very cold here at night. We're near the sea," he replied.

"Frankie, I don't see any hippies or girls. What's the story?"

"*Yuu,* this area is full of tourists. The hippies are in Union Square or Haight-Ashbury."

Hippies. Young people looking for a new way of life: their quest for freedom made them mystical to us.

"Let's go to Haight-Ashbury. I really want to see the hippies. Can we walk?"

"Frisco's a pretty small town, but the Haight is near Golden Gate Park, and that's pretty far." Frankie raised his hand to flag a cab.

In the summer of 1966, the hot spot of America was not Greenwich Village, but Haight-Ashbury. By 1969 Haight-Ashbury was a den of drug addicts and criminals, not the utopia of the hippies and the flower children. But when Frankie and I visited in August of 1966, the Haight was in its heyday; young people all over America believed that it was "happening." Six months later Haight-Ashbury held the Human Be-in, and hundreds of thousands of young people flooded in to enjoy a season of love filled with the prescribed flowers, dancing, singing, poetry, and, more famously, with sex, drugs, and rock 'n' roll.

San Francisco's Victorian houses were very different from the architecture in LA. Naturally Haight-Ashbury was filled with big houses whose owners rented out apartments to would-be hippies and artists.

"*Looku,* there's a hippie." Frankie was pointing. Although it was nearly ten at night, a crowd of people were hanging out in the street. Long-haired, bearded men in rumpled white clothing and women sat at tables outside, talking and embracing. It looked a little like Sunset Strip in Hollywood, only there were more people here. Young people were playing guitars and singing, and a man with a tangled beard stared up at the sky murmuring religious words. "God, God," was all I could catch. There didn't seem to be anything special going on. Most of the people were very young, and I had never seen young people hanging around like this at such an hour. They were wandering aimlessly, arms linked together, singing and talking.

I heard the familiar strains of a song from the radio.

"Frankie, that song, what is it? I've heard it a lot."

"That's Bob Dylan; he's supposed to be one of the greatest singers in this country. But I don't get protest songs. I like the Beatles, the Beach Boys, and the Stones better."

I walked through the hippie town looking around me like the bemused whites did in Chinatown. A man who was part of a group deep in meditation called out. He gave me the creeps.

Frankie explained. "He asked if we're Japanese and if we know Zen. If we do, we should come join them."

"What's Zen?"

"*Yuu*, don't you know Zen? I can't explain it too well, but you put your hands together like this, close your eyes, and pray. Japanese religion *yo*."

Frankie clasped his hands. Finally I got it.

"You mean *zazen*—Zen meditation? That's not religion."

"So what? The hippies want to learn Zen. Why don't you teach them?" At the time I didn't know that hippies were great admirers of Eastern religion. The group was gesturing for us to sit down.

"What are you gonna do? They're trying to get us to join in."

Frankie looked perturbed. One guy wore bead necklaces and bracelets. A woman picked up a hand drum and began tapping it with the flat of her hand. They looked more like followers of one of the new Japanese religious sects than practitioners of Zen. "*Nanmyō hō renge kyō.*" They were chanting a sutra that had nothing to do with Zen!

Were these people in their cheap, dirty clothing really interested in free sex? One young woman was lighting incense that smelled like mosquito repellent; imagine her having free sex with that perfume on her body.

Resignedly, we sat down with them, and the man who looked like their leader showed us how to cross our legs and position our hands. I had never done Zen before, even at home. Frankie who had no idea of what Zen was anyway acted curious; he crossed his legs as he had been told, placed his hands together, and closed his eyes. Who were they kidding? I hadn't come all the way to America to do fake Zen with hippies. All at once, I felt anger, sadness, and laughter welling up in my heart.

Everyone, including Frankie, was deep into "Zen" meditation by this time. There was nothing left to do except cross my legs, press my hands together, and shut my eyes. Moments later I opened my eyes feeling incredibly silly, but Frankie and the others were still meditating. Luckily, a man and a woman had lain down right near us and were kissing passionately. Here we go, I thought, free sex. In order to watch them more closely, I shifted my position slightly, squinted my eyes, and plunged into fake meditation.

Just beyond the kissing couple, five or six men and women were sitting in a circle smoking. One guy took a deep drag before passing the "cigarette" on to the woman next to him; she inhaled deeply and then passed it to the man next to her. The smoke mixed with the incense nearby, and a most peculiar smell drifted in my direction. The men and women puffed greedily on the cigarette, but nobody on the street paid any attention. I wondered if the two people kissing in front of me had smoked marijuana and whether they would have better sex because of it.

After our meditation session ended, Frankie and I resumed our walk through Haight-Ashbury.

"*Yuu*, pretty exciting, huh? The hippies think up their philosophies when they're meditating." Frankie was jubilant; I felt let down. Unlike me, Frankie was able to adapt immediately in these situations. We might both be Japanese living in America, but we were very different kinds of Japanese.

Late that night we returned to our cheap hotel, planned out the next day, and slept deeply.

For the next few days, we ate breakfast at the hotel and went sightseeing on the city buses and streetcars. All day long we explored the town, eyes wide with curiosity. We visited the Golden

Gate Bridge, historic houses, museums, and the University of California at Berkeley, where Jimmy taught. We stayed at Jimmy's one night, and went out at night to student hangouts on Telegraph Avenue.

Berkeley was so huge I found it hard to take in. Although it was summer, students bustled around campus carrying textbooks as fat as telephone books, or sat debating in groups on the grass. The American student movement had gotten off to a brilliant start here two years earlier with the Freedom of Speech Movement, and these students had an air of strength and determination about them.

Those of us who had been born in postwar Japan had been taught that American values were ideals to live by. Fighting for free speech and the end of racism meant striving for the triumph of an American notion of goodness, and it only confirmed my view that America was a great country.

The campus had its serious face, but many students sat lazily on the grass just talking with each other or kissing while squirrels frolicked around them. I was surprised by the love scenes being enacted before me without a thought that someone might be watching, and a wave of jealousy washed over me: these lovers made it look so easy.

At the same time, I was put off by their casual attitude. Frankie, however, was delighted by the students and so eager to transform himself it was painful. I realized that he had no choice but to act this way in this country, but I felt sorry for him, and it made me resent America for making him this way. Having never been accepted by the cool clique or been treated like one of the guys, I was quite the nationalist at this time.

On our fourth night, we were exhausted from wandering around and went back to the hotel early. Short of money, we were now sharing a double room. There was a bar and a dance floor in the back of the lobby, and after dinner we went there to have a beer. Couples were dancing to the music.

"Frankie," I said, "Frisco's been fun, but we haven't found any girls. And the hippies weren't that friendly. I guess free sex is harder than it looks."

"No, no. *Neba givu upu.* We still have a chance. Look!"

Frankie started winking and gesturing with his head to the right. A young girl was sitting there casually smoking a cigarette, and she smiled when we caught her eye.

"See, looks *alrigh. Goodo smilo.*"

"What're you gonna do?"

"*Yuu,* go over there. I'm givin' you a chance. Try!"

"No, I can't. I can't speak English."

"Well then . . . OK . . . I'll give it a try. *Alrigh* with you?"

Of course, I would have liked to approach her first if there had really been a chance. But I wouldn't have known what to say to her when I got to her table.

"OK, I'll try. *Ai wiru getto har,*" said Frankie, striding over to her table.

My eyes followed him, sure she would get angry, but she didn't. He said a few words to her and sat down smoothly at her table. The girl started talking and smiling at him. I felt a stab of jealousy.

I looked around the wide lobby, wondering if there wasn't anyone else. Frankie had all the luck—it wasn't fair. Then I caught sight of an Asian woman drinking by herself four or five tables away. She seemed deep in thought. Her face wore an unhappy expression, but she had finely cut features, an intellectual air, and looked under thirty. As I watched her movements, I realized that she was Japanese, perhaps a traveler or a nisei. I didn't care; I just wanted to talk to her, and, since we were on a trip, what did it matter? Burning with a feeling of rivalry with Frankie, I steeled myself and walked over to her table.

"Are you Japanese?" I demanded.

"Yes. What do you want?" Her answer came back in Japanese.

"Umm . . . would it be OK for me to sit down for a while? I'm all by myself. I just want to talk to you."

"With me? What about?" she asked, and then, perhaps because I was much younger than she or perhaps because the other guests were staring, she said, "Well, sit down. What's the matter—out of the blue like that?"

"Actually, I'm in San Francisco with a friend. That's him over there chatting up the American girl. I was all by myself, and I just wanted to talk to someone."

Never mind coming up with a good line! I sounded as though I

200

was begging as I told her about myself. She listened to me, sipping her beer, laughing periodically to reveal white teeth. She was beautiful.

"So you're a strawberry farmer from Los Angeles. Actually, I live there, too."

"Then you're here on vacation?"

"No, my ex-husband and his parents live here. My son lives with his grandparents. I came to visit him on my summer vacation."

"Umm . . ."

"No, it's OK. Don't worry about it."

She noticed that I was stuck for words and came to my rescue. Her ex-husband, she said, was an American, and their baby was four years old. Sometimes she saw the child in San Francisco, and sometimes her ex-husband brought him to LA. She had only arrived yesterday and was staying at the hotel.

"I am sorry."

Our discussion was getting rather involved, and I felt embarrassed, but as I made a move to go, she said, "No, it's OK. I'm here alone, too. Why don't we talk some more?"

I really hadn't wanted to leave. She was nice, and I felt comfortable with her, despite our ten-year age difference. About eight years ago, she told me, she had gone to study on a Fulbright scholarship at a university in the East; there she had met an American student, married him over the protests of his parents, and had a child with him.

"What were you studying?"

"English literature."

"And now?"

"We separated about a year ago. I decided to go back to school, and now I'm a part-time graduate student at UCLA. But didn't you say you're from Izu Ōshima? I went there when I was a student. Mt. Mihara and Habu Port. Now what was the name of that inn? . . ." she murmured wistfully.

She had a habit of glancing down, and at those moments she looked so beautiful that it caught at my heart. But all during our conversation baser thoughts were running through my mind—so,

201

you left your husband a year ago, maybe by now you're in the mood for a man . . .

"When I stayed in that inn in Ōshima, they gave me *kusaya*. You know, that smelly dried fish. It was my first time ever, and boy did it take me by surprise. But it was delicious."

"*Kusaya*, huh? If you really like it, I can get you some. Sometimes we get it from the island. I'll definitely bring you some. Please give me your address and phone number. I can bring you some strawberries and cauliflower, too, if you like."

Smiling, she stared at me as though trying to guess my intentions.

"Oh no . . . it's not like that. I just want to bring you some *kusaya*," I replied, flustered.

"You're a nice person. And maybe a little naive."

After more than a year in America, the only Japanese women I had met were the old women who had come over as war brides. Although this woman was ten years older than I, she seemed like the first real Japanese woman I had met. There was something of the older sister about her, yet she had the grace of a grown woman. I was very impressed. That such a beautiful Japanese woman had gotten divorced bothered me.

"Can I ask you something?"

"What?"

"Why did you get divorced?"

"Hmm . . ."

"My brother's about to marry a white girl. I'm not sure about mixed marriages."

"Mixed marriages, hmm . . ." She grasped her glass in both hands and sighed.

Her eyes had misted up, and I could tell that the alcohol was getting to her. I had read somewhere that if you make a pass at a woman when she is in this mood, you will have definite success. For a second I thought, This is my big chance. But she was still staring into her glass. During the gap in our conversation, I spun around to find Frankie standing there and his white friend leaving with another man. Her boyfriend had come to pick her up.

"Excuse me," Frankie said to my companion, then leaned down

202

to whisper in my ear. "*Yuu*, staying for a while? I'll be in the room."

Frankie seemed stunned by the sudden desertion.

"I'll go too," I said out loud, breaking the silence.

"Is this your friend?" she asked.

"Yes, he's the one I came with."

"Please sit down." She gestured to Frankie. "I've had a little too much to drink, and I'm going back to my room."

She stood up to leave. What an idiot Frankie was. Just as we had been getting somewhere. I couldn't just let her go like that. I chased after her.

"When I get *kusaya*, I promise to bring you some. Please give me your number."

"Here's my card from the company where I work part-time. We'll meet again." Her name was Iketani Naoko.

When we got back to the room, Frankie complained, "Makes me mad. *Fukku*. What a drag. It was perfect. She had a fight with her boyfriend, and, if he hadn't come tonight, she was breaking up with him."

"So that was her boyfriend after all."

"*Fukku*. Yeah. *Ai, ai*. I wanna go *homu yo*."

Frankie flopped on the bed. "I'm gonna sleep just like this, OK?"

After a few moments, I could hear Frankie snoring lightly. Carefully, I put Naoko's card in my bag and shoved it under the bed.

The next morning Frankie mentioned her. "*Yuu*, that girl you were with, was she Japanese? She's a beauty. But she looked old."

"Uh-huh, she's pretty, but it's too bad, she has a child."

"*Fukku*. We didn't get lucky."

I didn't tell Frankie that I had gotten her phone number. Secretly I thought that what had been bad luck for him might turn out to be good luck for me.

After a week in Frisco, we hadn't experienced free sex or marijuana and we sadly wended our way back to the farm. But on the day before we left we met two strange people in Union Square. We were wandering around when we caught sight of a black man and woman dressed in African garb asking for money. Naturally curious, we asked them what African country they had come from. At first they acted as though they couldn't speak English, but when they realized that we were Japanese, they spoke to us in black English and invited us to chat over coffee.

"*Yuu*, these guys are Americans. That's a Georgia accent," Frankie said, surprised.

It turned out that they were members of a black liberation group collecting money. According to them, sympathetic white people would give them money if they dressed up as Africans, but not a cent if they admitted to being black Americans. One day, they said, they were going to build a black America inside this country. Then they asked us to make a donation because we as Japanese were also victims of discrimination.

Their words unsettled me. I was aware of white attitudes, and it was natural for blacks to explain discrimination in this way— they had certainly experienced it in its worst forms. What shocked me was their plan to build a black America someday.

In those days the air reverberated with black power slogans. Blacks everywhere were riled up, but I had also heard similar sentiments from illegal Mexican immigrants. The Mexicans who would be arrested by immigration one day and back in America the next referred to this country as "el Norte"—or "the North." After all, the land had been theirs originally. Don't call us illegal aliens, they said. It's the Americans who are illegal aliens, and one of these days el Norte will be back in our hands.

Though America existed as a nation, different groups wanted to carve it up into their own little territories. In the same way that the Palestinians would never accept the Israelis who had arrived later, the Indians and Mexicans who had been pushed out of southern California would never forgive the white Americans. Nor would American blacks who had been brought to this country by force. The only way white America could atone for its sins was to allow each group the freedom to build its own version of America.

In order to arrive in Los Angeles by morning, we took the night bus. Gradually, the lights from San Francisco's high-rise buildings faded into the distance.

"Good-bye, Frisco, see you again," Frankie said wistfully. But with thoughts of Naoko, I whispered, "Good-bye. See you again in LA."

# 13

# Home and Family

A few days after I returned to the farm from my first long trip, Ted, Pete, and Charlie got back from San Diego. Of course we talked about "the night in Tijuana."

"The girls were more expensive than last year," Ted grumbled.

Jiisan, as usual, hadn't gone anywhere this year, staying home to plow his field with his ancient tractor that looked as though it might give out at any minute. Anchan had also stayed home to mess around in the field. We, too, had bought an old tractor from our profits. My brother loved machinery and had already plowed under all the old strawberry plants. Now we had to start tilling the field again.

At the end of August, my brother taught me how to drive the tractor. "If you can use this, you'll be a great farmer," he said, directing from the passenger seat.

It was much cooler to plow under the straw roof of the tractor than to swelter in the sun, and I felt great at the wheel. The previous summer, we had worked hard getting the field ready, but salt still formed on the ground, and we had too many stones. We also hadn't been completely successful in leveling the field. As a result, water distributed itself unevenly, and puddles formed between the rows. An even flow of water had an immediate positive effect on the plants. We had to be more careful about making the ground level this year, because of my brother's upcoming marriage. With a bulldozer borrowed from Frank, Anchan smoothed down the high spots and filled in the holes, then leveled the whole field with a rake that looked like a bear's claw and could loosen dirt a foot and a half deep. Sometimes we heard the sharp sound of steel striking underground rock, and the tractor would kick back. Day by day, our work progressed.

"Look how well strawberries and cauliflower grow in this soil. Coming from Japan, it's hard to believe," I said to Anchan one day, remembering how worried I had been about the dusty, sandy soil when we had been looking for a field the summer before.

"You're right. Japan's always wet, wherever you go. Any seed you plant sprouts in a few days. Here they'll die if you don't watch them every second."

"Anchan, do you want to stay a farmer? Will a white wife really help you with farming?"

"I didn't come here to be a farmer, I came here to succeed. Still, I don't know if I understand what success is. And I don't know what will happen when I get married. She is a white girl. I'm going to try my best."

After we had got a phone in May, my brother telephoned Sylvana every weekend. His "love calls," a jumble of English and Spanish, sounded pathetic from the next room. Could they really understand each other? I worried.

I had reason to worry. One day Anchan's girlfriend called when he was out, and I answered the phone in broken English. We sound the same, and she started talking as if I were Anchan. Face-to-face I could get an idea across, but on the phone it was impossible. I tried to tell her that he was out, but I couldn't find the words, and as she hung up she said, "Yes, I love you and I want you," and blew me a kiss. Not knowing what to do, I responded, "Umm. I love you, too." She never knew the difference.

Remembering what Jimmy's white wife had said about mixed marriages, I began to worry more about my brother's plans. Naoko's ambivalence echoed in my ears: "Mixed marriages, hmm . . ."

"If I marry an American," Anchan had explained, "I can become a citizen. That means my family can get green cards. Takita, Jiisan, the Mexicans, all of them are desperate for a green card. But when I'm a citizen you can have one. And not only you—anybody in our family can get one. That alone should qualify it as a success."

My brother loved his fiancée, but he was also tired of living alone in America. He was willing to be the pioneer who would bring his poor family to America and make them better off. In fact, Anchan's predictions were to come true: both my second oldest brother and my youngest brother would live in America for a long time.

Anchan had sometimes taken care of the rest of us in place of our parents. Born at a time when there was little food, he shared with other oldest sons of his generation a tendency to self-sacrifice. Although he had never lived with his first wife, he had legally been able to get a green card from that marriage. He could become a citizen from this one. By American immigration law, if one member of the family became an American citizen, immediate family members could apply for green cards. My brother wanted to open the road to America to us all.

Over twenty years have passed since then. Sometimes tears come to my eyes when I think of how much we owe Anchan. My brother got married the next year, had two children, and divorced again fourteen years later. The other members of our family departed one after another for America, leaving my mother with tears in her eyes.

"All I can do is try."

Although Anchan wanted to get married, he looked very grave whenever we talked about it. Selfishly, I wondered how I was going to act toward a white sister-in-law, and whether she might not change our lives drastically.

I thought about Frank, Pete, Hirata, Frankie, and all would-be Americans. Then I thought about Sylvana, Jimmy's wife, and all the students in my high school. They were born Americans but kept trying to prove it their whole lives.

Why did the people who were born in this country make such a big deal about being American? Immigrants could become Americans, so maybe the people who were born here only felt American after they, too, had learned the way of life. Nobody is excluded from the stage of the America drama, not the hundreds of thousands of illegal aliens, travelers, exchange students, nor the people who were born here. Another way to look at it is that there are no true Americans in this country—only would-be ones.

In September I went with Frankie to register at junior college. As my high school counselor had, the college counselor advised me to take subjects like gym and shop in the beginning, since my English still wasn't good. I was being told again to get myself accustomed to taking the same old subjects.

My brother laughed when he saw my course schedule. "*Yuu*, here you are in America and only taking gym, art, and shop. What do you plan to do? You can take gym in Japan. It makes you look like a bad student."

Although junior college was supposed to be higher education, I was commuting back and forth on my motorcycle to take courses that didn't belong in college. I had a language handicap, and I had to earn my own tuition—but I was getting more and more confused because I didn't know what I was doing in America. At nineteen I didn't find gym or shop challenging, and I led a gloomy existence on campus.

During Indian summer, in late September when the hot winds began to blow, a Filipino professor of philosophy, introduced himself to me. After finishing college in the Philippines, he had gotten his M.A. in America, gone to Japan to study Eastern philosophy, then returned to teach at the college. At the same time he was studying for his Ph.D. at UCLA. The professor understood Japanese well, and sometimes we had lunch together.

One day he invited me to attend his class. The sight of a small Asian man lecturing passionately about philosophy in a heavy Filipino accent to hulking white boys who had no interest in anything but girls was painful. The professor, on the other hand, was very confident of his successes in America, and said that one of these days he would become a citizen. Could he throw away his own nationality so easily? The professor was married to a beautiful white woman. When I was invited to their home, they gave me a guided tour.

"This is the living room. Come this way. This is my study, and that's my wife's. This is our bedroom," he explained. All such tours in America include the bedroom.

A big mirror hung close to the bed—probably for when they fooled around. The professor explained how much the house cost, what their mortgage payments were, and how they would buy a bigger house when they had paid off this mortgage, although they were satisfied with this house for now. Next I was shown to the garage, where he talked in detail about the makes and years of their two cars. This was his twelfth year in America, and he was on his second marriage; a child from the first marriage was doing fine with his ex-wife. Life was incredibly satisfying for him now. What he loved best was this house and his children from the second marriage.

That he would tell me—a mere student—so much about his private life and show me his house at first seemed a mystery. Finally I understood that he was showing me that, since he had succeeded here, I could, too, if I worked hard.

It struck me that people arrive on this continent naked, having discarded or run away from their homes and their families. Consequently, these are the first things that immigrants must acquire here, and they must build houses that are bigger and better. If not, they feel their losses have been for nothing.

Americans pay an inordinate amount of attention to their houses to prove how well they are doing. "Look at this wonderful bedroom I have, look at my big living room," they brag, proud of what they've been able to acquire here. The big houses in Beverly Hills are a physical manifestation of the American dream. Construction is used as an index of the American economy because a house is the fruit of the American dream. The housing index is a sort of sign of how many dreams come true each month, and this is important news. But the key to American life also lies in the family who lives in the house.

If you ask Americans what is most important to them, they will answer "my family." People who have left their mother countries behind and settled here can never run away from home again. To regain what you once had, only bigger and better, is what it means to be an American.

That American society is based on a social contract of free individuals only tells part of the story. As immigration policy shows, American society prizes the rights of the family.

The president and his cabinet—with its members chosen from the "best and brightest" in the land—stand as a more abstract symbol of the ideal family. Whenever a new president is elected, a photo is taken at the White House of the president as head of the household, his wife, and his cabinet members; the American public witnesses the rebirth of the ideal American family.

The White House itself also symbolizes the American dream. The American improves his lot by building a home and family: what begins as a shack in a field becomes the middle-class home in the suburbs, and is eventually transformed into the White House. As one of the best and brightest, one may begin at the shack and end up as a member of the president's ideal household. This is the American dream made flesh.

But why did so many tragedies and divorces occur in the home when Americans place so much value on it? I wouldn't understand the reasons for this until much later.

Back on the farm, the Mexican workers were organizing a boycott and a strike, the likes of which America had never seen.

Cesar Chavez, the leading Mexican-American activist, had changed the name of the National Farm Workers Union to the United Farm Workers Committee and given orders to all Mexicans working in California to strike and boycott. Both Mexican Americans and illegal Mexicans responded to the call, and a demonstration began in Delano, the headquarters of the organization, which involved walking 300 miles to Sacramento, the state capital, in twenty-five days.

Delano, about seventy-five miles from Fresno, is famous for its grapes. Chavez calculated that if they started in Delano and headed through the farm belt of central California, Mexicans working on farms along the way would leave the fields and join in the procession. Summer and autumn were the harvest season for central California. By striking at that time, he reasoned, they would force California to recognize how precious a resource the Mexican laborers were. Chavez's strategy succeeded beyond expectation. Two hundred thousand workers threw down the grapes they had picked and joined the walk.

At a time when the young people in Haight-Ashbury were

rebelling with flowers, rock, and marijuana, and the blacks were already on their way toward racial warfare on a national scale, the Mexicans—unable to speak English, stuck doing the lowest kinds of jobs, and living in fear of immigration—wanted to rebel, too.

That year the Mexicans went on strike, but there was no comparison between the 1965 strike and this year's in terms of scale and heightened emotions. Every day we watched the procession on the news. Many of the Mexicans carried placards that read CHICANO POWER.

"Me-*tachi*, we're lucky *yo na*. The Mexicans in San Joaquin Valley started this one. If this had started in San Diego or Imperial Valley, we'd have been in big trouble—we'd have been right in the path of the demonstration. If that had happened, *shee*, the *Mexis* workin' here would be sure to join in. Then *shinku whatto happun*. Me-*tachi's* field—*panicu*. No harvest. Terrible for the grape growers in San Joaquin. Everything will rot." Frank shook his head.

At that time we had nothing to harvest. About a month before, the California green front had moved up over the Tehachapi Mountains into central California and had stopped dead in the grape fields. The farmers in the San Joaquin Valley who were preparing for the harvest fell into panic. The newspapers and television reported daily the rising prices of grapes and vegetables.

At this point a Japanese American stepped in. A descendant of Japanese farmers, he described himself as a Japanese who had been born in this country. Harry Kubota decided to aid the frightened farmers. He put out a call for help to both nisei and first-generation Japanese immigrants, formed a rescue squad, and went to pick the grapes and lettuce that the Mexicans had abandoned. It was a form of strike breaking. About a hundred Japanese farmers worked on a harvest that normally demanded hundreds of men, and, by working to the point of collapse, they finished without mishap. As a result, Kubota's reputation grew even higher among the Japanese-American farmers of central California.

Later Kubota created an agricultural union, the Japanese-American Farmers League. Currently twelve hundred households belong to the league, making it the largest agricultural union in

211

the nation. Two-thirds of the members are actually white farmers, despite the league's name.

The Japanese farmers who took part in the strike breaking felt that it was time to show Americans how hard they could work. During the summer of 1966, the Japanese had also risen in a fervor, like the blacks, the Mexicans, and, to some extent, the flower children although they had expressed themselves differently. After this incident, Harry Kubota's name spread to southern California.

"See, Japanese are the good guys. We pick better than anyone else. I bet the white farmers appreciate him now." As Frank said, farmers all over were praising the Japanese strike breakers. Harry Kubota's success and his brilliance as a farmer were soon to be recognized; when Ronald Reagan became governor of California a year later, he appointed Kubota as his agricultural advisor.

"The whites are havin' to take another look at us. But you know, even though I understand what the Mexicans are feeling, they went too far, and the whites got mad. Call it civil rights, call it whatever you want, but whites get angry when Mexicans say those kind of things. You have to step pretty careful, or you get in big trouble," Frank told me.

I only came to understand how much meaning these words held for Japanese and their descendants who had lived before and during the war one afternoon after I had started college. We had finished planting strawberries on our 20-acre plot as usual and were getting ready to turn on the sprinklers when we saw Frank's prized car heading down the road in the field toward us. Frank got out, holding a newspaper in his right hand. His usually humorous expression had vanished. "Ishikawa, I'd like to talk with you."

"Yes, what is it?" I answered.

"Is this Ishikawa in the newspaper you?"

Frank opened up the newspaper; it was the Japanese *Rafu News* of Los Angeles. I couldn't believe it; there on the page Frank was showing us were words that I had written.

"*Yuu*, I don't think you should write these things. You're a student here, so you probably think a lot, but it's better if Japanese don't say these kinds of things," Frank said.

Ten days before I had read an article in the *Rafu News* by a minister in Chicago, something like: "America is fighting a just war in Vietnam. The country is now facing very difficult times. At just such a time Japanese living in America should pledge allegiance to America, support this war, and act like citizens of this wonderful and venerable country. These days some nisei are participating in the antiwar movement without knowing how much we first-generation immigrants suffered. They should think the whole issue through again." Reading this article had made me angry, and for the first time in my life I had fired off a letter in reply. The newspaper was always delivered to Frank's office, so I hadn't yet seen it.

I had written back: "Japanese shouldn't support the Vietnam War just because they live here. It would be far better for Japanese to support the antiwar movement. When you say that the parents of nisei should urge their children not to participate, what could be on your mind?"

When I explained this to Frank, he said, "You still shouldn't say those things. The isei suffered a lot. This minister, he's probably worried that if young people say anti-American things, they'll be called Japs by the Americans again—I'll bet."

As Frank and I were talking, Anchan came up, carrying a sprinkler pipe on his shoulder. He must have noticed something out of the ordinary.

"Daiku, I've been talking with you *braza* 'bout this," Frank explained, handing my brother the newspaper. Anchan understood and replied, "Boss, I'll talk to him."

"I'm not exactly mad. It's just better to keep these things to yourself. I don't want to cause any trouble here. By the way, Daiku, looks like *yuu-tachi's* plants have taken root. *Nexto yea mo,* you'll have a great crop. But you know, we had such a good crop this year, they're planting lots of strawberries in Orange County and Oxnard. Means we got to produce some great strawberries by Easter."

Frank got back in his car. As soon as he had left my brother started in: "*Yuu,* I don't really understand it, but America is fighting a communist invasion. If America didn't invade Vietnam, it would fall into communist hands. Hell, I don't know. That's

213

what everyone's saying. But really, what American is going to read what you wrote about Vietnam in a Japanese newspaper? Nobody listens to us."

With the heavy sprinkler pipes on our backs, we walked down the muddy path.

"Still, don't you think that guy in Chicago is wrong? I mean, saying that you have to listen to Americans because you live here . . . that you shouldn't say what you think. . . . No wonder we get called Japs. No wonder they make fun of us," I said excitedly.

"*Yuu*, what are you talkin' about?

My brother's tone had changed.

"*Yuu*, why do you think we're here? It's because the isei clenched their teeth when they were called Japs, and finally got accepted—that's why we can be farmers. Listen to me carefully. We're leasing our land, right? But Japanese couldn't even rent land, let alone own it, before nineteen fifty-four. And if that wasn't bad enough, we weren't even allowed to immigrate between nineteen twenty-four and nineteen fifty-four. Some guy named Fujii realized that the law prohibiting Japanese from owning land was against the American Constitution. He sued the state and won. Japanese were finally allowed to own land and then to immigrate.

"And that happened only ten years ago. Now, Kagoshima Construction is putting up a large building in Little Tokyo. The consulate's office will be there. But it's only because the Japanese Americans here fought so that Japanese outside the country can buy land, houses, and factories in California. What the isei are trying to say is, finally we can live peacefully in this country, so we should show that we are true Americans. And—"

"And what?"

"And I think that they're worried that if we draw too much attention to ourselves, terrible things could happen to us again."

I hadn't known that Japanese immigration had been prohibited between 1924 and 1955, or that Japanese hadn't been able to buy land in America before 1954.

"When you write things like that, the older Japanese get a bad impression. These days you see a lot of Japanese businessmen downtown and some are making fun of us, calling us immigrant laborers."

My brother was right. Compared with last year, there were lots more Japanese wearing suits in Little Tokyo. Older buildings had been razed to make way for new ones.

"It's not just the businessmen. The Japanese in the consulate give us a hard time, too. The other day when I went to find out how to change my citizenship, they asked me all about my last marriage. 'Is that why you're marrying an American woman,' they said, 'because you want to be an American citizen?' I've had it up to here," Anchan said angrily, "and I wasn't the only one it happened to. They really put the old immigrants through the wringer. Now we call them Nips!"

# 14

# No-Man's-Land

Soon after the uproar over my article, I went to see Naoko. I had
already phoned her once. Two weeks after we had gotten back, I
was in Los Angeles, but she couldn't see me. "Oh, it's you," she
said, "from that time in San Francisco. I'm surprised you still
remember me. Look, I have too much work to do today. Let's make
it another time."

The next time I contacted her because we had gotten some
*kusaya* from the island, and I remembered my promise to her.

"Really, you have some *kusaya*? You certainly keep your promises," she said happily. "Let's meet. But not in Japantown. Make
it somewhere else."

I rode my motorcycle to a restaurant on Wilshire Boulevard,
near the famous Ambassador Hotel. Her office, she said, was near
there and so was her apartment.

When I had first met her, Naoko had been wearing the casual
clothes of the traveler, but now, on her way home from work, she
was wearing a proper business outfit. Just by slightly changing
what she wore, she became almost a different person.

"I'm sorry about that time. I was by myself and had nothing to
do, so . . ." I apologized when I got to the table.

I had brought the dried *kusaya* in a paper bag, but the fish's
distinctive odor leaked out.

"That smell takes me back. But I bet it's bothering the other
customers," Naoko said, looking at an old couple at the next table
with bemused expressions on their faces.

"I also brought the newspapers that my mother packed it with. Please take them."

Whenever my mother sent us a package, she always enclosed a few newspapers, and, although they might have been a month old, I would devour them. I had brought them along thinking that somebody who had lived in America for a long time would like to read them. They had been all crumpled up, so the night before I had flattened them out under my mattress.

"You really think of everything, don't you? Thank you. But actually, the company I'm working for does business with Japan, and we get them sometimes. If you'd like to read them, I could send them to you. But if you read Japanese newspapers, your English won't improve," she said, sounding just like an adult.

Somehow, I couldn't think of how to bring the conversation around to *the* topic. From the beginning I was frustrated because things never seemed to go the way I secretly intended them to. But where should I begin?

"Do you work near here?" I asked.

"My office is on the eighth floor of the building just across the way. It's a consulting firm for Japanese companies here. I'm a translator," she explained, brushing the hair away from her neck with her hand. "You work on the farm and go to school at the same time, don't you?"

"Yes, to the junior college nearby. Part-time."

I didn't want to talk about school. Naoko had graduated from a famous university in Tokyo and then gone to a reputable school in the East on a Fulbright. It embarrassed me when people called the school I was going to college. Also, I didn't want her to know what subjects I was taking.

"What are your plans? Keep farming in California? Or maybe enroll in a four-year college in Japan?"

This was the last question I wanted to hear. Actually I had no vision of my future. "Before I came to America I had various plans, but after a year and a half here, I feel lost."

"I know. When I first got here I was thrilled, but after a few months of student life, I got very depressed."

"Why did you come here to study?"

217

Although this was only our second meeting, she began to talk to me much more openly than I had expected.

Naoko had attended a mission school and then gone on to college. Because her family was well-off and her father worked for a firm that had foreign investments, she had started to learn English and spend time with Americans in junior high school. Hers was an unusual home environment for postwar Japan. In her third year of college, she had fallen in love with another student, but, after he became deeply involved in the movement against the Japanese-U.S. Security Treaty, they began to drift apart. All of her women friends had also become stridently anti-American and anti–Security Treaty. Because she had been friendly with Americans since she was little, she couldn't adjust herself to the anti-American atmosphere, and, because her father had a close friend in America, she took the necessary exam and went to a university in Pennsylvania in 1959.

There were eight other Japanese exchange students at the school besides her, but she did her best not to associate with them, studied hard, and got her master's degree in literature. After three years she went back to Japan for another try with her boyfriend, only to find that he had failed in his cause and now seemed a completely different person. They broke up for good, and she came back to America thinking she wanted to study more. It was then that she met an American in a class and married him. After their child was born, she quit graduate school against her wishes. Her husband got his degree, and his work had brought them to San Francisco three years ago. They had gotten divorced last year. Now she wanted to start school all over again.

Having gotten married over the objections of her parents, she was now putting herself through school and living in her own apartment in LA.

"You might get mad at me for asking, but why did you get divorced? I think I mentioned that my brother is marrying a white woman next summer—his second marriage. I worry about him because he doesn't speak English very well. Do you think these marriages can work?"

"Hmm . . . I don't know your brother and his fiancée, so I really can't say, but in my case . . ." She paused to light a cigarette. Her face was illuminated by the small flame of the lighter, and she flinched slightly.

"I misunderstood him and I misunderstood myself. . . . Remember, I had come back to America again after ending my relationship in Japan, and I guess I was feeling a little desperate. School was hard. He started pursuing me when I was studying my hardest. He was brilliant, you know, and very popular. The kind of guy the girls would do anything to date.

"Slowly we got to know each other. Don't ask me why, but he started getting more serious. As for me, when we talked together, I don't know, I felt that we were really communicating. Not being able to talk to any of my old friends in Japan was very frustrating. Maybe that's why I felt I could talk to him about anything.

"But there was one thing I couldn't understand, even if we could communicate. Why did he fall in love with me, a Japanese woman? What was it about me that he loved? I mean, there were lots of American women who were brighter and prettier than me. And he could have had anyone he wanted."

"But you're beautiful, too," I interrupted, thinking I should say something.

"Oh, flattery will get you everywhere," Naoko replied, her tone softening.

"Anyway, after seeing each other for a while, we decided to get married. When I think back on it now, maybe I did it to feel superior. I had gotten the man all the other girls wanted. Me, a Japanese woman. We really weren't accepted back then. I was on a crusade. There I was, shorter than all the others, and I had gotten him—revenge was sweet. Oh, they treated me well enough on the outside, but inside I could feel their cold looks. I was also getting revenge on the friends I had broken with back home for not accepting me. And then I was used to the luxuries of America. I was just mixed up. Of course, I didn't know it—being able to talk to him was enough to make me happy.

"At first I was confident in my English and didn't feel at a disadvantage. It was no problem for me to lead my life in English— I thought. Later I realized that talking to him felt good because he knew how good my English was and spoke to me on my level. He knew how to make a woman feel good. I really thought we could

219

communicate, but I was wrong. When we started living together, he spoke in a language backed up by all of America. I was speaking a second language that I had learned as an adult. Later, his words overwhelmed me. I realized this when we got past romantic conversation and started to talk real life. Then I understood he was talking down to me."

"Even with your American education and perfect English, it didn't work because of language?"

"Language problems didn't lead directly to divorce. There were other things, too."

It would have been too rude to ask her any more about her divorce; it was time to change the topic. "Don't you want to go back to Japan?"

"That's what worries me most. I can't take my child back with me the way I am. I don't have the nerve to face my parents. . . ."

"I'm sorry to make you talk about this."

This was not why I had wanted to see her. I found myself angry for always being an attentive audience. I had come because I thought I had a chance, but so far our conversation was wholly focused on her own personal history. With Frank and the old man I also played the role of the audience, and now the same thing was happening with a woman whom I had knocked myself out to meet. Why did I always have to be the listener?

"It's OK. I really feel like talking."

Perhaps she was starved to speak Japanese. At any rate, she started again. "My parents were against the marriage. Especially my father. It shocked me. I mean, my father had lots of American friends, and he could read novels in English. For a man of his generation, he seemed unusually fond of America. But when I told him, he lost his temper. Seeing him angry like that, I decided that it had all just been a pose. He had fought America during the war. My parents did come all the way for the wedding ceremony, and they gave us their blessings, but my father looked very sad. We didn't talk much. It was the first time I had ever seen my father cry.

"When I went back to Japan to visit, though, I understood—I didn't have the confidence to go out with Japanese men. I was doing the only possible thing. It isn't easy to live in a foreign

220

country . . . If you don't know who you are, life will drift right by you, and one day you'll wake up and find yourself changed. It's very important to have a strong sense of self."

Naoko looked down. For the first time, her face looked tired.

"You've never been back since you got married?"

"I had a child so soon, no, I haven't gone back. . . . This sounds like a confession. I'm sorry."

She forcibly brightened and tried to sound cheery.

"Uhhhh"—I hesitated—"may I call you again sometime? I don't know English very well, and there are some things I'd like to ask you. And there's one other thing. Is there a reason you don't like meeting in Little Tokyo?"

"Japantown depresses me. It's all of Japan's shabbiness packed into one small space, and I can't stand it. Sometimes I get nostalgic and shop there, but when I'm done, I practically run out. And the answer to your other question is yes, it's fine. Call me. I'd just rather meet somewhere besides Japantown. You're very sweet, you know, taking all the trouble to bring me *kusaya*." When she expressed her gratitude, the happiness in her voice was no longer forced.

"I'll take you out next time to thank you," she offered.

That day on the way home, I leaned forward like the Hell's Angels on my prized bike and accelerated. And then, because no one could hear me, I tried out words in English that I would never use in front of anyone: "Baby, you are sweet! I wanna fuck you!"

Revving the motorcycle even more, I yelled again and again in English, then I yelled it in Japanese.

My yell didn't come from between my thighs, but flowed through my whole body until it reached my thighs. I was in love.

I took Naoko up on her word and often went to meet her, driving for over an hour on my motorcycle. Whenever we met, she treated me very well. She took me to Huntington Gardens in San Marino and out to eat at nice restaurants in LA. When I brought her strawberries the next spring, we had run out of things to say and it was time to take the next step.

By November, the strawberry plants had rooted themselves firmly in the ground, and little, robust green leaves were growing everywhere. Once we had gotten the plants to this point, and barring any extreme weather, we could expect a field of sweet, big strawberries before harvesttime. Until then we wouldn't be so busy.

I still commuted to the junior college on my motorcycle to take gym, art, and various other courses, though they weren't very interesting. Once a week I would visit Sensei and his wife and talk with them. One of my reasons for going was that whenever I took an English textbook that I didn't understand, Sensei would translate for me. I also met Naoko about once every three weeks. These two people gave me something to look forward to in my dreary life.

My brother's wedding was set for July in Port Jervis, not Niagara Falls, and he was going to New York for Christmas. I felt compelled to tell Sensei, because he had translated Anchan's love letters.

"Is that so? Congratulations. I must phone your brother and give him my blessings." Unlike Frank, Sensei was supportive of my brother's marriage.

"The boss of the farm says that white women are no good. My brother's been upset, but your approval will encourage him."

"I can understand how the boss feels. For the Japanese around here, marrying a white person's a big scandal. I have a story for you. Dear, when did Tamura publish his apology?"

"About his daughter? It was a good five or six years ago, I think," his wife answered, as she poured the tea.

"There was a pretty good poet named Tamwa in Los Angeles. He had written in the camps. His nisei daughter fell in love with a white man, and he was fiercely opposed to it. 'I won't allow you to associate with whites,' he told her. Even so, the couple eventually got married. He was powerless to stop them, but he did take out an ad in the Japanese newspaper to apologize to his fellow Japanese—a public apology to my contemporaries, was what he called it."

"Why did he have to go so far?"

"He probably had a lot of bad memories from the war, and he couldn't stand watching his beloved daughter marry a white man. A member of his own household joining forces with a white person—it felt like a betrayal."

"I didn't realize there were Japanese like that."

"His ad drew a lot of sympathy from the isei who had lived through the prewar period and the war itself. I myself thought he was going a little overboard. Still, when you think of the history of Japanese people in this country, you begin to understand him."

Today's Japanese and Japanese Americans probably laugh when they come across this story. But twenty-five years ago this topic was constantly bandied about in the Japanese-American community.

"It must have been hard for them." Not knowing how the Japanese had lived before or during the war, this was all I could offer.

"Although they weren't written by Tamura, I have some poems by his fellow poets. Perhaps you should have a look at them. Some of them clearly describe the way the Japanese in this country felt."

Sensei went to his study and bought me a mimeographed copy of a poetry collection from the camps. As I flipped through the pages, my eye was drawn to a poem, "My Loneliness," which I remember to this day.

> Now I know that
> it was sadness
> that made them drive us away with stones
> and I defend myself
> wanting only to be alone
>
> I live in no man's land
> Out of step with the world
> Gritting my teeth at the pain of life
> I focus my loneliness—
> a vein of gold
> laid bare in earth and rain

The people who "were driven away with stones" and who are "out of step with the world" are the Japanese who were despised by the Americans and thrown in detention camps.

Perhaps the poet was right. Anchan, Frank, Hirata, all of us were out of step with the world and, what's more, were living in the wilds of America—no-man's-land. But, the poet might have meant that being out of step with the world had brought us to America in the first place, and once we arrived we felt sorry for ourselves when stones were hurled at us and longed for our mother country.

But what was our mother country? If our mother country could only be the place we were born, what did Japanese immigrants feel when Japan started a war with America? The same author had written a poem at the beginning of the Pacific War, in 1941, entitled "Motherland!"

Somebody's walking across heaven
I hear their footsteps
Across oceans of flame
Footsteps of someone in pain.

The strife in my motherland
Reverberates to heaven
A country in distress
A country in decline
Footsteps echo
Chest aching, spirits sinking
Shaken to the depths of my being
Motherland!
I turn my face towards you
My pale face towards you
Body and soul weeping
I who can no longer be with you.

The Japanese in Japantown, the Japanese on the farm, even the businessmen selling electric rice cookers, all mourned because they had to live outside the country to which they were connected. It wasn't only the Japanese either; Italians, Mexicans, and all the other immigrants couldn't forget that they were far away from home.

Just before Christmas, Sensei and his wife organized an antiwar demonstration in Pasadena with scholars from the California Institute of Technology. At the time there were about ten Nobel laureates working at Cal Tech, known as the MIT of the West, and a few of them attended the demonstration along with a few dozen ministers and their wives. Some members of the religion department of Claremont College also took part; Sensei had taught there, and he had a strong connection to the school.

A number of the nisei and sansei children who were in their circle or who had been members of his church had gone to Vietnam, and this had upset Sensei a great deal. Whenever I visited him at home, the talk invariably turned to the Vietnam War.

"I feel that I must do something; this is my first demonstration," Sensei explained to me.

A more direct reason, however, was his and his wife's sympathy with the student movement. That year the students of Berkeley stepped up their tactics from gatherings and demonstrations to strikes and boycotts: they surrounded the administration building and stopped going to classes. Some even burned their draft cards. The news spread across the country like wildfire.

Up until this time, it had not been unusual for young people in America to protest, and at first the public was not very critical of the student movement. However, when students burned their draft cards in public and the scenes were replayed on televisions across America, the tide of public opinion turned. To make matters worse, students were surrounding their schools' administration buildings and acting in more and more extreme ways.

The public did not remain silent. There were demonstrations by people who urged that radicals be thrown off campuses, and critical editorials popped up in the mass media. The antistudent sentiment was evident at Berkeley—the hotbed of student activism—as well as in Ronald Reagan's dismissal of Clark Kerr, the president of Berkeley, who had been sympathetic to the students.

America became divided down the lines of "establishment" and "antiestablishment." Personal relationships were not immune; people argued fiercely on city streets and college campuses over whether they were part of the establishment or not.

Just knowing that there were Japanese like Sensei and his wife who attended antiwar protests helped me a great deal at that time. Unlike the people on the farm, some Japanese people stood up to America. I was very impressed with Sensei and his wife, because they had continued on their chosen path even though they were

225

getting old. There was no one like them on the farm; people there were deferential when it came to America. Adrift at the time, I had finally found "a place to be" in Sensei's way of life.

After almost two years in America, I was beginning to understand Japanese society in Los Angeles. Japan might have been defeated and occupied by the Americans, but these Japanese had been living as though they were victims since the day they stepped off the boat. It would take a long time before the Japanese could stop cowering and live with dignity. Even in today's prosperity, this is true.

Sensei's antiwar demonstration stirred the hearts of the nisei who were already leaning in that direction. Japanese and Japanese Americans began to form small clubs. Then, in 1969, the first antiwar demonstration of Asians was held in Little Tokyo. Sensei was at the head of the line; he got up on the platform and gave a stirring speech. I wasn't there, but a nisei professor at UCLA whom I would get to know later said to me, "I couldn't believe that a first-generation Japanese could make such a moving speech in English."

I often heard how much Sensei admired Henry David Thoreau. While Thoreau had been writing *The Maine Woods,* he had also been speaking on civil disobedience; Sensei was the Thoreau of the Japanese community, or at least he was following in the great man's footsteps. One often heard the words *civil disobedience* in those days, but I had learned what they meant from Sensei.

On New Year's Day, we phoned our parents for the first time. Although we had gotten our phone in May, one phone call a year to Japan was plenty, considering the price and our incomes. Anchan had already gone to New York and finally set the date and time of his wedding. He couldn't pull back now. Eight family members were gathered at home for the New Year's celebration, and we talked with each one. In those days the long-distance sound quality was poor, and the voices sounded very weak. This only reminded us how far away we were, and both of us shed tears. We were certainly living in no-man's-land. And that year my brother would go even further—into the world of white America.

# 15

# Arrivals, Departures, Good-byes

One day in February 1967, I stopped by the field after school, and my brother said excitedly, *"Yuu,* you were right about those people—they are Japanese. When I drove to the supermarket at lunchtime, this car started honking at me. I stopped, and a Japanese couple got out of the car. He's a gardener."

"Where are they from?"

"He's from Kagoshima. They have three kids: one in high school, two in junior high. All boys. He came here three years ago to get things ready, and the wife and kids joined him six months ago. He was growing flowers in Salinas at first, but it didn't work out, and he came here last December to be near a friend."

My brother was talking to me while he weeded, and I pitched in, too. My fingers were cold. I remembered spotting those people from the car many times since December.

"Anchan, see those people in that car, aren't they Japanese?" I had asked him.

*"Yuu,* what are you talking about? They're Mexicans. Gardeners, the two of them. If you can't tell the difference between Mexicans and Japanese yet, you're never going to make it as a farmer." My brother had laughed.

"I dunno. The woman was wearing a little towel on her head. Do Mexicans do that? They look Japanese to me."

"I'm sure Mexicans wear towels, too."

But now he had discovered what I'd suspected. "They'd seen us in the car a lot but couldn't figure out if we were Japanese or Mexican. So they decided to ask."

"What! I can see why they thought you were, but me?"

"You got it. You look more and more Mexican every day." After living and working with Mexicans for nearly two years, I probably *had* started to look like one of them. Our mother would be surprised when she saw us.

"Oh, by the way, they're all coming over at seven. They want to meet you, too."

At seven o'clock that night a big station wagon pulled up in front of our house. My brother introduced us.

"*Yuu,* this is the Yoshida family. Mr. Yoshida, this is my brother."

"We've seen you so often, but we didn't say anything because we weren't sure if you were Japanese. I hope we can be friends. The children just got here, and they don't know anything. Please teach them about America."

The mother and the father made little bows. Then the mother introduced the three children, who were tongue-tied and could only nod. They, like thousands of others, would spin their own version of the American dream. I took the hand of the oldest boy, a tenth grader.

One day just before harvest, I went into the strawberry field with a box under my arm. I was going to give Naoko a taste of the first batch of strawberries. Spreading apart the leaves of the plants, I searched for ripe ones. It wasn't easy to find big, ripe strawberries so early, but eventually, after searching from one end of the field to the next, I managed to gather about fifty.

Usually, picking was grueling work, but that day I felt light as air thinking of Naoko. Three days before, when the field had first been tinged with red, I'd called her and said, "The first strawberries will be ready on Saturday. How about it?" Luckily, she didn't have work or school that day, and she would be expecting me.

It was the second time I had been to visit her at home. Her apartment was very neat and organized. I still hadn't told my brother about her, and I made up a small lie as we ate lunch together. "Listen, Anchan. I'm going downtown this afternoon. I'm meeting this Thai friend of mine from school. If it gets late, I might stay over. Tomorrow's Sunday anyway."

228

"*Yuu* seem to be going downtown a lot lately. Is it a girl? I've noticed you always put on a clean shirt."

"That's not why. I don't want to look too dirty and make Japanese look bad," I said, startled.

Even though I didn't expect to stay overnight, a faint glimmer of hope had risen inside me.

"Strawberries fresh from the field," I said, when Naoko came to the door.

"They look delicious. You just can't find these in the stores. I'll try one now and save the rest for dessert. Please stay for dinner. I've made stew."

She took a strawberry and brought it to her lips. "Mmm, it's good, very juicy," she said, using English with me for the first time. Then she added, "It's such a nice day today, why don't we go for a drive before supper? I love driving by the sea. We can go around Santa Monica, Marina del Rey, and Venice Beach. Would you like to see the ocean?"

In fact, I hadn't been to the beach since the time I went to Santa Monica with Frankie and his friends my first summer in the States. We drove west along Wilshire Boulevard. Office buildings were lined up neatly on either side of the street in this commercial section, and tall pine trees had been planted between the buildings; it was a scene that often graced postcards. We passed UCLA, got on the freeway, and headed for the beach.

In late March, barely a soul was there, and the sea was quiet.

"It's cold, but it feels great," Naoko said, staring out to sea, her arms outstretched as she breathed deeply. "Japan's all the way across the ocean." She sounded unusually sentimental. Perhaps she really wanted to go back to Japan. I stared at her profile.

"Can you swim?" I asked.

"Yes. I used to be a great swimmer. Still, it's been years."

"We should come here in the summer. I was born and raised on an island, so I'm a good swimmer."

We walked by the waves, the salt air blowing gently over us. Then we went to Marina del Rey and Venice Beach. By the time we got back, it was nearly dark. The stew was delicious, and we toasted my brother and our harvest with wine. Dessert was coffee and strawberries.

"These strawberries are really delicious. One of these days, I'd like to come and see your field," Naoko said.

"Anytime you want. I'll show you how to pick. You have to bend down like this." I got up and showed her.

"You're very sure of yourself, aren't you?" she said, laughing.

I laughed too. Then I told her some of the funny things that had happened to me.

"Did I tell you I met the writer Henry Miller and talked about Ishizaka Yojiro with him?"

"What? No."

When I had told her the story from beginning to end, she said, giggling, "You told Henry Miller about Ishizaka Yojiro? You're too much."

Her laughter made me feel good, too, so I went on. "And Henry Miller gave me a picture and he signed it *Banzai Omanko*."

"Oh . . ."

She looked troubled. An uncomfortable silence grew up between us. Now I've blown it, I thought. But if I don't say it now, I'll never get the chance. My heart pounded, and my legs felt limp, but I mustered all my courage and stood up, saying, "I want to do it with you."

"What?"

"Fuck."

Her right hand, which held a cigarette, trembled and stopped in front of her mouth. A blush spread over her face. She seemed to be deep in thought for a second, then she rose slowly and took both my hands in hers.

"You're a little too sure of yourself, aren't you?"

"I'm sorry. I just really want you."

"Wait a minute, then follow me," she said huskily, and disappeared into the bathroom.

I could hear the sound of a shower. Then the door opened, and Naoko walked briskly into the bedroom wearing a bathrobe. Quickly I took a shower, too, and went into the bedroom wrapped in a big towel. She was lying down with the sheets up over her breasts, a red bedside lamp the only source of light. Holding the sheet with one hand, she guided me to her side with the other. Through the white sheet, translucent in the red light, I could see her breasts, and the sight set me on fire.

It was different from the time in Tijuana. I felt safer with Naoko because we had talked so much. And the darkness made me bold.

"I want you. I've wanted you since the day we met in San Francisco," I whispered.

In the reddish glow of the bed lamp, her face slowly moved closer to mine. "Make love to me," she said.

How long did I sleep afterward? I woke up feeling thirsty, headed for the kitchen, and popped a strawberry in my mouth. It crunched between my teeth, a little unripe, jolting me out of sleep. Planning to feed her a strawberry if she woke up, I brought a plate of them to the bedroom and climbed back into bed.

Later I woke up again, feeling a weight on my chest. She was reaching over me, trying to get a strawberry.

"Sorry to wake you. Did you bring them for me?" she asked, popping the red fruit in her mouth. Then, squeezing the strawberry with her tongue, she slipped the juice into my mouth and murmured, "Your strawberries were delicious."

My heart overflowed with happiness. When she said "strawberries" she didn't just mean the strawberries that we had just eaten.

From that time on, whenever I phoned her, she would say, "Hello, Mr. Strawberry." And, depending on her mood, she would call me "Mr. Strawberry," "Little Strawberry," or, when she helped me with English, "Strawberry Boy." Being called pet names by an older woman at that time in my life gave me security. I thought I had been rejected by both the Americans and the Japanese on the farm, and I wanted to be smothered with affection. Naoko's choice of nicknames addressed all the roles I played—the man, the boy, and the friend. I felt she'd given me a sign that we had crossed a bridge together.

It wasn't until I had made a confession, however, that I felt really sure. "It makes me happy when you say that. But I've been worried about one thing. You were married to an American, so I thought that maybe I wouldn't be good enough. I mean, American men are big, and they're supposed to be very good in bed. . . ."

231

"Silly thing. . . . You slept with me worrying about that?"

I thought I saw tears in her eyes. A blush spread over her face, and excitedly she lowered her body on top of me. "Make love to me again. I want you, a Japanese man. No, wait, I'll do it to you."

She peeled the sheet from our bodies, and soon I heard an unearthly cry come from her lips.

I opened my eyes to the rattle of china. She was bringing me coffee and was wearing her robe again.

"Did you sleep well?"

"What time is it?"

"Almost ten."

She opened the curtains, and the light streamed in.

"You were sleeping so peacefully, I didn't want to wake you," she said radiantly.

For some reason I felt embarrassed gazing at her in broad daylight, and I got up to take a shower. Engulfed in the stream of hot water, I went over the events of the previous evening in my mind.

"I want you, a Japanese man." Her uncharacteristic words lingered in my mind.

When I came out of the shower, the table was laid with coffee, eggs, ham, and more of the strawberries I had brought. A typical American breakfast, but you wouldn't find such a delicious meal anywhere. Watching Naoko eat strawberries with her slender fingers, I lost control again.

With the arrival of spring, the strawberries grew by leaps and bounds, and once again the red, ripe fruit sparkled under the relentless southern California sun. As usual, the pickers appeared out of nowhere, and the air grew pungent with sweat. My body felt boosted by the experience of that night, and I was able to work painlessly, the young farmer all the way.

One night in May, when we were at the peak of harvest, Takita, whom we had met at the Japanese-American picnic the year before, appeared from out of the blue. We had since eaten with him a couple of times in Little Tokyo. We were in the middle of dinner when he arrived, and my brother said, "*Yuu*, what's wrong?

232

Coming so far like this. If you'd called me, I could at least have met you halfway."

"No, no. I need some advice from you, so don't worry about it. But first, I took a look at your field before I came here. You've grown a beautiful crop. You're a real farmer now," Takita said.

"How 'bout a beer?" my brother asked, taking two cans out of the refrigerator.

"I have decided to go back to Japan," Takita announced.

"W-what? All of a sudden? You aren't getting along with your wife?" Anchan was shocked.

"No, that's not it. She wants to go back to Japan."

A year ago, Takita had only started seeing the woman because he wanted a green card. But in spite of their seven-year age difference and the very different lives they had led up until then, the two had fallen in love and quickly gotten married. My brother and I had attended the reception at a Chinese restaurant in Little Tokyo, and Anchan had said, "It's a good thing. In America, the more friends the better."

After the wedding, Takita had started working as a gardener.

"Tell me more about it," my brother spluttered.

"Yeah, well, suddenly she wants to go home. It came on after we got married and she started speaking Japanese again. Her last husband was a black American, you know, and I think she had a tough time with him with the language difference. I don't want to brag, but when we started living together, she said I made her happier than any other man."

"Hmph, I guess I can understand. Listen, she might get mad at me if she heard me say this, but she lived for a long time with an American, got divorced, and then started living with you—she's just discovering how good a Japanese man can be. Am I right? If you're happy together, why can't you just stay? Think about what you went through for a green card." My brother seemed shocked that one of his cronies from the old days was going home.

"You know, you're right, but when I think about my wife, it seems better to go back. She comes from a big farming family, and they don't have an heir. When she talked it over with her parents, they were thrilled. She's had to pay for marrying a black man and going off to America. Now that she's starting over again, she'd like to be near her parents. She'll be able to make peace with them."

"And you?"

"As for me . . . I'd prefer to stay here if I could, but I don't know the language, and if I'm going to spend my life as a laborer, I might as well be back in Japan. But forget about that—you're going to be getting married soon, right?" Takita was tired of being on the spot. "*Yuu*, is it going to be *alrigh*? I'm only saying that because I heard it from the horse's mouth—it's hard to be married to an American."

My brother's expression momentarily clouded over. The room felt close.

"It's hot. I'm goin' out for a breath of fresh air," I said.

Outside I took a deep breath, drinking in the sweet smell of the strawberries. I began walking toward Frank's field. Back there, in a shabby house in the middle of nowhere, two young Japanese men who had next to nothing in the world were tentatively making judgments about marriage. They had come to America believing that it was a land where dreams came true. How could everything turn out to be so hollow?

It had been incredibly hot that day. At work I had downed bottles and bottles of cola, but the heat had addled my brain all the same. I was having trouble thinking. I could hear Takita saying to my brother, "My wife's last marriage was hard for her. Now she's happy because she's married to somebody who speaks her own language."

Had he meant Japanese should stick with Japanese?

"I want you, a Japanese man," Naoko had said.

Naoko and Takita's wife had different backgrounds, different educations, different ex-husbands, yet they were saying the same thing. Something else Naoko had said the last time we met nagged at me: "You can't say it about everyone, but most Americans who marry us are losers. I've been here for eight years. I've met a lot of Japanese women married to Americans, and all their husbands are losers."

"I don't get it. Why?"

"You probably don't know this yet, but America is a very harsh culture, especially when business and society interact. If you're

234

not tough enough mentally and physically, you can't survive. It's something I've just come to understand: the ones who can't make it marry Japanese women or women of other races. I don't like to say this, but why do you think so many Japanese women married blacks and came to live here?"

"Probably because Japan was poor after the war," I replied, remembering the *onlys* strolling on the arms of black soldiers on our island.

"That wasn't the only reason. Why do you think so many black men brought back Japanese brides? Because they wanted someone even lower down the social scale than themselves. And they found them in Japan."

"I still don't get it."

"A Japanese woman doesn't speak English. She has to depend body and soul on her husband. Had American black men ever met anyone who depended on them utterly? No. Blacks were downtrodden in America. They wanted to escape the stigma. You could say the same thing about white men. Maybe not all of them, but many white men in this cruel, competitive society who feel at a disadvantage marry Japanese women.

"It seems inconvenient—a man and a woman who can't communicate living together. But subconsciously American men like their wives to have a language handicap. Why? Because dominating their wives gives them a taste of success even when their own lives have been a failure. . . . They seem so kind to us because they are permanently superior in terms of language, physical strength, and, of course, national strength. To put it another way, we may feel that they're being nice to us, but actually it's discrimination. Marriage in America is politics."

"So you mean that black Americans brought back lots of Japanese women because they wanted to enslave them as they had been?"

"No, not enslave them. Subconsciously, they wanted to create a class below them, but no one could fill that role in America. In a defeated nation like Japan, they got what they wanted."

Perhaps Naoko was speaking from experience. Anyway, her words made my stomach churn.

The words kept coming back to me: Americans who marry

235

Japanese are losers. It struck me, then, that maybe she herself was a loser. Just like the black men who had brought back Japanese brides, wasn't she subconsciously trying to make me—ten years younger and at sea in this country—into a pet?

She had also said, "People always say that American society is a struggle for survival and that only the fittest make it. But the struggle isn't in the society; it's between men and women. In America, the man wants to pass on his sense of failure to someone else, like in a game of Old Maid. Sometimes the man wants to stop being a failure and rise in the world, but if he can't, then he longs to have an utterly dependent creature below him. It's the clash between the desire to succeed and the desire to dominate that creates a struggle for survival in America."

And my brother was about to set foot in this unknown territory.

I continued walking along the moonlit road through the field. When I looked behind me, I saw a faint light in Jiisan's windows. He would be alone, resting on his ratty sofa. The old man didn't watch television; instead, after dinner he lay down with the Japanese newspaper and drifted off to sleep. I wondered if he was doing the same thing tonight. Although I had seen him in the morning on the farm, I was seized with a sudden urge to visit him. I went back to the house, got on my motorcycle, and set off in his direction.

"Were you asleep?"

"*Oi*, was wonderin' who it was at this hour—*yuu ka*?" The old man had nearly been asleep, and he came out into the hallway, rubbing his eyes.

"Isn't it hot?"

"*Hotto na yoru yo na.* So hot I can't sleep." The old man tightened his bathrobe around him.

"It's a little cooler out here."

We sat down on a bench outside.

"An old friend of my brother's from his trainee days, Takita, is at our house right now, and he's asking my brother's advice on going back to Japan. They're talking mostly about marriage, and since I can't give an opinion on that, I came to see you."

"Is he taking his wife back to Japan? I see. . . . I knew guys like

236

that. Dying to get to America, but once they get here they find they aren't cut out for it, and back home they go."

"Are there many like that?"

"Yup. Some of them get used to this country after a few stays. Some can take it from the beginning. Takes all kinds of people. But the ones who don't like it, they go back to Japan, and then they're back here a few years later. Human beings just keep movin' till they find their own place, I guess."

"Is this your place? Is that why you've lived here for so long?"

"Even at my age, I don't feel America is my home. I just wanted to go overseas; Okinawa was poor and . . . Anyway, I wanted to work. . . . That's why my brother and I boarded that boat. The only reason. That's what made me what I am today."

"Do you regret coming to America?" I asked timidly. It was a question that I had been wanting to ask him for a long time.

"Regrets, eh? . . . I'd be lying if I said no. But I would have had regrets if I stayed in Japan, too . . . I don't know," he replied, closing his eyes.

Sometimes I doubted whether my brother, Takita, Frank, Jiisan, Naoko, or even Sensei and his wife were happy here. Of course, compared with Japan, America had incredible material wealth. And nobody would complain if you spoke loud, or bother you about what you wore or how you behaved. It was certainly a much easier place to live than Japan. If you could get used to American idealism and the burning sun, it wasn't bad at all. The beach at Santa Monica where Naoko and I had gone that afternoon and the modern buildings along Wilshire Boulevard were very pleasant. If you stayed here, the material wealth, the personal freedom, and the pretty scenery could be yours. The Japanese and Mexicans on the farm had the faces of men who worked hard, and I liked this, too.

But something was missing. Even if you got everything you wanted, there was still that one thing. It was difficult to pinpoint, but I felt that as long as you had that one thing, you could survive even if you lost everything else. And when I tried to give it a name, it was the past.

We immigrants have no past. Although we can reinvent a present and a future faster in this country than anywhere else, we can't re-create our past here no matter how rich we get. When we come to America, we have to discard our past—and we give up a great deal. Some people immigrate because they want to forget who they are, to be rid of their old selves. But they don't admit it, and say instead that they have come to build a future. To them a change of place seems enough to ensure a better life.

Many people find their own pasts repulsive, but they are misguided. The future doesn't spring from nowhere; rather, it grows out of both the past and the present, and it is this sense of continuum that makes our lives whole. The past soothes our hearts. Anchan's and my past lay in our relationships back in Japan, and it was because we missed them that we felt empty in this country.

"If we could only live like this on Ōshima," my brother had said. When Naoko had said, "I want you, a Japanese man," I think this was partly what she meant. Jiisan, too, had been trying to express something similar: "There's nothing in America that I value or feel nostalgic for."

A car pulled out of our driveway. It must have been Takita on his way home. He was serious about going back to Japan. The car made its lonesome way down the road, headlights pushing away the darkness. Eventually Takita would go home with his wife, but five years later he would be back again, alone, on a tourist visa. Apparently he still hadn't found his own place.

"*Yuu no buraza*, gettin' married soon. . . . The three of you goin' to live in that house?" the old man said, looking down at our shack.

At least temporarily we were going to kick the Mexicans out and I was going to move next door while Anchan and his wife stayed where we were now. Eventually, they'd probably rent an apartment, but this was our immediate solution.

The lights in the house went out. Anchan, upset by Takita's news, must have turned in early.

"Oh yeah, Jiisan, there's a new Japanese family here. They came from Kagoshima."

"Is that so? From Kagoshima, you say? People do move around." He seemed to be speaking to no one in particular. In America, where people constantly were coming and going, Jiisan had probably spent his life saying good-bye. And he had run into many people like Naoko, who couldn't make up their minds one way or the other.

Sylvana would be coming to live with us in two months' time. The old man and I stared down at the darkened house under the blue light of the moon that was dancing down strawberry road.

# 16

# The Point of No Return

The boss was disappointed by prices that season. Toward the end
of the harvest in late June, I went to his office to ask him about
some work and found him bent over the accounts with his book-
keeper.

"Yup, *oba producto dattan ka nō*. Prices just won't go up. We're
losing five cents a box compared to last year. And fertilizer and
seedlings went up this year, too. We're not goin' to make much of
a profit. What a waste."

The night before, Anchan had been telling me the same thing
as we looked at our accounts: "We probably won't suffer too big a
loss, but it's not going to work out the way we thought. And we
worked so hard. . . ."

Strawberries had fetched a good price the year before, and
farmers both near and far—in Orange County and Oxnard—had
switched from vegetables to strawberries. With regular weather
and plenty of pickers, thanks to a slowdown at immigration,
southern California had produced an unprecedented strawberry
crop this year, and prices had plummeted.

"*Shee*, just producing something good doesn't mean you're going
to *meku mane*. Farming's a gamble." Frank began his usual sermon.
"But that don't mean we grow something else next year. We keep
growin' the same thing. That's what makes a good farmer. *Shee*,
watch the white farmers. Next year they'll be tired of this and
move on to something else. That's why they're no good—they
*chanji mindo shite shimau*. We'll grow the same old strawberries
next year, too. We got staying power."

Perhaps Frank was right. Japanese farmers had been successful in this country because they were tough, they improvised, and, even more important, they loved what they grew.

"*Yuu-tachi* can't give up now. Work hard, and it'll be *alrigh* next year," he added.

With my brother getting married soon, we could have used a little profit. Still, there was nothing to be done about it. We had given our all.

Back in the field picking strawberries again, I watched a red station wagon pull up and a familiar figure get out. It was my high school English teacher. He marched into the field, extending his hand for a handshake. "Ishikawa, long time no see. Just as I thought. You've turned into an excellent farmer. That's great!"

A year ago the same words had made me very angry: how thick can this guy be, telling me to be a farmer when there are so many things I want to do, I had thought. Maybe he's just making fun of me because I'm Japanese. But after two years here, I had learned that most Americans are not prejudiced about professions, and will wholeheartedly encourage a young person who starts down a new path. Americans put no limits on a person's potential. But can you imagine a Japanese person seriously encouraging a boy who works in a noodle shop to become a great ramen chef? I resented some parts of America, yet I was very drawn to the straightforward character of its people.

"Please pick as many strawberries as you like. The season's almost over. Go ahead."

"Mmm, good, very good. Juicier than last year." He popped three strawberries into his mouth at once.

"I don't know what I'm gonna do yet," I said, responding to his earlier comment. "I've got one year of junior college left, but I don't know if I can graduate by then. I'll probably keep farming with my brother for a while." My first year of junior college had ended the week before.

"One of these days I'm going to buy land and become a farmer. When I do, please teach me everything you know," my teacher requested.

He was about to go off on a summer vacation with his family, he said. As the two of us were chatting, my brother drove by in

241

our truck, stuck his head out the window, and yelled, "*Yuu*, that's it for today. I'm going home to make dinner. We're having steak."

I arrived home to find González, Antonio, and my brother in a big fight. My brother was screaming at them.

"What's the matter?" I asked.

"Matter? These idiots ate our steak. I could forgive them for that but *goddamu*, they ate it and took a shit on the plate."

"What?"

I went inside and came right back out. A bad smell filled the air.

"Anchan, you're right. How do you say 'eat shit' in Spanish?"

"Don't say such stupid things," my brother growled.

"But do you really think González and his buddy did it?"

"Who else would come into the house?"

"What do they say about it?"

"It wasn't them, they just got home. How could they do something like that when we've lived together for three years? I want to believe them. . . . But who else could have gotten in?"

"It wasn't González. One of the pickers probably broke in, saw the steak in the refrigerator, and ate it. But taking a shit afterward, I don't know . . ."

"*Eniway*, we can't do anything about it. Let's eat out. *Goddamu yo na*. Somebody takes a shit in my house, and my bride's gonna be here any day." Anchan cleared up the mess on the table.

"Anchan, let's not eat together tonight. I'm going to grab some hamburgers and go visit Sensei and his wife—it's been ages," I said, mounting my bike.

Since I had started seeing Naoko, I had fewer chances to go to Sensei's house, and I had a lot to talk with him about. I passed the Yoshidas, the family from Kagoshima, and saw their two junior high–age sons sitting in the front garden. I stopped to visit with them.

"Hey, getting used to America yet?"

"I can't speak English yet—it's no fun," the older one said sullenly.

Then I heard the father yelling inside the house: "How dare you say that? I'm trying my best, aren't I?"

Next came the sobbing voice of the mother: "I came, because

you kept asking me to. But it's so different from your letters. If it's going to be like this, I'd rather be poor back in Japan. I'll never make friends here. The kids are lonely, too. Please, let's go home."

I wondered if they fought like this all the time and decided not to linger. I grabbed two hamburgers at a stand along the way, and went straight to Sensei's house.

As I arrived there, a car was pulling out, and I wondered who it could have been.

"I'm sorry it's been such a long time. I've been so busy with work and school. I brought you some of our strawberries." It had been two months since I had last come. "Did you have a guest? I just saw a car leaving."

"It was Mr. Yamaoka, who used to come to our church. He dropped in unexpectedly from Long Beach. A very interesting man."

Sensei's wife poked her head out of the kitchen—apparently she was cleaning up after the guest. Lighting the stove, she said, "Long time no see. How are you? We're seeing lots of old faces tonight. Oh, strawberries, they look delicious. Would you like green tea or coffee? I got some good tea from Japan, so let's have that."

"The international situation is tense," Sensei commented, scanning the newspaper. "The summit meeting between America and Russia hasn't exactly been a success."

I had missed hearing Sensei's views on world politics. That year, 1967, a summit meeting was held between the USSR and the United States in Glassboro, New Jersey, to discuss the precarious world situation—the escalation of the Vietnam War and disruptions in the Mideast. A large photo of Johnson and Kosygin was in the paper in front of me.

It had recently come to light that the National Student Association had received funds from the CIA for activities overseas; this set students against students, students against universities, and universities against business. Then, on April 4, Martin Luther King, Jr., issued a statement urging young people to become conscientious objectors to the war. In answer to his call, young men eligible for the draft fled to Canada, Mexico, or as far afield as India and settled there.

"Times have changed. Up until now, I never dreamed I'd see young people leaving this country. America's a place to *come* to. But I guess some of them are fed up with the war and have decided to leave for good. It's a significant change," Sensei commented.

"Why?"

"America's a country of immigrants. People only go to a new country because it's more stable or wealthier than their own. They have to believe that bigger and better things await them.

"It's a mistake to say that America *is* the richest country in the world. What you have to say instead is: America *has to be* the richest country in the world, it *has to be* the freest country in the world. Do you follow me? Say somebody comes to work here. He won't come unless he can make more money here. Or take a political refuge. He won't immigrate if the political situation is less stable here than it is at home. America isn't allowed to just *be,* it's a country that *must be* better. People live by that. But now some people have run out of love for their country."

"Didn't anyone leave before now?"

"Of course. After World War One, many Americans went to Europe. But they didn't go there because they hated America. They went because they had a complex about Europe and needed to discover who they were. But people are leaving now because they're fed up. It could be a very serious problem."

"Why doesn't America stop the war?"

"Because they're fighting for ideology."

"Ideology? I don't understand."

"America isn't fighting over territory or capital, but for justice. Do you understand? Justice. No other country in the world could afford to do that. But this stubborn pursuit of so-called justice is ruining this country."

Sensei now launched into an impassioned speech. Although he seemed to be leading a quiet, retired life, when conversation turned to the state of society, he got all riled up.

"You are a busy man, aren't you? Just a minute ago you were having that discussion with Mr. Yamaoka, and now you're on about the Vietnam War," his wife said, pouring tea.

"What kind of person is Mr. Yamaoka?"

"Yamaoka came here from Kumamoto after the war with the

244

help of the Displaced Persons Act. Wouldn't you say that he's around forty now, dear? Anyway, he married a white woman in our church, and he was so persistent that he had English down pat in five years. He came into the church and started attending the nisei Bible class in English."

"What was his wife like?" I asked, curious on my brother's behalf.

"We had an isei gardner in our church. She was the daughter of one of his customers. Very pleasant but quite shy. Yamaoka didn't come from a very good home, and he planned to settle in America, so he wanted to marry an American. We watched him become more American day by day; sometimes he left us speechless."

"It's true. Sometimes we thought he was a nisei—his way of talking, his gestures," Sensei's wife added. I busied myself with bean cake and tea.

Sensei continued: "Eventually they had a child. Yamaoka didn't give the child a Japanese name, which was unusual. He said the baby wouldn't need it in America. They seemed very happy after the baby; I remember them cuddling her at a church picnic. Frankly, we were impressed. We hadn't seen many mixed couples look that happy. I thought that things had really changed for the Japanese here. But then . . ." Sensei took a sip of tea and sighed deeply. He seemed to be tired of talking.

"When the child was two, she broke out in a high fever and suffered brain damage. It was painful to watch the agony that couple went through. Yamaoka started to brood. His father had died in the war, and his mother had brought him up, but during those terrible days she had been a prostitute. He had rejected his mother and committed many petty crimes when he was young. In fact, I don't think he could've stayed in Japan; he had to fake his refugee status to get in here. When he got here, he turned over a new leaf, seeing that he could make a new life for himself. But when his child got ill, he began to believe that the sins of his past had been visited on her. He decided that he would spend twenty-four hours a day with her and abandon the idea of getting rich if only she would live.

"But his wife thought differently. She went around to hospitals

245

and government offices, searching for a place that could treat the baby. And she told her neighbors and her friends that her child was retarded but that they were going to bring her up the best they could. She tackled the problem head-on, because she's an American, and everyone in this country is entitled to equality— even a retarded child.

"It was very touching to watch the mother. But Yamaoka couldn't stand it. He must have thought that the three of them would live discreetly by themselves and not go out much, the way it would be done in Japan. Yamaoka had been on his way to becoming an American, but now he slipped back into the role of a Japanese father.

"But more than being a wife and a mother, Mrs. Yamaoka was an American with ideas about how the world should work. And she was going to put up a struggle. Gradually things got worse. They started to have bitter fights and eventually separated. To us it had looked like such a happy marriage. And they didn't break up for lack of love. But these kinds of things happen in America. After the separation, Yamaoka stopped coming to church. Tonight he dropped in on us unexpectedly."

Sensei took another sip of his tea. "Well, I've talked myself blue in the face. Isn't your brother getting married soon? I hear the wedding's being held in New York. If you have time, you should visit Syracuse University. The president is a classmate of mine from BU."

"You've given me food for thought. I need time to sort all this out," I answered, blundering my way out of Sensei's house.

It was ten o'clock. The air outside was chilly, and I pushed down hard on the bike's accelerator, to lose myself in speed. I came to a little road that led through an orange field. Down here I won't have to worry about cars, I thought, and went even faster. Then I saw a red light in my mirror growing bigger and bigger. A patrol car. When I stopped, two big cops with pistols jumped out and came up to me. One held his gun and made me put my hands over my head while the other searched me. Then they asked for my driver's license, which they peered at by flashlight, comparing my face with the photograph.

"Mexican?"

"No, no, I am a Japanese farmer!" I said emphatically.

"Go see America by bus before the wedding. I'll fly in once I've finished up the field and bought some furniture," my brother suggested, as his wedding date drew closer. "It'd be fun to go cross-country. When you get to Middletown, you call Akiko, and she'll come pick you up. Stay with her until I get there."

Having finished work early that day, we were sitting around the house talking. A map of New York State was spread on the table. Sylvana lived in a small town called Port Jervis. There New York, New Jersey, and Pennsylvania came together, so it was also called the "Three-Point Town." It had a small population and was two hours away from New York City by car. Akiko would pick me up from Middletown, the closest Greyhound bus station.

"From LA you go through Las Vegas, Salt Lake City, and Wyoming—see, here's Cheyenne on the map—straight into Chicago," Anchan continued. "Then circle around the Great Lakes and down into Middletown. How many miles is it, I wonder. A round trip from the tip of Hokkaido to Kagoshima, maybe more."

As it turned out, I took two weeks to get to the wedding; it was my longest trip yet in America.

"Hey the boss gave me a little something for you to travel with. So did Ted," Anchan said, showing me some money in an envelope. "You should thank them tomorrow."

There was still plenty of light outside. The Mexicans were taking a breather after work before starting home. Infrequently we could hear the rumble of trucks going up and down the farm roads. Then we heard the sound of a car pulling up at our door and a knock. It was Hirata, the man who had tried to sell us the graves, and two of his Mexican employees.

"Hot today," Hirata said to Anchan. "I heard *yuu no braza* was going East, so I wanted to catch him. Here's a little something."

Hirata had also brought money. I had gotten some from Sensei and his wife as well. Nice people, all of them.

"Ishikawa, congratulations on your marriage. When you get back, please bring your wife over. My daughter speaks good English, and I think they'd get along."

"*Sankyu yo* for remembering my brother. We'll be over as soon as we can. All this will be new to her, so I'm counting on your help. How about a beer?"

"Forget me, but how about one for García here? It was very hot today, and he's a thirsty man."

My brother handed García a beer, and the two exchanged a few words. Then Anchan said something odd: "Hirata, have you been teaching this guy *shigin*? He said that you've been making him memorize old Japanese songs."

"That's right. We spend lots of time in the car on our way to the next customer. That's where I teach him. Mexicans are usually good singers, but this guy is fantastic. Let's have him sing one."

Oh no, I thought, here we go again, as Hirata turned and said, "García, *singu shigin*."

García looked at us blankly.

"García, *cantaré*."

"*Nogii maresuke-e saaku-u kinshujo-o sa-ansen-n somoku-uu utataa-aaa koryo-o . . .*"

My brother was never surprised by anything the Mexicans did, but now his eyes grew wide.

"Pretty good, huh? A lot of Japanese can't do it that well. When he gets a little better, I'm going to recommend him to the club and get him an artistic name. He'll sing "Takasagoya" for you at your wedding reception in Little Tokyo."

Hirata then started on me: "*Yuu* should try it. See how good a Mexican can be. *Yuu Japanesu yangu.* You could be even better."

Ten years later, when I came back to live in America for the third time, I joined Hirata's club and got the artistic name Ishikawa Ryosei. It had taken ten years for Hirata to convince me, but once I had my certificate, it became one of my treasures, along with the diploma I had received for art and gym classes. I found myself inexplicably pleased by it. Perhaps the certificate was a symbol of being accepted in a country where immigrants normally didn't take kindly to newcomers.

"It'll be nice for us, you marrying a white woman. Now we'll know someone in the white community," Hirata had said revealingly.

\* \* \*

The day before I was due to leave, I visited Jiisan. Visiting an old person is a surefire way to calm down.

"*Sō kaa? Yuu* goin' to New York, too? I been in this country for forty years, and I ain't never been to New York. But you're *yangu,* you can go lots of places. Take care of yourself," he said, giving me twenty dollars out of a paper bag in the closet. "It's a long trip. Save this for when you run out. Stop off at Vegas—there's no better place. But you're too *yangu,* so no gambling. Once you get the taste for it, it's all over.

"One time I took my savings with me. Came home with barely the shirt on my back. But if you make money, you can't wait to go back. Lots of Japanese have been ruined—lost everything and turned into blanket men," he said emotionally. "Anyway, when your brother's wife gets here, we'll celebrate."

I returned to Japan in the summer of 1969. By the time I came back to America in 1975, Jiisan had quit farming and had entered an old-age home in Little Tokyo. I ran into him in a bookstore there, and he congratulated me on my return: "*Yuu,* back again?"

I never saw him again. He died in 1976 and was buried in Evergreen Park, also known as the Japanese cemetery, in East LA.

On the day of my departure, Ted drove me to the bus terminal in Los Angeles. I put my luggage in a locker and walked toward a hotel to meet Naoko for lunch.

When I walked into the lobby, I saw her chatting with another man, and I felt a little jealous. When she saw me, she said something to the man and walked over in my direction.

"A friend?"

"Somebody I know from work. Sometimes we do things together. I never thought I'd run into him here."

"He isn't a boyfriend, is he?"

"I think I already have one of those."

I didn't know if she was telling the truth. But she had said she wanted a Japanese man. I mumbled under my breath.

"Hey, Mr. Strawberry, you're thinking strange thoughts. I see it in your eyes," she teased. "Anyway, let's have lunch. My treat."

She walked toward the restaurant.

The Biltmore Hotel. I had never eaten lunch in such a fancy place before.

She looked over the menu. "I'm going to have wine. Strawberry Boy?"

"No, thank you. Umm, it's not a big deal, but would you stop calling me Strawberry Boy?"

"Oh, are you still mad?"

"No. But if those Japanese guys over there hear us, what're they gonna think?" There were two tables of Japanese businessmen nearby.

"All right, I see. There have been lots more Japanese here recently. I'm busier at work, but I don't feel like spending much time with them," she said, glancing over at their table.

As she had said, the number of Japanese businessmen in the Los Angeles area had risen dramatically over the past two years. The bank that had come to collect deposits on the farm two years ago now had more than five branches. New buildings were being built in Little Tokyo with Japanese capital, the aftereffects of an economic boom in Japan. Naoko worked for a consulting firm that helped Japanese firms expand, so she knew well how much Japanese exports to this country had risen.

"I can't believe it. When I came here eight years ago, there weren't any Japanese products on the shelves. And when you did find them, Americans made fun of them because they were cheap and broke easily. Something must have happened over there." Listening to her made me feel that perhaps I had been left behind, not only by my friends but by Japan as well.

We must have looked like an odd couple—a beautiful older woman and a student—the Japanese businessmen kept stealing glances at us.

"I wonder why Japanese men only look at women one way," she said, starting on the meal that had just been set before us.

"What do you mean?"

"I could never stand the way Japanese men look at women. This might bother you, being a man and all, but a Japanese man only looks at a woman as a sex object. I was very relieved to find that American men—not all, mind you, but some American men— treat women as human beings. They know how to associate with a

250

woman without making her feel self-conscious, like drinking tea together, talking, or asking for advice. Japanese men are always on the make."

"Did I look at you like that?" I asked.

"Umm, . . ." she said, and then giggled. "Why is it that you always take things so personally?"

"It sounded like you were accusing me."

"OK. Confess. *Did* you look at me like that?"

"Yes," I said softly. "But there were other reasons."

"See?" She brought her napkin to her lips.

"So, you find American men attractive after all."

"I don't care if they're American or Japanese. I just want to be with someone who knows how to treat a woman. And I have the feeling that there are more American men who do, that's all."

"I'll treat you well. What should I do?"

"You're impossible," she said in disbelief. "What time is your bus?"

"In forty-five minutes."

"And how long will you be gone?"

"I'm taking two weeks to travel. Then I'll come back through the South. So it'll be three weeks, maybe a month."

"New York, eh? That takes me back. When I was first a student, I landed in Los Angeles and had to fly to New York City to get to school. A friend of my father's who lived in New York came to meet me at the airport. I remember being amazed by the streets of Manhattan from the airplane, and, without realizing it, I exclaimed, 'We're in New York!' " Her voice was sad.

"I wish I could take you with me," I said.

"Why?"

She was listening to me intently.

"I don't speak enough English to go by myself."

"Is that all?"

"And . . . if we went together we could do it every day."

"You silly thing." Her face was turning red. "I'll drop you at the bus terminal."

When we got in the car, she turned on the radio, and we heard the strains of an old Japanese song.

251

"Impossible. I never dreamed that one day I would hear Japanese songs on American radio. Do you know this Sakamoto Kyū song?"

"Yes. But why do they call it 'Sukiyaki' here?"

She was humming to herself. We drove into the parking lot of the terminal.

"Well, here we are, *itte irrashai*."

"Take care of yourself. I'll write."

"It's odd."

"What is?"

"When Japanese say good-bye, I said it, too—*itte irrashai*."

"Why is that?"

"Well, it means 'You're going but you will come back.' 'Come back' becomes part of saying good-bye. I wonder if you find the same thing in other languages. Take English, for example. 'Good-bye,' 'so long,' or 'see you again' don't have that meaning."

I remembered my mother saying *irrashai* when I left the island, and a lump rose in my throat. My parents had also said *irrashai* to Anchan, fully expecting him to return. But now I was headed to a ceremony that would ensure that he would not. In fact, all the people on the boat had been sent off with the word *irrashai* ringing in their ears. So had Jiisan, Sensei, his wife, and thousands of others. Naoko probably had too.

But how many of them could have said, "Yes, I will be back"? Some, like the old man, would never go back. And think of the foreign service employees, the exchange students, the immigrants, and the businessmen who had died far away from home. Depressed, I stared at Naoko.

"I'll never get used to saying *itte irrashai,* but I hope you get a good look at your brother's 'point of no return.' And . . . *itte irrashai,*" she said, gripping my hand and making as though to push me out of the car.

I got out and spoke to her through the window, and, when she turned to wave, I thought I saw tears in her eyes.

GIs, blacks, Mexicans, and hippies milled around the terminal, and the bus itself was full. Next to me sat a middle-aged black woman who really talked up a storm. She was on her way to see her son in Atlanta after three years, she said; he had sent her a

252

round-trip ticket, and she was very proud to have a son who did so much for his mother.

When we got out on the freeway, the bus picked up speed. Although the speed limit was 65, our driver accelerated to 75 mph, and we whizzed past the passenger cars.

Three hours out of LA, there were fewer homes and the scenery changed: we were now in the Wild West. Through mountains and valleys, the road was straight as far as the eye could see, a freeway cutting through rock. I was amazed by the expanse and wondered how the pioneers had gotten their wagons up and down the mountains. I remembered Horace Greeley's phrase, but changed it to "Go east, young man" to fit my own adventure.

The other passengers must have been used to the scenery; they were busy reading, or staring at one another.

As the horizon turned a reddish purple with evening, the mountains and the cactus took on a light purple cast. The sky was an incredibly deep blue, and the wild, hostile land glowed in the dying light. Eventually we saw lights shining ahead of us—electric lights, proof that people lived in this unfriendly territory. The farther we drove, the brighter they got, and then we were in Las Vegas.

Frank had once told me, "You won't find any clocks in Vegas. They distract the gamblers. Like when I go there, if I look at the clock, I think, 'Oh no, it's so late, got to go home or the wife will get mad.' It's bad for the dealers. The house always wins because it has money. If you keep on playing, the one with money always wins. So they try to make you forget time."

He was right; there were no clocks in the casinos, and every one was more fancy than the last. I had imagined gamblers as threatening characters with scars on their faces, but these were elegant ladies and gentlemen in formal dress, as if we were in a first-class hotel lobby. Bunny girls were serving drinks at the tables, their big breasts jiggling as they moved. Las Vegas looked just like the movies.

I had reserved a motel room for one night near the bus station, and, after depositing my luggage there, I had a look around. Besides real casinos, the smaller businesses had slot machines. In fact, the whole town was one big casino. There was no ceiling to the amount one could gamble, but neither was there a floor, and I found penny slot machines. The poor and the rich congregated together; democracy at work.

I decided to try a little gambling myself and sat down at a slot machine. When a row of the same little pictures lined up, real money would pour out of the machine. I could see how this could become a habit. A woman at a machine across from mine had just hit the jackpot—one hundred dollars. She was screaming and jumping up and down, and the machine was beeping and flashing.

I remembered another of Frank's stories: "About ten years ago I took a Japanese couple to Las Vegas; it was their first time, and I taught the wife how to play the slot machines. Well, she was doing it all by herself when she lets out a yell and bursts into tears. So I go over and ask her what's wrong, and she says that she broke the machine. Actually she had hit the jackpot, and all these dimes had come pouring out."

The bunny girls kept asking me if I wanted to order something, and when I did they were very quick about it, but their tips cost more than the bill itself. You can't be stingy with bare-breasted women who wait on you. The big winners at the poker table gave them five- and ten-dollar tips without blinking an eye. Behind the poker table, women in low-cut thigh-high dresses stood eyeing the winners, call girls waiting to attend to men who had won big and were on a high. Greed, the great social leveler.

The next afternoon I left Vegas. The bus moved across a huge plain, where there was nothing but the sky and the horizon. It felt as though we were silently being absorbed into the vast loneliness of nature. I took a map out of my bag to see where we were. The distance we had traveled so far was no bigger than a grain of rice on the map. I beheld the vastness of America, and it made me feel how alone in the world Anchan and I were.

The bus went through Salt Lake City, city of the Mormons, and into Cheyenne, Wyoming. Finally the bus stopped at a scenic vista above the plain. Never in my wildest dreams had I imagined that I—born and raised on the Izu islands of Japan—would be deeply moved by this land. The view might have sprung straight from one of the westerns I had seen at the base.

I spent the next night in Cheyenne, stayed three days in

Chicago, and made stops in Detroit and Cleveland as I wended my way east. Two weeks after leaving Los Angeles, I arrived in Middletown, New York, and phoned Akiko.

"I've been waiting and waiting for you. I kept wondering when you'd get here. I'm on my way. Stay where you are, OK?"

Thirty minutes later she showed up.

"You're so big I didn't recognize you. How many years has it been? How is everybody at home? What does the island look like?" Akiko asked impatiently. "I feel so relieved. I haven't spoken Japanese for ten years, and I wasn't sure I could anymore."

Akiko remembered me well, but all I could remember about her were her visits to our house with her future husband, Bob, and, of course, the big fight with Bob.

"You've done so much for my brother, what with all the arrangements and now the wedding," I said, getting in her car. "What's Sylvana like?"

"She's outgoing and cheerful and Italian, so she's good with people. This is an Italian neighborhood. She's of Italian descent, and I'm sure it's going to work out," Akiko declared, proud of her role as matchmaker.

We drove along a densely forested mountain road, dramatically different from dry southern California.

"Look over there. See that church. That's where they're getting married."

I looked in the direction she had pointed in time to see a cozy church.

"Everybody's talking about it. They say it's the first time a Japanese has married one of the local girls," Akiko chirped happily.

Akiko seemed more enthusiastic about the wedding than my brother. When we got to the house, Bob and the kids were waiting for us. Bob remembered my parents and asked after them. Even in this small, isolated town somebody knew my hometown. All roads lead to America, I thought, musing on how my brother and I had gotten here.

"Oh, I must phone Sylvana. She's been looking forward to your arrival, and so have her parents. I'll just invite them over now—they're very close."

"I feel kind of embarrassed. Maybe I could meet them with

255

Anchan when he gets here." My brother was due to arrive in two days.

"What are you talking about? She's going to be a member of your family."

Before long we heard a car pull up, and Sylvana and her parents arrived. Akiko introduced me. The father gave me a hug.

"This is your new sister-in-law." Akiko took the girl by the hand and introduced us. She was beautiful. We each gave our names again and shook hands. Then we pecked each other on the cheek and embraced lightly.

So this would be Anchan's wife . . . Perhaps Anchan was meant to stay in America after all. At any rate, he had reached the point of no return. I shook hands with my brother's bride-to-be, and she looked deep into my eyes.

# 17

# Crossing Over

My brother was met at the airport by the McBanes, cousins of his fiancée's mother. Many of Sylvana's relatives lived in downtown Manhattan, Brooklyn, or Queens, while her mother's Italian parents had moved nearby. For the grandfather, the wedding was the perfect opportunity for a family reunion, and he had issued an order for the whole family to gather.

That night a rehearsal dinner was held at a restaurant. The father's relatives did not attend; he was the bride's stepfather, and none of his family lived in New York. Sylvana's real father had been of German descent; he had died ten years earlier. Her mother was the third daughter in an immigrant family of eight.

I spotted several Italian faces, which resembled those of the Mexicans on the farm. The bride's Italian grandparents couldn't speak English at all, so her mother sat next to them and translated. Here were white people who had lived in America for fifty years and couldn't speak English; I was relieved to discover that it wasn't only the Mexicans, the Chinese, and the Japanese who grappled with the language barrier.

Sylvana took Anchan by the hand and started introducing him to people, whereupon Akiko grabbed my hand and did the same. Everyone was friendly. When we got to Grandpa, as they called him, the old man stood up slowly, embraced me just like a Sicilian mafioso in the movies, and said something in Italian, which the mother promptly translated into English. "Grandpa says he's very happy to welcome Japanese into the family."

Lots of grandchildren came up to greet the old man, and each time he rose and gave them that same hug. I felt uneasy being welcomed into the family by someone who looked like a retired Mafia don. Then Akiko explained: "The old man came from Milan and worked as a shoemaker in Little Italy. In the old days, there was lots of discrimination against Italians. When Grandpa turned fifty, he left New York and retired here."

"Was it so tough for the Italians?"

"Yes. In New York the Italians were called wops." Akiko mouthed the last word quietly.

"What does that mean?"

"It means 'without passport.' "

"So they were illegal aliens too?"

"That's right, Italy was so poor, many of them landed without passports. Over time, the name stuck," Akiko explained as we wandered around.

Led by his fiancée, who wore a frilly blouse and a ribbon in her hair, my brother stopped to greet each person in the room. I noted his sunburned face, his stubby fingers, and his thick arms bulging out of his short-sleeved shirt, which was now linked in the arm of a virginal white girl, and I felt sorry for him, because his rough looks seemed out of place. What an odd couple.

"Is Anchan OK?" I asked, watching his stiff movements.

"He's doing fine. Anybody can get married," Akiko answered.

"No, I don't mean that. I mean marrying an American." I had asked the question that had been on my lips all week, even though the wedding was the next day.

"*I* married an American. It's hard sometimes, but I'm happy," Akiko said.

But I couldn't take her words at face value, and I turned to study her. Akiko, a Japanese woman, had married an American more than fifteen years ago, and by now her expressions and her gestures were 100 percent white American. But what bothered me was the impression I had gotten of her when she picked me up at the bus station. I had seen a number of Japanese women married to Americans, and gradually these women's faces began to look more and more like those of foreign women. It had gotten to the point where I could spot the Japanese wife of a black man in Little Tokyo. Japanese women seemed to take on the sexuality of the men they had married, white or black—something that Japanese men could never grasp.

I wondered if marriage would Americanize Anchan's features as much as it had Akiko's.

Tapping a young man on the shoulder, Akiko said to me, "Let me introduce you. This is Antonio. He only came from Italy a year ago. And he's your age."

Antonio shook my hand. He couldn't speak English very well.

"He's not used to America yet," Akiko explained, "and he's having a hard time. He says he got here 'cause he's a distant relative of Grandpa's."

Antonio was munching potato chips alone, looking uncomfortable. Watching him reminded me of myself. His community was probably like ours, with its own versions of Jiisan, Sensei and his wife, Frank, and Hirata—all players in the human comedy. Like the Chinese, the Koreans, and even the Armenians, the Italians were certainly expending an absurd amount of energy on becoming Americans. Antonio was going to have to work hard to find his own niche here. Three generations of an Italian family, with the grandmother and grandfather at its center, chatted away happily at the party. Meanwhile, one young man who hankered for the things they had was about to start out. Antonio would eventually have his own family, and, when he got married, the whole clan would gather again to give their blessings. In the final analysis, American history could be broken down into the fortunes of individual families.

But if this is true, how do people here function as members of a nation? Especially since being American involves showing others that you lead an attractive life-style.

America broadcasts its selling points and its ideals to the world, and Americans talk about the country as though it were paradise.

The door to America had opened gradually in many countries, and each war had opened it a little wider—World War I, World War II, the Korean War, the Vietnam War. I pictured the twentieth century as a tug-of-war between people trying to get more access to America and those trying to stem the tide of immigration. This tug-of-war is particularly relevant today. Nestling up to America, postwar Japan kept the door between the two countries wide open, but now there are movements afoot to shut America out. Japan's future depends on how we will settle the issue of the open door. And it is up to the postwar generation to do it.

The church sat by itself in a field outside town; the green grass shimmered under the July sun. Anchan and I were waiting in the basement for the ceremony to begin. He was dressed in a white tuxedo, and I was wearing a suit that Sylvana's parents had gotten for me.

"Mom and Dad would never dream that we'd be wearing these clothes and that I'd be getting married in a little American church out in the country like this," Anchan said nervously. He had been swigging glasses of water one after another.

"*Oi, yuu,* go up there and take a look."

"They'll be down soon to get you."

"But before that go and check out the people and the setup," he ordered. "I can't exactly sneak up there myself and spy on the enemy camp."

I climbed the stairs. Dozens of people in their Sunday best were already seated. A buzz rose when I appeared—they seemed to mistake me for Anchan. Outside, just as Akiko had said, many of the locals were standing around, curious. It was the first Italian-Japanese wedding in the town. In their hands they held little flowers and, strangely, rice.

Mistaking me for the groom, a cute little girl asked, "Where is Japan?"

"*Yuu go aru za way to Californi ando cross za bigu Pacificu Oshan,*" I replied.

The townspeople chatted with me amiably. Summer in New York was humid, and I could feel the sweat running under my suit. Everything looked newly green.

Grandpa arrived in a large station wagon and embraced me as he had the night before. Next came the bride in her parents' car. Her pure white dress shone as it trailed over the grass. She gave me a little wave, then disappeared into the church with her parents.

The service was about to begin. I ran back to the basement.

"The place is full. Some of the locals are waiting outside," I reported.

"*Oi.*"

"What's wrong?"

"*Yuu,* let's get out of here."

"Eh! What do you mean?"

"I'm getting cold feet."

"Now?"

I could understand what Anchan was feeling. He had been down here brooding while I had been gone. Maybe he had remembered my mother's words when he left the island: "If you marry an American, you'll become one in the end."

Or maybe it finally hit him that he was marrying a woman he couldn't talk to.

My brother had already crossed the border between Japan and America. But now he would have to cross a whole new border. Most of the immigrants I had met until then, including my brother, had made the transition to a new land. However, these immigrants soon discovered that although they now lived in America, there were still countless smaller, unforeseen barriers that lay ahead. Most of these barriers, however, were limited to the externals of work and life and they could always retreat into themselves if life became too painful. But when an immigrant married somebody who spoke a different language and had different customs, the barriers were in place twenty-four hours a day—there was no avoiding them.

When people leave their native lands to become Americans they have two hurdles to cross—the national border itself and the borders between different languages and customs. In order to become an American—by definition, a person who has transcended borders—one must confront a world filled with obstacles and submerge oneself in it. In fact, Americans seem to inhabit many separate spheres but feel that they should tear down the walls between them; thus, they end up thrashing about somewhere between a borderless world and a bordered one. My fear of becoming that kind of American had made me cherish such a secluded life on the farm.

Once in a while my brother had told me about his anxieties.

261

"With the English I have now, I can't talk to my wife. Still, I guess if I speak with her long enough, I should get better. But how are we going to communicate? It worries me. . . ."

Anchan wasn't worried about whether he and Sylvana could communicate in English; rather, he was worried about whether she could understand who he was before he had to explain himself in English. Or maybe he did just wonder whether they could converse.

Living in a foreign country, I came to feel intuitively that human relationships depend on words. Men and women grow apart if they don't talk to each other. As Naoko had said, once two people get married, they must go beyond romantic conversation into real life. Worried though he was, Anchan seemed to feel a missionary zeal to open the door to America for the rest of us, and he forged ahead into battle.

Akiko came down to tell us the ceremony was about to begin.

"*Yuu,* be nice to her," Anchan ordered me, and then, slapping his cheeks like a sumo wrestler getting revved up for a match, he squared his shoulders and marched up the steps.

The people in the church greeted our entrance with applause. Anchan stood by the minister. Then Sylvana, swathed in white lace, walked slowly up the aisle. They turned to face each other in front of the minister.

The minister began to speak; then he asked my brother a question to which he answered "yes," and he asked the same question of the bride, and she also replied "yes." Next Anchan took the ring and placed it on her finger. They kissed. Loud applause rose from the pews, and, at that very moment, the doors opened and the July light streamed into the dim interior of the church.

As bride and groom linked arms and moved slowly toward the light, people on both sides of the aisle rose, still clapping. A red carpet had been laid down the aisle, and on top of that a length of white cloth. To Anchan, walking the white cloth symbolized becoming an American, but to the parents who had sent their sons and daughters off to America, the cloth might as easily have been a trail of tears. Displaying its riches and its liberties, America had snatched many away from their native lands.

When the couple left the church, townspeople showered them with flowers and rice. Grains of rice scattered about Anchan's head, a symbol of fertility in this country, too. Then the church bell began to ring. Long after their car had left, it rang out over the lush field. Listening to it, I felt that I should be happy and wish them my best, but instead I felt lonely—America had stolen my brother. I suddenly had the illusion that the people in the car that grew smaller in the distance were actually Naoko and an American man, and found I longed for her.

The next day Anchan and Sylvana left to drive back to southern California. After Akiko and her family had seen the couple off, I made my good-byes as well and got on the bus. I was setting out on my trip down south. First, though, I planned to stop in New York for a few days. When I got on the bus, all the exhaustion of the journey and the night before caught up with me, and I fell into a deep sleep.

When I opened my eyes a crack in the hot bus, we had left the lovely green town and were about to enter a city. Out the window I could see red clouds above a setting sun. As the bus climbed a hill, a wide panorama of dozens of skyscrapers, the tallest ones soaring into the evening sky, opened on the right-hand side.

The scene jogged my memory. That was it. It looked just like the shiny photos in the magazines I had picked out of the garbage on the military base. Ah, New York, I thought. Finally I'm in America.

Which America was the true one—the America of the photos, the America before my eyes, or the America of the farm? I sat riveted, a kaleidoscope of images flashing before my eyes. For an instant I was struck by an odd fancy that America exists only in the mind.